Negotiating Financial Agreement in East Asia

Every international negotiation bears a risk of collapse, as even among like-minded countries, different players often have different priorities and interests. This can result in conflict as states clash over certain agreement details, and their disputes can escalate and founder the entire negotiation, missing an opportunity to realize potential initiatives. However, other circumstances have witnessed the cases of successful deals. This begets a puzzle: what did these states do to salvage their talks and seal their deals?

This book examines East Asian financial negotiation processes and seeks to explain why some negotiations are successful despite the risk of bargaining failure. Using the Chiang Mai Initiative Multilateralization (CMIM) talks as a case study, the book analyses how states with little prior experience at dealing with certain aspects of an agreement manage to avert negotiation failure and successfully conclude their final deal. Using extensive archival research, in-depth interviews with involved negotiators and experts, and a process-tracing method, it reconstructs the making of the CMIM agreement. The multi-country analysis reveals the roles played by key actors, namely, China, Japan, South Korea, Indonesia, Malaysia and Thailand, in shaping the agreement terms. The book goes on to argue that preventing a stalemate or succeeding in concluding arrangements like the CMIM is a product of various strategies and tactics employed by negotiators. These include employing bargaining strategies and tactics that help avoid a negotiation deadlock and assessing the conditions under which such strategies and tactics are likely – or unlikely – to achieve the objective of avoiding bargaining failure.

As a study of East Asian economic negotiation processes, this book will be of huge interest to students and scholars of East Asian cooperation and regionalism as well as finance, international business, international relations, and international political economy.

Kaewkamol Karen Pitakdumrongkit is Assistant Professor in the S. Rajaratnam School of International Studies, Nanyang Technological University, Singapore.

Routledge Studies in the Growth Economies of Asia

Negotiating Financial Agreement in East Asia

Surviving the turbulence

Kaewkamol Karen Pitakdumrongkit

Routledge
Taylor & Francis Group

LONDON AND NEW YORK

First published 2016
by Routledge
2 Park Square, Milton Park, Abingdon, Oxon OX14 4RN

and by Routledge
711 Third Avenue, New York, NY 10017

First issued in paperback 2017

Routledge is an imprint of the Taylor & Francis Group, an informa business

British Library Cataloguing in Publication Data
A catalogue record for this book is available from the British Library

Library of Congress Cataloging-in-Publication Data
Pitakdumrongkit, Kaewkamol Karen.
   Negotiating financial agreement in East Asia : surviving the turbulence / Kaewkamol Karen Pitakdumrongkit. — 1 Edition.
      pages cm. — (Routledge studies in the growth economies of Asia ; 128)
Includes bibliographical references and index.
   1. East Asia—Foreign economic relations.   2. Negotiation—
East Asia.   I. Title.
   HF1600.5.P58 2015
   332'.042095—dc23
   2015022099

ISBN 13: 978-1-138-49465-7 (pbk)
ISBN 13: 978-1-138-80752-5 (hbk)

Typeset in Times
by Apex CoVantage, LLC

Contents

Figures

Tables

Boxes

Abbreviations

ABMI	Asian Bond Markets Initiative
ACU	Asian currency unit
AFDM+3	ASEAN+3 Finance and Central Bank Deputies' Meeting
AFMGM+3	ASEAN+3 Finance Ministers and Central Bank Governors' Meeting
AFMM	ASEAN+3 Finance Ministers' Meeting
AFMM+3	ASEAN+3 Finance Ministers' Meeting
AJCEP	ASEAN–Japan Comprehensive Economic Partnership
APEC	Asia-Pacific Economic Cooperation
ASEAN	Association of Southeast Asian Nations
ASEAN+3	ASEAN and China, Japan and South Korea
ASEAN5	Indonesia, Malaysia, the Philippines, Singapore and Thailand
batna	best alternative to no agreement
BSA	bilateral swap arrangement
CEPA	Closer Economic Partnership Agreement
CLMVB	Cambodia, Lao People's Democratic Republic, Myanmar, Vietnam and Brunei
CMIM	Chiang Mai Initiative Multilateralization
EMEAP	Executives' Meeting of East Asia–Pacific Central Banks
EPA	economic partnership agreement
ERPD	Economic Review and Policy Dialogue
EU	European Union
FDI	foreign direct investment
FTA	free trade agreement
GATT	General Agreement on Tariffs and Trade
GDP	gross domestic product
IMF	International Monetary Fund
JIEPA	Japan–Indonesia Economic Partnership
JMEPA	Japan–Malaysia Economic Partnership

JTEPA	Japan–Thailand Economic Partnership
NDA	net domestic asset
NEER	nominal effective exchange rate
NIR	net international reserve
VAT	value-added tax
WTO	World Trade Organization

1   Introduction

When most of us hear about the conclusion of an international negotiation, a contract-signing ceremony comes to mind. Country leaders come on a stage and give a speech on how fruitful a relationship among them is. Then they proceed to sit on a table and ink the agreement. What usually follow are shake hands and smiles to a camera. These are the common pictures of celebrations. But how many of us have ever wondered how a negotiation is conducted? How do governments, with their different priorities and interests, manage to bargain and seal their deal?

This book is about negotiation processes of financial cooperation among East Asian countries. It will walk you through how international agreements, especially economic ones are made. The actual processes are usually quite far from handshaking and smiling displayed in the media. They are often bumpy, involving several twists and turns. Shifting stances, wavering opinions, siding with particular parties, concealing one's agendas and bluffing are prevalent in international bargaining. Therefore, at each stage of a negotiation, there always exists a potential risk of deadlock.

This risk heightens especially when countries are negotiating certain agreement details which they have neither before adopted nor familiar with. Because countries possess little knowledge about these "new" elements, and they become uncertain whether to proceed with a negotiation and strike a deal. However, we have witnessed in several occasions that states were able to reach their deals. The Chiang Mai Initiative Multilateralization (CMIM) agreement is a prime example such a success story. CMIM is a financial arrangement among the finance ministries and central banks of ASEAN+3 countries together with the Hong Kong Monetary Authority. ASEAN+3 is a forum that coordinates cooperation among the ten member countries of the Association of Southeast Asian Nations (ASEAN)[1] and the three Northeast Asian nations of China, Japan and South Korea (the +3). CMIM is aimed to set up to be a regional mechanism that provides financial support to members in crisis times.

As mentioned earlier, this book will delve into the processes of international negotiations. However, the bargaining dynamics of financial cooperation in the context of East Asia have so far been under-examined in the recent literatures. Most extant studies tend to examine factors that *initiated* East Asian financial cooperation (Rajan 2002; Grimes: 2009; Sohn 2005; Sohn 2007), or suggests ways to enhance the *functioning of certain regional mechanisms* such as Chiang Mai Initiative (CMI) and Chiang Mai Initiative Multilateralization (CMIM) (Kawai 2005; Kawai and Houser 2007; Sussangkarn and Vichyanond 2007). Another line of research attempts to explain negotiation outcomes by relying on *the three traditional levels of analysis in the field of International Relations* (Waltz 1959; for examples, see Sohn 2005; Grimes 2006). This research strand does shed some useful insights, but its explanatory power is somewhat limited. This is mainly because the three levels of analysis can at best set a wide range of possible outcomes, but they are unable to determine which choice states finally selected among the possible options to evade bargaining deadlock. In short, what has been lacking in the recent literature regarding East Asian financial coopera-tion is a study of micro-processes, namely analysing bargaining strategies and tactics negotiators use to achieve agreement outcomes. Such scholarship neglect yields substantive practical implications. Without knowledge concerning bar-gaining dynamics, negotiators may not know how to break a negotiation logjam or save the talk from falling apart, which can obstruct efforts to further regional cooperation.

Unlike these previous studies, this book will fill important intellectual gaps by examining the making of the CMIM agreement through the lens of bargaining strategies and tactics, which can provide lessons for policy makers to enhance financial cooperation in East Asia and other regions. To tell the story of how states employed such strategies and tactics to prevent negotiation failure, this study chooses to focus on the Chiang Mai Initiative Multilateralization (CMIM).

The case of the Chiang Mai Initiative Multilateralization (CMIM)

Speaking about East Asian financial cooperation, CMIM comes to mind. The mechanism is significant to East Asian financial cooperation mainly because it is the most advanced form of such cooperation to date, containing several new fea-tures that have never been adopted by the regional states previously. For example, CMIM sets up a regional fund to provide its members with financial or "liquidity" support in crisis times. Second, it set up an independent surveillance unit called the ASEAN+3 Macroeconomic Research Office (AMRO) which oversees the members' economies. Third, CMIM is the first time that regional states agreed to use a weighted-voting system to govern the decision-making processes, namely the decision to disburse financial assistance to borrowers. The adoption of a weighted-voting system was unprecedented in the history of East Asian financial cooperation. As one expert puts it,

> One of the most striking innovations of CMIM is the introduction of weight voting for lending decisions. This development has been exciting for [Asian Monetary Fund or] AMF proponents, who have long assumed that a voting procedure would be a necessary element of an autonomous regional funding mechanism.
>
> (Grimes 2011a: 95)

The fact that these new elements were included into the CMIM framework in turn enhances the importance of studying CMIM negotiations. Doing so, we can extract additional insights into how East Asian economic cooperation might evolve in the future as these features, such as the use of a weighted-voting system, may be applied into other regional agreements to come.

As CMIM contains significant new-fangled features never embraced by the regional states before, it bears a high risk of a negotiation collapse. It is because these stakeholders might be uncertain about how to handle such new details or clash over the issue which could ultimately break down the whole negotiation. Yet, against the odds, ASEAN+3 states in the end succeeded in concluding the deal. How did these countries managed to ride the turbulence and arrive at the most advanced financial agreement? Therefore, examining the CMIM negotiation will help shed light on a broader question: how do states with little prior experience at dealing with certain aspects of an agreement manage to avert a negotiation failure and successfully arrive at their final deal? In the sections and chapters that follow, this book will explore: (1) bargaining strategies and tactics that help break out of a bargaining deadlock, and (2) the conditions under which such strategies and tactics are likely (or not likely) to achieve the objective of avoiding bargaining failure. In other words, I will demonstrate that CMIM was neither created in a vacuum nor it could emerge naturally. Rather, the facility came into being because of these states' efforts to prevent a potential stalemate. The success of such arrangement is a product of various strategies and tactics employed by the involved negotiators.

Members' financial contributions and their voting power

Although the making of the CMIM agreement involved negotiations over several aspects, this study chooses to primarily focus on the two issues of members' financial contributions and voting power. They were chosen because the conclusion of CMIM negotiations largely hinged on whether states succeeded in cutting their deals on these components. As one source highlights, the participants regarded these matters as the most important under negotiation and bargained hard accordingly (Henning 2009; Rathus 2010).

One may wonder, what makes the two features of members' financial contribution and vote shares so significant that the life and death of the whole CMIM negotiation leaned on them? This was because financial contributions and voting power are linked. Some of the countries' vote shares are proportionally calculated based on the amount of contributions they make to the CMIM reserve pool. States contributing more to the CMIM fund have a larger share of votes, which can be used to influence certain decisions such as approving financial support to crisis economies. The CMIM votes can also be used to extend states' clout beyond the facility itself. For example, the members with greater voting power may force their counterparts requesting to borrow from the CMIM mechanism to make certain concessions in other areas outside the CMIM (e.g. trade) in exchange the former's votes to approve the lending. Unsurprisingly, "[i]t took a long time before the amount of contributions from the various countries in the current CMIM can be agreed upon, as the contributions are related to the weight, and hence influence, of the country in the CMIM" (Sussangkarn 2011b: 14).

It should be noted that although the centre of this study was on examining how the CMIM members arrived at their contribution amounts and voting power, I will also explore how bargained to arrive at some other CMIM aspects, namely the decision to multilateralize CMI and the selection of the first director of the ASEAN+3 Macroeconomic Research Office (AMRO). These additional intellectual exercises are purposed to shed further shed light on the negotiation processes of East Asian financial cooperation.

History of the Chiang Mai Initiative Multilateralization (CMIM)

Cooperation in East Asia is not a new phenomenon. However, the process of regional financial cooperation does not have a long historical mileage because it did not actually begin until the late 1990s. Before this period, the governments exhibited little interest in such cooperation at a region-wide level. For example, ASEAN was initially aimed to be a security organization, with a focus on dealing with international security issues such as the impacts of the Vietnam War on the region. Economic cooperation, including the area of finance, was not the organization's original main focus.

The 1997–1998 Asian financial crisis (AFC) fostered a new interest in East Asian cooperation as the event exposed the vulnerability of the region's banking and financial systems, which "seemed to suggest that the cost of defending diverse national currencies was, for most regional governments, becoming too high to bear" (Cohen 2003: 285). The AFC started in Thailand after its central bank's attempt to defend the value of the country's currency, the baht, against market speculations failed. It was at first viewed that the problem would be contained within Thailand and did not spread. However, the opposite occurred. The contagion soon swept the region. The collapse of the Thai baht in July 1997 triggered a financial panic leading to a series of currency devaluations in other East Asian economies. Bangkok resorted to the International Monetary Fund (IMF) for liquidity assistance and was put under the Fund's programme in August. Thailand's financial turmoil sent out repercussions and put pressure on the Indonesian rupiah and South Korean won. Both countries soon found themselves walking on the same path as Thailand. Jakarta and Seoul eventually got financial help from IMF in November and December 1997, respectively. For those countries that did not resort to the IMF facilities, they too experienced severe economic downturn or recessions. The Asia's financial meltdown in the late 1990s heightened the realization of economic interdependency that "East Asian economies were inextricably linked to each other and could not afford to ignore what was happening elsewhere within the region" (Sussangkarn 2011a). Therefore, it became necessary for regional states to pursue financial cooperation for the purpose of preventing and/or managing such crises in the future.

Another reason why the idea of regional financial cooperation gained a momentum in East Asia was due to the effects of the IMF rescue packages on the regional economies. The programmes were mainly crafted by the Fund, with major influence of the US Federal Reserve and Treasury. East Asia viewed that Washington was to some degree behind the IMF's bailouts and hence the conditionality details reflect certain US interests.

The IMF imposed on the borrowing states the conditionalities which was heavily criticized as ill-suited for East Asia. For example, Jeffery Sachs (1997) discriminated the East Asian crisis from the previous ones where the problem was triggered by the actions of the public sector, namely governments with budget deficits choosing to print out money to finance themselves. Hence, the IMF's former "patients" were characterized by inflation with a weakening currency and foreign-reserve depletion. In contrast, East Asia's experience was quite different. In regard to Indonesia, Malaysia, the Philippines and Thailand, the governments had been doing well before the crisis. They usually ran budget surpluses, or even accumulating foreign reserves into their central bank's vault. The major culprit this time was actually the private sector which used short-term borrowing to fund its long-term investment in non-exporting sectors such as real estate. Therefore, the same bailouts of slashing the budget deficit and imposing restrictions on a central bank's lending to the public sector could not be applied to these economies. Sachs (1997) then concluded that the Fund's structural adjustment programme was indeed "the wrong medicine for Asia."

In sum, the IMF-championed policies turned out to be wrong-headed. As a result, the situations in countries such as Thailand and Indonesia were exacerbated. Their market confidence worsened and their economies faced recessions. The Fund's ignorance of different situations in East Asia ultimately came back to hurt itself. Not only that the "one size fits all" approach undermined its programmes' effectiveness, the IMF's reputation and legitimacy were jeopardized. As one expert posits, a "nation's desperate need for short-term financial help does not give the IMF the moral right to substitute its technical judgments for the outcomes of the nation's political process" (Feldstein 1998). Some East Asian governments also felt that the developed countries, namely the USA, had behaved opportunistically by taking advantage of the IMF's conditionalities to purchase local banking and industrial assets at discounted prices (Phongpaichit and Baker 2004: 8–9). In short, AFC and its aftermaths gave East Asian states a strong impetus to pursue regional financial cooperation and build more effective lender-of-last-resort facilities of their own.[2]

As a result, a series of regional initiatives has been rolled out since AFC. In September 1997 at the Group of Seven (G-7) meeting in Hong Kong, China, the Ministry of Finance of Japan proposed the establishment of what was considered to be an "Asian Monetary Fund" (AMF), which would have served as a reserve pool which funds could draw upon to sustain their economies in crisis. This entity, if comes into fruition, would have involved Japan, China, Hong Kong, South Korea, Indonesia, Malaysia, Singapore, Thailand, the Philippines and Australia.

But, the AMF turned out to be a stillborn. One reason was due to the inappropriate timing of the proposal. The idea came in when AFC had widely spread. The Philippines and Indonesia already floated their currencies. These were also some controversies "over a proposal to significantly reform the structural dynamics of the international financial institutions" (Lipscy 2003: 94). Other factors explaining why the AMF project failed to take off included Washington's and IMF's opposition and China's withholding of support (Altbach 1997).

Washington's opposition was partly based on the ground that the AMF's membership excluded itself, and the original draft contended that the facility would not need to coordinate with the Fund (Lipscy 2003: 95). In contrast, the absence of China's backing was explained by the fact that Beijing was not consulted by Japan and did not have an idea of AMF-like mechanisms at that time.[3] This was partially because the time when the AMF idea came was at the height of China's negotiations to join the World Trade Organization (WTO) (Amyx 2005). The AMF proposal came during the 1990s which was when the Chinese elites' legitimacy was at stake. The policy makers hence viewed the country's accession to the WTO as necessary for the regime's survival which could only be sustained by the foundations of long-term economic growth (Morrison 2000). Additionally, Beijing was also reported to suspect that the AMF was Tokyo's effort to forge its own hegemony in the region (Huotari 2012). For the reasons cited earlier, it came with no surprise that Tokyo's proposal was quickly dismissed.

The failure to launch the AMF did not prevent East Asia's pursuit of regional alternative mechanisms to address the crisis. Another regional initiative named the Manila Framework was coined at the Meeting of Asian Finance and Central Bank Deputies in Manila, the Philippines on 18–19 November 1997. It was later endorsed at the Finance Ministers' Meetings of ASEAN, Australia, China, Hong Kong, Japan, South Korea and US, in Kuala Lumpur, Malaysia, on 2 December 1997 (APEC 1997). The framework aimed to achieve four objectives: (1) creating a regional economic surveillance mechanism to complement the IMF's global surveillance; (2) enhancing cooperation in strengthening domestic financial systems and regulatory mechanisms; (3) strengthening the IMF's capacity to respond to financial crises; and (4) supplementing the IMF's resources. However, this mechanism fell short of addressing regional financial issues. For instance, it did not help alleviate the situations in Indonesia and South Korea. Meeting twice a year to review the economic development issues was insufficient to monitor financial crisis conditions. Moreover, the entity was weak on surveillance, as it had no permanent secretariat. In their report, a study group on "Economic Surveillance and Policy Dialogue in East Asia" noted that without a "secretariat and board members from outside the region . . . [the Framework is] not suitable for the region" (IIMA 2005: 3). Hence, this entity eventually met its demise. The Manila Framework ceased to exist in 2004.

The day 15 December 1997 marked another historical milestone in East Asian financial cooperation. The Southeast and Northeast Asian countries convened the 9th ASEAN Summit in Kuala Lumpur, Malaysia and the ASEAN+3 was born. At the 1st ASEAN+3 Summit, the leaders discussed the future of East Asian development and cooperation. The major outcomes under the ASEAN+3 cooperation include the Chiang Mai Initiative (CMI), the Asian Bond Markets Initiative (ABMI),[4] and the Economic Review and Policy Dialogue (ERPD).[5] The structure of ASEAN+3 financial cooperation is summarized in Figure 1.1.

The Chiang Mai Initiative (CMI) was a logical response to the shortcomings surfacing during the AFC. A consensus at that time was that the success of speculative attacks on the currencies of regional states triggering AFC was due to the fact the affected countries' foreign-exchange reserves were insufficient to cope with capital outflows. As a result, ASEAN+3 agreed to develop a regional mechanism that would supply money to crisis economies. Consequently, the CMI was formed on 6 May 2000 at the ASEAN+3 Finance Ministers' Meeting (AFMM+3) in Chiang Mai, Thailand. According to the Joint Statement, the governments

> recognized a need to establish a regional financing arrangement to supplement the existing international facilities . . . [and] agreed to strengthen the existing cooperative frameworks among [their] monetary authorities through the "Chiang Mai Initiative." The Initiative involves an expanded ASEAN Swap Arrangement that would include ASEAN countries.

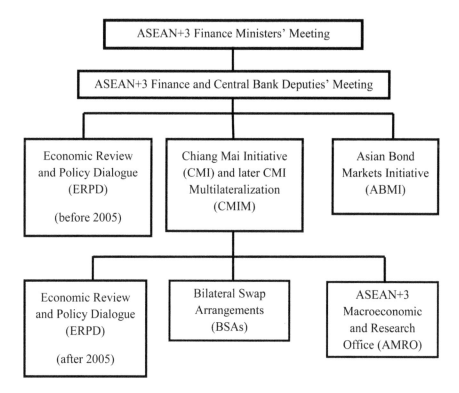

Figure 1.1 ASEAN+3 financial cooperation structure

As stated earlier, CMI was constructed to support the existing facilities, such as the IMF. As a result, the idea was welcomed by the USA and Fund. As Deputy Secretary of State Richard Armitage expressed Washington's approval of this regional initiative (Central Banking Publications 2001). The IMF also gave its "green light," praising that the region's determination to work with the Fund (Fischer 2001; Henning 2002).

Moreover, unlike the stillborn AFC, China lent its enthusiastic support to the CMI project for the following reasons (Jiang 2010: 609). First, thanks to the flexible nature of CMI, Beijing deemed that its participation would unlikely jeopardize its own sovereignty. As the CMI's swap contracts were to be negotiated bilaterally between lenders and borrowers, China felt that it needed not to compromise its own interests when joining CMI (Jiang 2010: 611). Moreover, the country during that time was more worried about Washington's influence in the region than Tokyo's (Rapkin 2001). What drove Beijing's concern was the 1999 US involvement in Kosovo. This incident left the former with a feeling that the latter was being more aggressive which could potentially undermine certain Beijing's interests (Bowles 2002). On the contrary, China became less against Japan's roles in regional financial cooperation, reflecting that the positive-sum view of financial cooperation began to replace the previous zero-sum mindset (Sohn 2008).

CMI's main purpose was to provide liquidity assistance through a network of currency swaps. A currency swap is a contract to "exchange [a credit line] for another and to reverse the transaction at a date in the future" (Henning, 2002: 16). It should be highlighted that swap arrangements are different from loans because the former are exchanges of assets and have no collaterals. The CMI's swap arrangements consisted of two main elements: an expanded version of the pre-existing ASEAN swap arrangements (ASAs),[6] and a new network of bilateral swap arrangements (BSAs) between ASEAN countries and the +3 nations. The size of the ASAs[7] was expanded from US$ 200 million to US$ 1 billion in 2000, and to US$ 2 billion in 2005.

The BSAs usually take a form of swap networks between the US dollars and local currencies of participating countries. As of 2009, 19 BSAs had been negotiated. After eliminating double-counting,[8] the total net amount was approximately US$ 60 billion (Henning 2009: 2–3). However, some amount available to the CMI borrowers was tied to the IMF program. For example, at the 3rd AFMM+3 in May 2001, it was agreed that 90 per cent of the amount of financial assistance would require an IMF agreement as a precondition while the other 10 per cent (the so-called "IMF de-linked portion") would not. In other words, member countries could draw from the facility up to the 10 per cent of the agreed amounts without accepting an IMF program. However, the remaining 90 per cent would be disbursed only when the borrower accepted the Fund's conditionalities. In May 2005, at the 8th AFMM+3, the finance ministers decided to increase the de-linked portion from 10 to 20 per cent. Again in May 2012, it was increased to 30 per cent. Owing to the IMF linkage, the money available for actual lending may not be as large as the swap size appeared to be, especially when countries do not sign on to the IMF package.[9]

Beside setting up a network of bilateral currency swaps, CMI also addresses the issue of surveillance. In May 2005, the finance ministers agreed to incorporate the ASEAN+3 Economic Review and Policy Dialogue (ERPD) into the CMI framework to perform surveillance functions such as assessing global, regional and national economic conditions, monitoring capital flows and currency markets and analysing the macroeconomic and financial risks in the region.

Despite major developments, CMI contains particular shortcomings, leading critics to doubt the mechanism's ability to manage and prevent a crisis. Some major limitations included modest liquidity amount made available, high IMF dependence and inefficient conduct of swap arrangements (Asami 2005; Sussangkarn 2011b). For instance, the IMF linkage meant that less than half of the borrowed amount would be immediately accessible by crisis economies, while the rest would be released after the borrowers accepted the IMF package. "In general, IMF programmes are not negotiated until crisis has already occurred" (Sohn 2007: 3). This means that once the agreement with the Fund was in place, the financial help might come in too late to manage the crisis, undermining the CMI's main purpose.

Another limitation lies in the inadequacy of the liquidity assistance provided by CMI. As John Ravenhill (2002: 187) points out, the facility might fail to serve as a source for alternative bailouts because its swap lines unmatched the reality. Although this might be hard to assess, the estimation of CMI's capacity could be gauged by looking that the scale of liquidity assistance the crisis countries sought during AFC. Take Thailand for example. Bangkok in 1997 needed US$ 17 billion to cope with its economic turmoil. If this event occurred after the CMI was formed, Bangkok would be able to secure only US$ 7 billion from the mechanism, clearly far from the amount it needed. Also, the ASEAN+3 monitoring mechanism, the ERPD, merely served as an information-exchanging platform, and was tainted with feeble peer review with policy coordination (Menon 2012).

Furthermore, because CMI borrowers had to negotiate separate swap contracts with each of its lenders individually, if the lenders demanded different contract terms and conditions, concluding the swaps might take longer and the borrowers might not be able to get money to sustain their economies in time. In short, bilateral negotiations might end up being laborious and obstructing quick disbursements of financial support. As a result, CMI would cease to be an efficient mechanism.

Aiming to address the CMI's weaknesses, ASEAN+3 countries decided to upgrade the mechanism into CMIM. For example, the 9th AFMM+3 in May 2006 set up a task force to explore the modalities of multilateralizing CMI. With inputs from the task force, ASEAN+3 governments decided to multilateralize CMI at the 10th AFMM+3 in Kyoto, Japan in May 2007. The Joint Statement states that ASEAN+3

> unanimously agreed in principle that a self-managed reserve pooling arrangement governed by a single contractual agreement is an appropriate form of multilateralisation . . . [and] instructed the Deputies to carry out further in-depth studies on the key elements of the multilateralisation of the CMI

including surveillance, reserve eligibility, size of commitment, borrowing quota and activation mechanism.

Comparisons: CMI vs CMIM

The difference between CMI and CMIM swap arrangements are outlined in Figure 1.2.

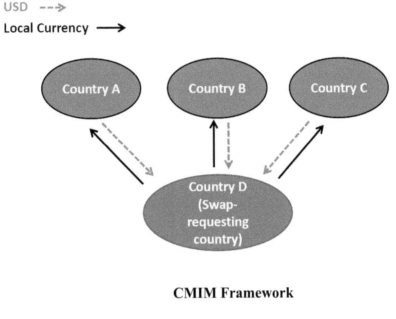

CMIM Framework

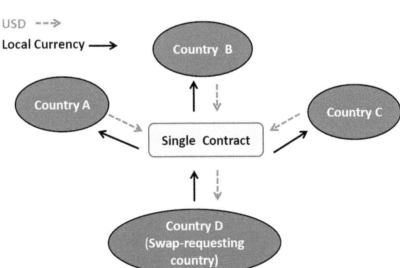

Figure 1.2 CMI vs CMIM framework

As shown previously, under the CMI framework, Country D (or a swap-requesting/borrowing country) had to conclude separate swap contracts with each of the three lending states. By contrast, under the CMIM agreement, Country D can conclude a single contract with all the lenders at once.

It should be highlighted that according to the Kyoto agreement, CMIM as a "reserve pool" does not result in real transfer of foreign reserves from the members' vaults to a central pool. Members by and large had authority to manage the fund. As Henning (2009: 4) noted, "the phrase 'self-managed' qualifies 'reserves' [means] that the reserves would not in fact be physically collected in a common fund but would instead be held and earmarked by national central banks." Instead, cooperation under the CMIM took a form of capital commitment.

After the Kyoto meeting, the ASEAN+3 governments began negotiating the key aspects of the agreement. For example, they decided in May 2008 that the CMIM reserve pool was to be at least US\$ 80 billion and the proportion between the contributions of the +3 and ASEAN states was to be 80:20.

The 2008 global financial crisis (GFC) did accelerate the CMIM development. Even though the GFC has not put CMIM into a real test because South Korea and Singapore did not tap on the mechanisms' resources but instead turned to secure their liquidity support via bilateral credit swaps with the People's Bank of China, Bank of Japan and the US Federal Reserve. Nevertheless, the GFC bolstered the advancement of East Asian as it pressed regional states to immediately launch the CMIM (Wheatly 2009).

Against the backdrop of global economic downturn, the governments convened at the Special AFMM+3 in February 2009, which was three months before the usual AFMM+3 took place in May 2009. ASEAN+3 decided to take concrete actions to further enhance CMIM to ensure regional market confidence and stability. For example, the members decided to expand the CMIM size from US\$ 80 to US\$ 120 billion. The meeting also agreed to establish an independent regional surveillance unit (later named the "ASEAN+3 Macroeconomic Research Office") to monitor the members' policy behaviour and economic development and support the decision making. Moreover, the ASEAN+3 countries pledged for further reducing the IMF de-linked portion "after the above surveillance mechanism becomes fully effective in its function" (ASEAN+3 2009a).

The 12th AFMM+3 took place in Bali, Indonesia in May 2009, in which ASEAN+3 states "reached agreement on all the main components of the CMIM, including the individual country's contribution, borrowing accessibility and the surveillance mechanism." (. The focus of the discussions had shifted from determining the distributions of members' contributions and voting power towards the operational phase of CMIM, as the finance ministers tasked the "Deputies to work out the operation details and implementation plan, particularly the legal documents that will govern the CMIM" (ASEAN+3 2009b).

It should be emphasized that at the Bali meeting, only major elements of the CMIM agreement were settled. The process of working out the other CMIM details took about eight months after the talk. Finally, on 24 December 2009, the members signed the CMIM agreement. CMIM officially entered into force on 24 March 2010.

After CMIM was in operation, some of the agreement details were altered. The ASEAN5 countries – Indonesia, Malaysia, Philippines, Singapore and Thailand – made some contribution adjustments among themselves at the 13th AFMM+3 in Tashkent, Uzbekistan in May 2010. In addition, the members agreed on all the key elements of the CMIM's independent surveillance unit called the ASEAN+3 Macroeconomic Research Office (AMRO). In the following year, the AMRO started its operation in Singapore on 1 May 2011. The surveillance unit's main tasks include monitoring the ASEAN+3 economies, facilitating the early detecting of risks and problems and supporting CMIM decision-making process.

On 4 May 2011, another AFMM+3 was convened in Hanoi, Vietnam. At the meeting, the ASEAN+3 countries endorsed the "Operational Guidelines for Enhancing Effectiveness of CMIM" outlining how swap arrangements are conducted. The idea of creating crisis-prevention measures was also seriously considered. This emerged from the rationale that financial instability in certain countries can be prevented from spreading to other states or escalating into a full-blown regional-wide crisis. As a result, the Deputies were tasked "to initiate a study on the design of a possible crisis-prevention function for CMIM, including the size" (ASEAN+3 2011).

In May 2012, the 15th ASEAN+3 Finance Ministers and Central Bank Governors' Meeting (AFMGM+3) convened in Manila, the Philippines on 3 May 2012. At this meeting, some developments were made in regards to the total CMIM size, IMF-delinked portion, the length of the renewal of the borrowed amounts and the crisis-prevention mechanism. For example, the fund size was expanded to US$ 240 billion and the de-linked part was raised to 30 per cent. In May 2013, at the 16th AFMGM+3 in Delhi, India, the ASEAN+3 governments agreed to transform AMRO into an international organization. On 10 October 2014, at the sideline meeting of the IMF/World Bank Group Annual Meetings in Washington, DC, USA, the CMIM members completed the signing of the "AMRO Agreement" which upgrades AMRO to an international organization (MOF Japan 2014).

A year later, in May 2014, the 17th AFMGM+3 announced that the "first full set of indicators of the "Economic Review and Policy Dialogue (ERPD) Matrix" which consists of various economic and financial indicators of all ASEAN+3 members" was created (ASEAN+3 2014). The Matrix was aimed to evaluate the members' qualification for utilizing the CMIM crisis-prevention mechanisms.

Table 1.1 presents some major CMI and CMIM outcomes and the meetings' chairs/co-chairs.

CMIM features

Before delving into the breakdowns of the members' financial contributions and voting power, it is worth-mentioning that the CMIM agreement also outlines other important features.

Table 1.1 Selected major outcomes of CMI/CMIM and chairs/co-chairs

Dates	Events	Negotiation Outcomes	Chairs/Co-chairs
6 May 2000	The 2nd ASEAN+3 Finance Ministers' Meeting (Chiang Mai, Thailand)	The Chiang Mai Initiative (CMI) was formed.	H. E. Pehin Orang Kaya Laila Wijaya Dato Haji Abdul Aziz Umar, Minister representing the Ministry of Finance, Brunei Darussalam
9 May 2001	The 3rd ASEAN+3 Finance Ministers' Meeting (Honolulu, USA)	The finance ministers agreed that 90 per cent of each bilateral swap line required the IMF loan agreement as a precondition, while the other 10 per cent did not.	H. E. Tun Daim Zainuddin, Finance Minister, Malaysia
15 May 2004	The 4th ASEAN+3 Finance Ministers' Meeting (Jeju, Korea)	The finance ministers agreed to explore the ways of enhancing the effectiveness of CMI.	H. E. Mr Lim Hng Kiang, Minister in the Prime Minister's Office and second Minister for Finance, Singapore
4 May 2005	The 8th ASEAN+3 Finance Ministers' Meeting (Istanbul, Turkey)	The finance ministers agreed to enhance the CMI's effectiveness, such as by integrating the ASEAN+3 surveillance mechanism into the CMI, concluding new swap contracts and raising the IMF-delinked portion from 10 to 20 per cent. The governments also "tasked the Deputies to study the various possible routes towards multilateralizing the CMI."	H. E. Chansy Phosikham, Minister of Finance of Lao PDR
4 May 2006	The 9th ASEAN+3 Finance Ministers' Meeting (Hyderabad, India)	The Deputies were tasked to form a "new task force" to further study modalities towards multilateralization.	Senior Minister Keat Chhon, Minister of Economy and Finance of the Kingdom of Cambodia

(Continued)

Table 1.1 Continued

Dates	Events	Negotiation Outcomes	Chairs/Co-chairs
5 May 2007	The 10th ASEAN+3 Finance Ministers' Meeting (Kyoto, Japan)	The members "unanimously agreed in principle that a self-managed reserve pooling arrangement governed by a single contractual agreement is an appropriate form of multilateralisation."	H. E. Chalongphob Sussangkarn, Minister of Finance of the Kingdom of Thailand and H. E. Jin Renqing, Minister of Finance of the People's Republic of China
4 May 2008	The 11th ASEAN+3 Finance Ministers' Meeting (Madrid, Spain)	The finance ministers agreed the proportion of the amount of CMIM contribution between the +3 and ASEAN to be 80:20.	H. E. Vu Van Ninh, Minister of Finance of the Socialist Republic of Viet Nam and H. E. Fukushiro Nukaga, Minister of Finance of Japan
12 February 2009	Special ASEAN+3 Finance Ministers' Meeting (Phuket, Thailand)	The finance ministers agreed to increase the size of CMIM from US$ 80 to US$ 120 billion. It was also agreed to set up an independent regional surveillance mechanism and work on the future reduction of the IMF de-link portion after such surveillance mechanism "becomes fully effective in its function."	H. E. Korn Chatikavanij, Minister of Finance of Thailand and H. E. Jeung-hyun Yoon, Minister of Strategy and Finance of the Republic of Korea
3 May 2009	The 12th ASEAN+3 Finance Ministers' Meeting (Bali, Indonesia)	The finance ministers agreed on all CMIM main components, including the individual country's contribution. Within ASEAN5, Indonesia, Malaysia, Singapore and Thailand contributed US$ 4.77 billion each, while the Philippines contributed US$ 3.68 billion. The Deputies were instructed to work out the operational details and implementation plan for CMIM unit he finance ministers also welcomed Hong Kong's participation in CMIM.	H. E. Korn Chatikavanij, Minister of Finance of Thailand and H. E. Jeung-hyun Yoon, Minister of Strategy and Finance of the Republic of Korea

Date	Event	Ministers
28 December 2009 24 March 2010		The CMIM agreement was signed. The CMIM entered into force.
2 May 2010	The 13th ASEAN+3 Finance Ministers' Meeting (Tashkent, Uzbekistan)	The contributions of Indonesia, Malaysia, the Philippines, Singapore and Thailand were adjusted for them to contribute equally to CMIM. The finance ministers agreed on all key elements of the regional surveillance unit called "ASEAN+3 Macroeconomic Research Office (AMRO)."	H. E. Vu Van Ninh, Minister of Finance of the Socialist Republic of Viet Nam and H. E. Xie Xuren, Minister of Finance of the People's Republic of China
1 May 2011 4 May 2011	The 14th ASEAN+3 Finance Ministers' Meeting (Ha Noi, Vietnam)	AMRO started its operation in Singapore. The finance ministers endorsed the "Operational Guidelines for Enhancing Effectiveness of CMIM" and "instructed the Deputies to initiate a study on the design of a possible crisis-prevention function for CMIM."	H. E. Agus D. W. Martowardojo, Minister of Finance of the Republic of Indonesia and H.E. Yoshihiko Noda, Minister of Finance of Japan
4 May 2012	The 15th ASEAN+3 Finance Ministers and Central Bank Governors' Meeting (Manila, the Philippines)	The members increased the size of CMIM from US$ 120 to US$ 240 billion, increased the IMF de-linked portion to 30 per cent, lengthened the maturity and supporting period for the IMF linked and de-linked portions, and introduced a crisis-prevention facility called "CMIM Precautionary Line (CMIM-PL)."	H. E. Keat Chhon, Deputy Prime Minister and Minister of Economy and Finance of the Kingdom of Cambodia, and H. E. Bahk, Jaewan, Minister of Strategy and Finance of the Republic of Korea

(*Continued*)

Table 1.1 Continued

Dates	Events	Negotiation Outcomes	Chairs/Co-chairs
3 May 2013	The 16th ASEAN+3 Finance Ministers and Central Bank Governors' Meeting (Delhi, India)	ASEAN+3 agreed to transform AMRO into an international organization and reached consensus on the draft of "AMRO Agreement." The governments tasked the Deputies to continue working on the CMIM Operational Guidelines.	H. E. Pehin Dato Abd Rahman Ibrahim, Minister of Finance II at the Prime Minister's Office of Brunei Darussalam, and H. E. Zhu Guangyao, Vice Minister of Finance of the People's Republic of China
3 May 2014	The 17th ASEAN+3 Finance Ministers and Central Bank Governors' Meeting (Astana, Kazakhstan)	The development of the first full set of indicators of the "Economic Review and Policy Dialogue (ERPD) Matrix" was finished. The Deputies were tasked to continue developing the Matrix and ponder how it "will be used to assess a member's qualification for the CMIM crisis-prevention facility."	H. E. U Win Shein, Union Minister of the Ministry of Finance of the Republic of the Union of Myanmar, and H. E. Taro Aso, Deputy Prime Minister and Minister of Finance and Minister of State for Financial Services, Japan
10 October 2014	A sideline meeting of the Annual Meetings of the International Monetary Fund and the World Bank Group (Washington, DC, USA)	The AMRO Agreement was signed.	
3 May 2015	The 18th ASEAN+3 Finance Ministers and Central Bank Governors' Meeting (Baku, Azerbaijan)	The governments welcomed the strengthening of CMIM Operational Guidelines such as conducting Test Runs and peace-time preparation exercises, and assigned the Deputies, in cooperation with AMRO, to continue working on these exercises. The members also encouraged AMRO to cooperate with other relevant international financial institutions.	H. E. Dato' Seri Ahmad Husni Hanadzlah, Minister of Finance II of Malaysia, and H. E. Kyunghwan Choi, Deputy Prime Minister and Minister of Strategy and Finance of Korea

Sources: Joint Ministerial Statements of AFMM+3 and ASEAN+3 Finance Ministers and Central Bank Governors' Meetings

Size of the pool

The CMIM size had been expanded a few times since its inception. In 2008, the total size was agreed to be at least US$ 80 billion. In 2009 and 2013 the members decided to increase the total size of the CMIM pool to US$ 120 billion and US$ 240 billion respectively.

Purchasing multiples

The borrowed amount is determined by a "purchasing multiple" or a number used to multiply with the members' contributions to calculate the maximum amount they could borrow. The multiples determine the actual quota each member can borrow from the CMIM fund. Each CMIM member could draw from the CMIM fund up to the predetermined multiples of the amount it contributes.

As Table 1.2 illustrates, the multiples are higher for those contributing less to CMIM. For example, China's and Japan's borrowing multiple is 0.5, meaning that they can borrow up to only half of their financial contributions. In contrast, the borrowing multiple of Cambodia, Lao People's Democratic Republic, Myanmar, Vietnam and Brunei (CLMVB)[10] is 5.0, which allows these countries to borrow five times as much as their contributions. One explanation behind this set-up was that CMIM aimed to help out countries which are likely to require financial assistance during the crisis.

Table 1.2 The CMIM purchasing multiples (by member)

Members		Financial Contribution (billion USD)		Purchasing Multiple	Maximum Swap Amount (billion USD)
China	China (excluding Hong Kong, China)	76.80	68.40	0.5	34.20
	Hong Kong, China		8.40	2.5	6.30
Japan		76.80		0.5	38.40
Korea		38.40		1	38.40
Plus 3		**192**			**117.30**
Indonesia		9.104		2.5	22.76
Thailand		9.104		2.5	22.76
Malaysia		9.104		2.5	22.76
Singapore		9.104		2.5	22.76
Philippines		9.104		2.5	22.76
Vietnam		2.00		5	10.00
Cambodia		0.24		5	1.20
Myanmar		0.12		5	3.20
Brunei		0.06		5	3.20
Lao PDR		0.06		5	3.20
ASEAN		**48**			**126.20**
Total		**240**			**243.50**

Source: The Joint Statement of the 15th ASEAN+3 Finance Ministers and Central Bank Governors' Meeting, May 2012

IMF linkage

The IMF de-linked portion is the amount the borrower can draw from the CMIM facility without being put under the IMF programme. This de-linked part was initially set to be 10 per cent under the CMI framework. That meant the members could draw up to the 10 per cent of the agreed amounts without being put under the IMF program. In February 2009 and May 2012, the de-linked part was enlarged to 20 and 30 per cent respectively.

Decision-making structures and procedures

1. CMIM decision-making bodies

CMIM decision-making structure consists of two tiers: ministerial-level decision-making body (MLDMB) and executive-level decision-making body (ELDMB).

a. Ministerial-level decision-making body (MLDMB)

MLDMB consists of ASEAN+3 Finance Ministers. The entity makes decisions on policies and sets the framework of CMIM fundamental issues such as the size of the CMIM reserve pool, and members' contributions and voting power. These issues are determined by consensus. It should be emphasized that the CMIM agreement excluded the Monetary Authority of Hong Kong, China from MLDMB. Thus, Hong Kong cannot cast votes on the fundamental issues.

b. Executive-level decision-making body (ELDMB)

In contrast to MLDMB, ELDMB consists of deputy-level officials of ASEAN+3 Finance Ministries and their central banks plus Monetary Authority of Hong Kong, China. ELDMB makes decisions on executive issues such as approving the disbursement of financial support and the renewals of borrowing terms. These issues are determined by a two-thirds (2/3) supermajority voting rule.

In ELDMB, if votes from finance ministry and central bank by one country are the same, it is counted as one vote from a country. If finance ministry and central bank of one country diverge on their vote, it is considered as no vote from a country. However, these rules are inapplicable to the Monetary Authority of Hong Kong, China. Hong Kong's vote must be combined with Beijing's vote and counted as a single vote from China.

2. Determination and activation processes

Because CMIM is purposefully set up to provide financial assistance to crisis economies, the processes of determination (i.e. approving the swap) and activation (i.e. actual disbursement of the fund) are among the most crucial steps under the agreement.

As Figure 1.3 illustrates, the determination and activation processes begin when a crisis country (or a swap-requesting country) lodges a swap request to coordinating countries. Coordinating countries refer to the two co-chairs of the AFDM+3 of a particular year (one from the ASEAN and the other from the +3 countries). It is agreed that two co-chairs automatically assume the role of coordinating countries under the CMIM framework. For coordinating countries by year, see Table 1.3.

The coordinating countries, within two days after receiving the request, inform ELDMB about the request and supply the latter with other relevant information. ELDMB then undergoes a determination process. To decide whether to approve a disbursement, ELDMB reviews the economic situation of the requesting country based on relevant data such as the country's plans to cope with its problems and studies by regional surveillance units and international financial institutions.

During the determination process, CMIM members may opt out from participating in providing financial support to the crisis party by invoking an "escape clause." The Annex I of the Joint Ministerial Statement of the 13th AFMM+3 outlines conditions which an escape clause is allowed:

> In principle, each of the CMIM parties may only escape from contributing to a swap request by obtaining an approval of the Executive Level Decision Making Body. In exceptional cases such as an extraordinary event or instance of force majours and domestic legal limitations, escape is possible without obtaining ELDMB approval.

In other words, the members can use an escape clause under the following circumstances: (1) when a country is a swap-requesting country itself or is at risk of becoming a crisis country; (2) when a country faces national emergencies such as civil wars or natural disasters which render it unable to make financial contribution under the CMIM agreement; or (3) when a country has domestic legal limitations restricting contributions under the CMIM agreement. However, when countries use this clause, they in turn cannot vote in a determination process.

Table 1.3 Coordinating countries (by year)

Year	ASEAN	Plus-3
2009	Thailand	South Korea
2010	Vietnam	China
2011	Brunei	Japan
2012	Cambodia	South Korea
2013	Indonesia	China
2014	Laos PDR	Japan
2015	Malaysia	South Korea
2016	Myanmar	China
2017	Philippines	Japan
2018	Singapore	South Korea
2019	Thailand	China

Within two weeks after the determination process starts, ELDMB casts their votes. If 2/3 or more of the total votes are in favour of the swap, lending is approved. ELDMB then moves on to conduct the activation process of disbursing the fund to the requesting country. The respective amount will be disbursed transferred from the providing parties to the requesting ones, in accordance with the terms and pro rata allocation provided in the CMIM agreement. This process is to be completed within one week after reaching the voting results.

Surveillance mechanism

The agreement also sets up the ASEAN+3 Macroeconomic Research Office (AMRO), which serves as the independent regional surveillance unit to support CMIM decision-making process. During peace times, the AMRO assesses and prepares reports on the macroeconomic situations of individual member economies and the ASEAN+3 region as a whole. It also conducts annual consultations with member countries. During crisis times, the AMRO assists ELDMB by preparing recommendations on a swap request based on its macroeconomic analysis of a swap-requesting member. It also helps monitor the use of the funds once the swap request is approved. The AMRO was established as a company limited in Singapore in April 2011.

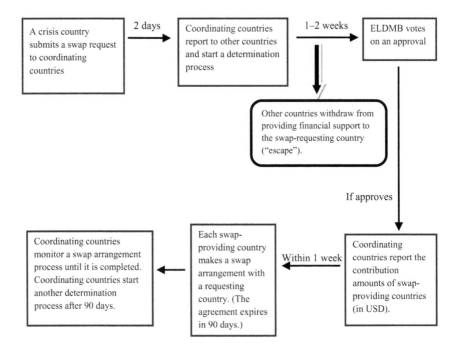

Figure 1.3 CMIM determination and activation processes

Breakdown of the members' financial contributions and voting power

Financial contributions to the CMIM fund take a form of a commitment letter whereby the members continue to manage their own reserves. Members' contributions would not result in an immediate deposit of the amounts to the CMIM pool and the amounts were to be held at national central banks and released when a currency swap occurs. In short, the implementation of the CMIM does not involved immediate depletion of members' reserves. Rather, the contributions are earmarked for use when needed.

The share of the reserve pool to be contributed by each member was determined on a *pro rata* basis or in relation to a formula that weighs several economic variables. The *pro rata* basis is commonly utilized to compute countries' contributions in several international organizations. For example, IMF members' quotas are calculated from a formula consisting of a variety of economic variables such as GDP per capita, the size of an economy and shares in regional trade.

The contribution ratio among the +3 (including Hong Kong) and ASEAN had not been adjusted since it was agreed in May 2008 at the 11th AFMM+3 in Madrid, Spain. According to the Joint Statement, the +3 (including Hong Kong) together would contribute 80 per cent of the total CMIM size while ASEAN would cover the rest 20 per cent.

Within the +3, China (including Hong Kong) and Japan would make equal contributions to the fund while South Korea would contribute half of the former's amounts. Within ASEAN, it was agreed that ASEAN5 would make more contributions to the CMIM pool than CLMVB countries.

Unlike the proportion, the absolute amount of members' contribution had been changed a few times during the negotiations. In 2009, to make up the total of US\$ 120 billion, the +3 was responsible to contribute US\$ 96 billion. ASEAN, on the other hand, was to together put in US\$ 24 billion. In 2012, the total CMIM size was doubled, and so as the members' absolute contributions. Hence, the +3 and ASEAN were to contribute US\$ 192 billion and US\$ 48 billion respectively.

The actual contribution amounts of ASEAN5 were also adjusted among themselves. In 2009, Indonesia, Malaysia, Singapore and Thailand was to each put in US\$ 4.77 billion. However, the Philippines was responsible for a lesser amount of US\$ 3.68 billion. The rest will come from CMLVB. In contrast, at the 13th AFMM+3 held in May 2010, the financial contributions of the ASEAN5 were aligned so that they will all make an equal contribution of US\$ 4.552 billion. This means the Philippines' amount increased from US\$ 3.68 to US\$ 4.552 billion. The contributions of Indonesia, Malaysia, Singapore and Thailand were hence reduced from US\$ 4.77 to US\$ 4.552 billion.

Each member's total votes consist of (1) basic votes and (2) votes based on contributions. Basic votes (3.2 votes) are given to all member (except Hong Kong), regardless of their contribution amount. In addition to basic votes, each member gets one vote per each US\$ 1 billion contributed. Regarding CMIM voting system, the members agreed to adopt a 'no veto' rule in which no one single party has power to block a collective decision on its own.

Table 1.4 The CMIM contribution and voting power distribution

Members	Financial Contribution		Basic Votes	Votes Based on Contribution	Total Voting Power	
	USD (billion)	(%)	(no. of votes)	(no. of votes)	(no. of votes)	(%)
China — China (excluding Hong Kong, China)	68.4 } 76.8	28.5 } 32	3.2 } 9.6	68.4	71.6 } 80	25.43
China — Hong Kong, China	8.4	3.5	0	8.4	8.4	2.98
Japan	76.8	32	3.2	76.8	80	28.41
Korea	38.4	16	3.2	38.4	41.6	14.77
Plus 3	**192**	**80**	**9.6**	**192**	**201.6**	**71.59**
Indonesia	9.104	3.793	3.2	9.104	12.304	4.369
Thailand	9.104	3.793	3.2	9.104	12.304	4.369
Malaysia	9.104	3.793	3.2	9.104	12.304	4.369
Singapore	9.104	3.793	3.2	9.104	12.304	4.369
Philippines	9.104	3.793	3.2	9.104	12.304	4.369
Vietnam	2	0.833	3.2	2	5.2	1.847
Cambodia	0.24	0.1	3.2	0.24	3.44	1.222
Myanmar	0.12	0.05	3.2	0.12	3.32	1.179
Brunei	0.06	0.025	3.2	0.06	3.26	1.158
Lao PDR	0.06	0.025	3.2	0.06	3.26	1.158
ASEAN	**48**	**20**	**32**	**48**	**80**	**28.41**
Total	**240**	**100**	**41.6**	**240**	**281.6**	**100**

Source: The Joint Statement of the 15th ASEAN+3 Finance Ministers and Central Bank Governors' Meeting, May 2012

Like the contribution amounts, members' absolute voting power was adjusted when the CMIM fund size was enlarged. For instance, the +3 (including Hong Kong) together used to have 100.80 votes in May 2010 when the total CMIM size stood at US$ 120 billion. However, their amounts doubled to 201.60 votes in 2012 when the CMIM size was raised to US$ 240 billion. Likewise, ASEAN countries together got 40 votes in 2010, but 80 votes in 2012.

It should be emphasized that although the members' absolute voting power was altered, the proportion of their votes remained the same since May in 2010. The +3 (including Hong Kong) together have 71.59 per cent of total votes, while ASEAN get the rest 28.41 per cent.

Among the +3, China (including Hong Kong) and Japan has equal percentage votes – 28.41 per cent of total CMIM votes each. China's votes come from Beijing (25.43 per cent of total CMIM votes) and Hong Kong (2.98 per cent of total CMIM votes). South Korea was able to get 14.77 per cent of total votes, which was half of what China and Japan secured. Within ASEAN, ASEAN5 each have 4.369 per cent of total votes. Vietnam, Cambodia, Myanmar, Brunei and Laos PDR have 1.847, 1.222, 1.179, 1.158 and 1.158 per cent of total votes, respectively.

With regard to determining executive decisions, at least two-thirds (2/3) super-majority vote from the deputy-level officials of ASEAN+3 finance ministries and central banks is required. For example, a decision to disburse financial support to the borrowers is approved when at least two-thirds or 66.67 per cent of total votes are in favour of approval. Hence, countries with larger vote shares can wield more influence over these decisions than the others with lesser voting power. The finance ministry and central bank of an individual country tend to vote the same which could be counted as votes from the country. However, in cases that ministry and central bank of one country vote differently, it is considered as no vote from a country. This rule is not applied to the Monetary Authority of Hong Kong, China. The number of Hong Kong's votes must be combined with those of Beijing and they together are counted as China's vote. Table 1.4 presents CMIM members' financial contributions and voting power.

Steps in dividing members' contributions and voting power

As earlier posited, members' contribution and voting power were contentious issues. How did the CMIM participants decide on the distributions of these elements among themselves and prevent the discussions over these matters from toppling the whole negotiation? The first step of splitting the members' contributions and vote share started with discussions between the +3 and ASEAN states to determine their contribution proportion. Then, each of the two groups – the +3 and ASEAN – held discussions among themselves to figure out how to divide up their individual contributions and voting power.[11]

Figure 1.4 depicts the steps of dividing the CMIM members' financial contributions and voting power. The numbers outside the parentheses denote members' financial contributions. The figures in the parentheses indicate the participants' vote shares.

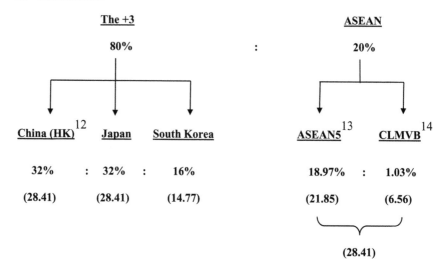

Figure 1.4 The steps of dividing members' contributions and voting power

Source: Author's illustration

Summary of the main findings

Through the analysis of the CMIM parties' actions during the negotiations, this book reveals that the members employed several strategies and tactics to help them prevent CMIM talks from collapsing and finally conclude the negotiations, as well as shape the agreement terms favourable to themselves.

First, states took advantage of a disparity in their sense of urgency to prevent a bargaining gridlock and bring the negotiation to a close. If the talks were to collapse, regional states would have lost a mechanism to provide financial support should another crisis erupt. This risk could create a sense of urgency for certain vulnerable states as it tempted them to reach an agreement at the current negotiation rather than wait for a settlement at subsequent rounds. This book uses the concept of a "discount rate" – how much one values the present vis-à-vis the future – as a proxy for the sense of urgency that stems from the risk of no settlement. An actor with a strong sense of urgency is considered to possess a high discount rate and vice versa.

A sense of urgency turned out to alter states' bargaining behaviour and outcomes. An actor with a strong sense of urgency (i.e. a high discount rate) values the present negotiations more than subsequent ones. As a result, he feels he cannot afford to wait longer and hence may accept an agreement at the present negotiation even if he has to make unilateral concessions to his opponents. By contrast, a player with a low sense of urgency (i.e. a low discount rate) assigns more value to future negotiations than the present one, and hence can afford to let a current round collapse in hopes of achieving better agreement terms in the future.

This study discloses that the +3 countries relied on the gap of a sense of urgency between themselves and ASEAN states to prolong negotiations and force the latter to conclude the deals with less favourable terms than the former. Also, a higher sense of urgency to conclude the CMIM agreement explains why South Korea eventually acquiesced to China and Japan to contribute to the CMIM pool less than the latter.

Second, the quality of an alternative course of action or a back-up plan that a player can pursue if no agreement is reached appears to have affected the CMIM terms. This book follows convention in using the term a "better alternative to no agreement" (batna) to refer to such alternative course of action. States with a better course of action or back-up plan are found to influence outcomes. For example, realizing that it possessed a better back-up plan than did South Korea, Japan was able to convince Seoul to make smaller contribution (and thus receive lesser voting power) than itself. Likewise, without an effective back-up plan available or a better solution than CMIM, Indonesia, Malaysia and Thailand felt obliged to make concessions to the other ASEAN states in order to prevent the negotiations from collapsing.

This study also finds that states with better information pertaining to the negotiations made use of informational advantage to unlock the negotiation stalemate. Informational advantage can be achieved in two ways: (1) by knowing other actors' preferences or (2) by knowing the issues being negotiated ("expertise"). Owing to their knowledge about other parties' preferences, states were able to develop or adjust their strategies and tactics accordingly which in turn salvaged the CMIM talks from collapsing. This study reveals that South Korea used this kind of knowledge to settle a China–Japan conflict over Hong Kong participation and shape the decision to distribution the CMIM contributions among the +3. States with better knowledge about issues being negotiated (expertise) can make their counterparts accept the validity of technical knowledge they provide. With greater expertise, these countries were able to reduce possible clashes that might arise and conclude the negotiations. The book's analysis reveals that by diligently study technical details such as the internal procedures of CMIM operations, the Japanese negotiators were able to enhance their expertise and then influence the overall negotiations. Similarly, resorting to professionals who excelled at writing legal documents helped South Korea reduce conflicts over the drafting process which might otherwise have tanked the negotiation.

Moreover, countries, via the position of a co-chair, could influence CMIM bargaining dynamics and outcomes. The analysis reveals, for example, that the South Korean co-chair, reconciled conflicts among the stakeholders and ultimately shaped the design of the two-thirds (2/3) supermajority voting system.

In addition, employing issue linkages enabled states to evade bargaining stalemate and conclude their CMIM deals. Linking issues were conducted by trading their concessions on specific agreement terms they cared less about in exchange for the others' concessions on matters that were more critical to them. For example, Japan strike a deal with China concerning Hong Kong inclusion into the CMIM by linking this issue with Beijing's financial contribution and vote shares. Moreover, as Tokyo relied less on Indonesia, Malaysia and Thailand in the areas of trade and investment than vice versa, it used its advantage economic relations to gain an upper hand in CMIM talks vis-à-vis the latter.

Finally, preventing a group from creating a coalition is found to have enhanced one country's influence over the others which in turn enabled it to conclude the negotiations. By choosing to side with neither China, Japan nor ASEAN but instead playing a role of a balancing player, South Korea successfully persuaded the former to accept its proposal of voting rules.

Overview of the book

The book is organized as follows. Chapter 2 introduces a conceptual framework which helps explain how countries prevent a negotiation from collapsing. Several bargaining strategies and tactics useful for evading a negotiation logjam and methodology are discussed. The findings are presented in the following four chapters reporting on the evidence to explain how each of the six countries (China, Japan, South Korea, Indonesia, Malaysia and Thailand) influenced the final outcomes. Country chapters were arranged for the purpose of highlighting how individual states' bargaining strategies and tactics enabling them to prevent the negotiation failure and steer outcomes in their favour. Chapter 3–5 presents the findings about the roles played by China, Japan and South Korea, respectively, in shaping the final agreement details. Chapter 6 reports on how Indonesia, Malaysia and Thailand managed to alter the CMIM results. This book concludes with Chapter 7, which revisits the research puzzles to show how the main findings shed some light on answering the questions. It also offers generalizable lessons for policy makers and scholars, particularly the implications of this research on the study and practice concerning the East Asian economic negotiation and cooperation. Suggestions for further research are also provided.

Notes

1 The ASEAN members are Brunei, Cambodia, Indonesia, Laos, Malaysia, Myanmar, the Philippines, Singapore, Thailand and Vietnam. The ASEAN was established on 8 August 1967 by Indonesia, Malaysia, the Philippines, Singapore and Thailand. Since then, membership has expanded to include Brunei, Myanmar, Cambodia, Laos and Vietnam.
2 For an entity to function as an international lender of last resort, it must be to provide liquidity quickly and in any amount on demand. A world central bank would be an example of an international lender of last resort.
3 Interview with C1, 13 May 2014.
4 The ABMI was aimed to develop efficient local-currency bond markets to enable both private and public sectors to raise and invest long-term capital in the region in order to alleviate a "double mismatch" problem. Double mismatch is composed of (1) maturity mismatch – a disparity between debt maturities as a result of using short term borrowing to finance long-term investments, and (2) currency mismatch – a mismatch between the denomination of debts as debts are denominated in foreign rather than local currencies (Balboa et al. 2007: 5). The double mismatch problem was considered to be a main culprit in the Asian financial crisis. East Asian economies invested a significant part of their savings in foreign currency-denominated assets, especially the US dollar-denominated

assets. They borrowed the money back in forms of short-term US dollar-denominated loans and bonds, and then directed the money to longer-term domestic investments which returns were in the local currencies. The use of short-term, foreign-currency-denominated liabilities as a financing source created a double mismatch problem.

5 The ERPD functions as a forum for information sharing and analyses financial and macroeconomic policies and conditions of the ASEAN+3 economies in order to identify economic vulnerabilities and appropriate policy responses accordingly. The ERPD process consists of two phases. The first one constitutes unofficial fora where surveillance reports, including the ones from the IMF and Asian Development Bank (ADB), are presented to the AFDM+3 (held twice a year). The second stage concerns with the discussions of matters relating to the policies of AFMM+3 (held on an annual basis as the sidelines of the ADB Annual Meeting).

6 The ASEAN Swap Arrangements (ASA) began in August 1977 when the when five ASEAN nations – Indonesia, Malaysia, the Philippines, Singapore and Thailand – signed a Memorandum of Understanding on the ASEAN Swap Arrangements. The ASA's objective is to provide instant short-term foreign exchange liquidity for the members in times of short-term liquidity problems. Each member contributed US$ 20 million, totaling the ASA's size to US$ 100 million. In 1978, the size increased to US$ 200 million.

7 In the expanded CMI, Brunei, Indonesia, Malaysia, the Philippines, Singapore and Thailand each contributed US$ 150 million. Cambodia, Laos, Myanmar and Vietnam contributed US$ 15, $5, $20 and $60 million respectively. The ASA members could unconditionally draw from this arrangement twice the amount they contributed to the pool. The borrowed amount is to be repaid within six months and may be renewed for a maximum of six months. The ASAs were used only five occasions – US$ 20 million by Indonesia in 1979; US$ 4 million by Malaysia in 1980; US$ 80 million by Thailand in 1980; and the total of US$ 340 million by the Philippines in 1981 and 1990. However, during AFC, the ASA was not activated (Henning 2002: 14).

8 In the existing literature, the CMI swap size varies, depending on the author's calculation. The amount of $60 billion presented here might be lower than other sources because it was computed after eliminating double-counting.

9 The terms and conditions of the BSAs under the CMI framework are as follow. The non-IMF-linked portion could be drawn for a period of 90 days and renewed once. The IMF-linked part could also be drawn on a 90-day basis, but renewed up to 7 times, for a period of 2 years at the creditor's discretion. Moreover, the interest rate was the London Interbank Offered Rate (LIBOR) plus a premium of 150 basis points for the initial drawing and the first renewal. The premium would rise by an additional 50 basis points for every two additional renewals, but not to exceed 300 basis points.

10 CLMVB consists of Cambodia, Laos, Myanmar, Vietnam and Brunei.

11 Interview with T11, 20 December 2013.

12 HK indicates the Hong Kong Monetary Authority.

13 ASEAN5 refers to Indonesia, Malaysia, the Philippines, Singapore and Thailand.

14 CLMVB refers to Cambodia, Laos PDR, Myanmar, Vietnam and Brunei.

2 How countries evade negotiation stalemate

Assumptions of the conceptual framework

Why do states make deals instead of letting their talks collapse? Before delving into a conceptual framework analysing negotiation processes, two assumptions this book adopt should be highlighted. The first assumption is that negotiators are rational in the sense that if an agreement is reached, they can walk away with better deals than non-agreement (Fisher and Ury 1991: 100). Otherwise, a negotiation would simply break down. Why wasting time and other kinds of resources to conclude a deal which makes you less better off than having no deal at all? If alternatives to a "no talk" are more superior than a deal itself, rational actors will not spend more time negotiating. The second assumption is that individual negotiators face a common dilemma at the bargaining table. The dilemma is the tension between their desire to gain more than others – to get a bigger piece of the pie, on the one hand – and the risk of no agreement, on the other. If a negotiator pushes his agenda too hard in hope that doing so will allow him to get more favourable terms, he is simultaneously increasing the probability of an impasse as other parties may disagree with his agenda or insist on outcomes more favourable to themselves. Therefore, an individual bargainer is likely to be careful and self-restrained due to the risk of stalemate. When negotiating, he must achieve two things at the same time: (1) to reap concessions from his counterparts to get as much as he can and (2) to prevent a negotiation from collapsing.

Because different countries have different priorities, concerns and interests, there is a high tendency that they clash with one another over agreement details. How do they work out their differences and finalize their deals? Will the disagreement which arises out of a conflict of interests ultimately tank the entire negotiation? A short answer is: it depends. Admittedly, disagreements usually emerge from different preferences, but they do not always result in a deadlock preferences, although different, are sometimes reconcilable. Countries can work out their deal, evade the stalemate and reach the deal. In short, an agreement does not emerge naturally, it takes effort by involved parties to reconcile and decide on particular details that they can agree upon.

To better illustrate the preceding, let us explore a hypothetical case in which two states are negotiating a bilateral trade agreement with each other. State A has only one export commodity which is automobile, and it desperately wants to boost its car sales abroad. State A calls on State B to reduce the tariffs or taxes on

A's exported cars into B. It is because reducing the tariffs can somehow lower the price of A's cars sold in B, helping the former increase its exports as it hopes for. State B, on the other hand, is interested in raising its rice exports into A, but is also reluctant to welcome more A's cars in its markets, as the influx of A's automobiles may outcompete its domestic car producers and drive the latter out of business. Consequently, after listening to A's initial offer, B gave a flat 'no' and a negotiation is stuck.

How does the stagnancy unfold? Does this conflict lead to the end of their negotiation? The outcome depends on how both parties figure out solutions to the problem. If no common ground can be reached, no deal is strike. However, if A and B compromise, then the negotiation can be concluded. For instance, B presents a counter-offer, saying that it will reduce tariffs on only some models of A's car imports into B except the ones B's domestic car producers dominate the market. In return, A must lower its taxes on B's rice exports. At the end, A accepts the counter-offer and both parties walk away with the new agreement that in some ways makes both of them better off.

However, it is rare that when an agreement is reached, each negotiating country walks away with equal gains. Differences in the distributions of benefits usually result. Some states can get better deals than their counterparts from the same negotiation. Let's revisit the hypothetical case from earlier. The final agreement posits that A has to open up its rice markets to receive more B's exports. However, welcoming B's rice in A's domestic market makes the latter's farmers less competitive because they produce lower-quality rice. This is not what A initially wants out of the deal. However, A accept B's counter-offer anyway as it desperately needs to increase its car sales in B's market. In contrast, getting some models of A's cars into B does not hurt the latter's domestic automakers. In this scenario, we can see that B walks away with more favourable outcome than A.

Elements of bargaining influence

What actually do states do to evade stalemate and shape agreement details, like the preceding one? By definition, what determines negotiation outcomes is relative to bargaining influence. "Who gets what in a negotiation is a function of who has the capacity and leverage to force the opponent into making concessions" (Clark et al. 2000: 71). Strategies and tactics are means to ends, which are preventing a talk from collapsing and getting the most favourable deal possible. Determined to shape final outcomes as they desire, negotiators have been found to utilize various strategies and tactics to enhance their bargaining influence (Schelling 1960: 28–35).

The discount rate

Most negotiations involve the issue of time and bargainers tend to experience some kind of time pressure. Otherwise, the negotiation cannot be close as no one desires to reach an agreement. Time puts pressure on bargainers because time creates costs that they must pay as every minute goes by until an agreement is settled (Moore 2000). The costs incurred on the negotiators can come from several sources. For example, particular national constituencies (e.g. rice farmers, steel producers) may press the government to seal the deal quickly. Delaying the agreement may generate some revenue loss to the economy or instigate social unrests. Simply, temporal pressure can just result in other opportunity costs. These situations affect actors' perception that potential benefits from the agreement may be unrealized or negative consequences will result if the deal is not concluded (Stuhlmacher et al. 1998). Hence, negotiators are required to close even though the agreed outcomes may not best serve their interests (Carnevale et al. 1993). As a result, negotiators generally have a "discount rate" when they are bargaining. A discount rate indicates how much one values the present vis-à-vis the future.

A discount rate is not to be confused with a "shadow of the future" (Axelrod and Keohane 1985). This notion posits that repeated interactions among actors shape their behaviour as players take into account factors, namely the possibility of retaliation which one-shot interactions do not have. In the area of international negotiations, a shadow of the future has been used to explain the likelihood of reaching an agreement. For instance, James Fearon (2003) argued that a shadow of the future could undermine the successful conclusion of negotiations. Because of a long shadow of the future, countries realize that they will be constrained by the agreement details over a long period of time as repeated interactions open a probability of them getting punished by their counterparts in case of non-compliance. This in turn tempts states to bargain hard and delay agreements in hope that they can get a better deal from the start. In other words, due to a shadow of the future, countries' concerns over strict implementation of the agreement makes them reluctant to conclude a deal in the first place.

Parties' discount rates have been found to affect players' bargaining behaviour, negotiation dynamics and outcomes. An actor with a higher discount rate has a stronger sense of urgency – a greater need to reach an agreement at the current negotiation – than parties with a lower discount rate. A high discount rate forces a negotiator to settle an agreement quickly as he feels that he cannot afford to wait longer, even though he has to acquiesce to his counterparts (Pruitt 1981: 233–234). As Henderson et al.'s (2006) laboratory experiment demonstrated, time-urgent persons exhibited heightened interests in making costly concessions. Moreover, players under temporal constraints cannot employ their preferred strategies and tactics to be executed during the time allowed. For example, as Pruitt and Drews (1969: 45) posit, greater time pressure heightens the importance of reaching agreement and renders "less workable the tough strategy of holding out in order to discourage the other negotiator, because this strategy takes time to take effect." Additionally, time limits curb an actor's aspiration. He is likely to lower or soften his demands, concede more quickly and conclude agreements faster (Hamner and Baird 1978; Smith et al. 1982).

With respect to the frequency and size of concessions made, Stuhlmacher and Champagne (2000) found that players with a higher discount rate made more and larger concessions than those with a lower discount rate The study confirmed that when time pressure was unequal among parties, those incurring greater costs tended to offer a higher number of concessions and settle a deal for less favourable outcomes than those with less costs (Komorita and Barnes 1969). Likewise, Yukl et al. (1976) found that time-urgent actors tended to get less well-off agreement terms than the latter.

In contrast, a party with a low discount rate values the future more and is therefore more willing to wait for a better deal, or even let a present negotiation fail in hopes of obtaining a better deal in the future (Komorita and Barnes 1969; Rapoport et al. 1990). With a lower sense of urgency, he is less likely to give concessions (Henderson et al. 2006). He sometimes uses his lower discount rate to his advantage by intentionally delaying or threatening to postpone a settlement if their counterparts refuse to yield to the former's demands. "Time-buying" is often a tactic employed by those who can afford to wait in order to force the others to capitulate (Lewicki et al. 2000). For example, Goldman and Rojot (2003) documented that Middle Eastern countries deliberately stalled negotiations when dealing with Western states in order to make the latter impatient and consequently concede. As a result, players with a lower discount rate can extract additional concessions from those with higher rate (Cohen 1980).

In the realm of international economic relations, disparities in actors' discount rates were found to shape bargaining results. For example, Cameron and Tomlin's (2000) study of the North American Free Trade Agreement (NAFTA) negotiations shows that Washington, while negotiating with Canada in 1992, was under time pressure due to domestic considerations. US law required the President to wait 90 days after the conclusion of an international agreement before formally signing it. The Bush Administration wanted the NAFTA agreement to be settled by 5 August 1992 so that the text could be signed prior to the Presidential election in November of that year. Faced with a rising discount rate, Washington finally made unilateral concessions to Canada, such as agreeing that the latter could maintain its right to screen foreign investment.

Beside determining the distributions of gains from an agreement, a temporal constraint in some circumstances can help parties evade bargaining stalemate and bring a negotiation to a close. As time passes and temporal pressure mounts, mediators were likely to intervene more actively to settle conflicts among disputants in order to conclude a deal (Carnevale and Conlon 1988; Wall and Rude 1991). Also, when deadlines were imposed, conflicting players were observed to act more rationally and pragmatically, which in turn increased the probability of agreements (Zartman and Berman 1983: 195). It is a main reason why a mediator sometimes, deliberately and arbitrarily, imposes deadlines as a tactic to extract compromises from rivalling parties. As a result, negotiators sometimes undertake "deadline diplomacy" or a notation that due dates impose upon disputants beget time pressure tempting them to be more cooperative with one another and search for ways to resolve their conflicts and break a deadlock (Nathan 2006: 17). One example is President Jimmy Carter's usage of deadlines during in the Camp David talks to help conclude the negotiations between Egypt and Israel in 1978 (Touval and Zartman 1985). As time pressure or temporal constraints help states wrap up deals and reap gains at the expense of the others. The first hypothesis hence is as follows:

> *Hypothesis 1: States with a lower discount rate in the CMIM negotiations were likely to close a deal with more favourable terms than countries with a higher discount rate.*

Attractiveness of non-agreement alternatives or best alternative to no agreement (batna)

Non-agreement alternatives or best alternatives to no agreement (batna) are actions or back-up plans a party can pursue should a negotiation break down. Batna has been found to shape players' behaviour and bargaining outcomes. Illustratively, countries having a larger internal market size possess a better batna than their counterparts with a smaller market. Because greater market size can serve as the former's back-up plans if no bilateral trade deal is concluded, the former do not need to seal the deal with the latter if the agreement terms are not in the former's favour. In addition, countries with a larger market can bargain hard to ensure that they get the terms they initially want. Likewise, states having preferential trade agreements (PTAs) with third parties were observed to possess a better batna than their equivalents with no such alternative ties (Mansfield and Reinhardt 2003). Having in place PTAs enables the former to bear less cost of no agreement than those without such conditions. If no agreement can be reached, the former can still rely on their market or other PTA markets while the latter cannot.

Insights from da Conceição-Heldt's (2011) research revealed that WTO members with a prospect of inking outside trade agreements with their major trading partners possessed a good batna, exhibited strong bargaining stances and conceded less than their equivalents without such pending deals. Likewise, as Busse et al. (2000) discovered, the European Union (EU) was able to gain leverage over Mexico in their bilateral trade negotiations because the former was at that time negotiating other PTAs with Chile, MERCOSUR[1] and South Africa. The deal would provide the EU with alternative markets in case that the EU–Mexico FTA failed to materialize.

It should be emphasized that batna is different from the previously mentioned concept of a discount rate, although both are related. Discount rates involve temporal constraints the actor is facing during a negotiation, while a batna concerns with the quality of back-up plans he has when negotiating. The two concepts are in some cases related in a sense that the quality of an actor back-up plan can be one of the sources of his discount rate. When a bargainer has better-quality back-up plans, his discount rate may be lower as his alternative permits him to wait a bit longer for the future talks to conclude deals favourable to himself. On the contrary, for the actor who possesses worse back-up plans or lacks any plan at all, his discount rate may rise as he has no choice but to do anything to salvage the current negotiation, even though he has to accept some agreement terms not favourable to himself.

Let's examine the following hypothetical scenario to better understand the preceding logic. Suppose countries having alternative PTAs or smaller internal market (i.e. better batna) are negotiating a new trade pact with their equivalents without such pre-existing agreements (i.e. worse batna). As a result, the former, thanks to their better batna, are in no hurry to secure the trade deal, and thus tend to adopt a status quo position and wait longer to strike more favourable deals. In contrast, the latter's worse batna inflicts them with a higher discount rate as they are dependent on the others' markets to sustain their economies. This forces these states to be more desperate in concluding the current deal.

As a result, batna shapes negotiation results. When their alternatives to no deal worsen, players tend to be more willing to work together to resolve their conflicts. They hence employ cooperative tactics which help break stalemate and can even reach an agreement with greater joint gains (Thompson 2001: Chapter 4). Hurd's (2005) study of the United Nations (UN) sanctions on Libya revealed that after the Pan Am flight 103 bombing incident of 1988, the UN imposed economic sanctions on Libya and the US and UK adopted a no-compromise position until Libya complied with UN resolution demands. However, by 1998 the sanction coalition was falling apart due to defections by several small states, jeopardizing the legitimacy of the UN Security Council. Seeing their batnas worsened, Washington and London agreed to suspend the UN sanctions in return for fewer Libya's concessions than they had initially demanded.

As far as the distribution of the benefits is concerned, parties with a more attractive batna tend to arrive at more favourable agreement terms than those with a less attractive batna (Fisher and Ury 1991; Lax and Sebenius 1986; Moravcsik 1998). Moreover, countries with relatively "attractive alternatives . . . with lower loss associated with the failure of negotiations, are more likely to be influential in claiming a larger share of the value being distributed within negotiations" (Hopmann 1996: 119). Laboratory research suggested that individuals with a better-quality batna are more likely to gain the upper hand in bargaining. For instance, Brett et al.'s (1993) study revealed that negotiators with a strong batna tended to have greater dyadic gains than those without a batna. Also, Pinkley et al. (1994) found that players with high-quality batnas to the current negotiation were able to acquire a larger share from the negotiation than their equivalents with low-quality batnas.

Real-world scenarios confirm the experimentation results, indicating that batnas shape bargaining results more accurately than countries' relative power. Illustratively, Wriggins (1976) perused a negotiation between the United Kingdom and Malta. In 1971, the Britain wanted to renew its naval base lease in Malta. Aiming to get more British compensations than before, the latter worsened London's batna by rejecting its offer and instead tried to cut deals with Libya and the Soviet Union. As a result, the British made more concessions to Malta despite the former's being more powerful than the latter. Likewise, Hopmann's (1978) analysis found that in the Conference on Security and Cooperation in Europe in 1974–1976, states having the least to lose from non-agreement – that is, having a better batna – were able to obtain more favourable terms than those with more to lose.

Regarding international trade bargaining, countries with larger internal markets to fall back on if no deal was struck gained an upper hand in a negotiation (Drezner 2007). Enia (2009) has demonstrated that after signing a free trade agreement with Singapore, Japan's batna was better than Mexico's, enabling Tokyo to negotiate with the latter from a relative stronger position and walk away with more favourable outcomes than the latter. Additionally, Cameron and Tomlin's (2000) analysis of the North American Free Trade Agreement (NAFTA) negotiations has revealed that Canada and the USA possessed more attractive batnas than Mexico because the former had signed Canada–US free trade agreement (FTA) prior to the NAFTA talks, and Washington was more interested in pursuing GATT than NAFTA. In contrast, Mexico at that time had no other tracks beside pursuing NAFTA. As a result, the country conceded to both Ottawa and Washington in several areas such as agriculture and financial services.

Batna in other circumstances also helps states break bargaining impasse. For instance, actors with a worse batna are likely to be more cooperative with others and proactive in finding a compromise solution where interests converge and an agreement is concluded. At WTO talks, when the EU and US viewed that their batnas deteriorated after the 1999 Seattle Round failure, the two powers became more cooperative with each other, which partly resulted in their agreement afterwards (Odell 2009).

These examples suggest that having a more attractive batna (e.g. a better back-up plan) enables states to wrap up their deals, and in some cases allows them to bargain hard, reap concessions from other parties and walk away from a negotiation table with a more favourable deals that the latter. This is formulated as a hypothesis as follows:

Hypothesis 2: Parties in the CMIM negotiations with a more attractive batna were likely to close a deal with more favourable terms than those with a less attractive batna.

Informational strategies (exploiting informational asymmetry)

Thomas Schelling (1960) once regarded bargaining as the strategic use of information. Informational strategies refer to using information or knowledge relevant to negotiations in order to avoid bargaining gridlock or gain an upper hand during talks. It is because actor can use the information to develop new ideas, make important decisions and find solutions to the problems. In most cases, states do not have equal access to information relevant to bargaining – some states are likely obtain more of such data than the others. The result is informational asymmetry.

Informational asymmetry usually comes from two sources: (1) knowledge about other actors' preferences and (2) knowledge about issues being negotiated (expertise).

Other actors' preferences

Knowing other parties' preferences can affect bargaining dynamics and outcomes (Fisher and Ury 1991; Raiffa 1982). Under the condition that preferences are similar, this knowledge allows actors to aggregate their preferences, facilitate bargaining processes and reach an agreement (Walton and McKersie 1965; De Dreu et al. 2008). In cases of conflicting preferences, a negotiator who knows his opponent's preferences can utilize such data to craft optimal results for both of them (Raiffa 1982). It is because in most negotiations, actors' different interests are not entirely incompatible (Neale and Bazerman 1992). There exists room that interests can be reconciled.

Furthermore, knowledge about others' preferences has been found to affect the distribution of outcomes among players. Schoemaker (1990: 1187) contends that informational asymmetries create opportunities for exploitation. Individuals with more information about their counterparts can use this knowledge at strategic moments in order to reap concessions from the latter (Wolfe and McGinn 2005). In other circumstance, bargainers with more of such data utilized it to shape agreement terms more favourable to them than their less-informed counterparts (Milgrom and Roberts 1987). As information asymmetries beget opportunism, parties sometimes conceal information about their own preferences given to the others in hope that they would gain an upper hand in negotiations (Murnighan et al. 1999).

Empirical research confirmed that parties with more information regarding others' preferences were able to obtain a larger part of the pie (Schei and Rognes 1993; Pinkley 1995). For example, Cameron and Tomlin (2000) studies climate change talks between the North and the South. They discovered that when the Southern countries took advantage of asymmetrical information by withholding their preferences from the North. The former gained more bargaining leverage over the latter. A key condition under which such strategy worked out successfully was that no Southern states defected by cutting private deals with the North. Furthermore, in his study of the international trade conflicts from 1961 to 1980, John Odell (1985) found that South Korea utilized asymmetrical information about other preferences for its own gains. Seoul decided to let Hong Kong and Japan negotiate with the USA over textiles before it actually did. After the USA exposed its preferences in its negotiations with Tokyo and Hong Kong, Seoul was able to utilize such information to ask for more favourable deals in its own negotiation with Washington.

In short, knowing others' preferences enables states to reconcile their differences and conclude a negotiation, gain more bargaining leverage and walk away with more favourable outcomes than others. This is formulated as a hypothesis as follows:

Hypothesis 3.1: States in the CMIM negotiations that had more knowledge on other actors' preferences were likely to close a deal with more favourable terms than those that had less knowledge.

Expertise

International bargaining sometimes involves negotiating complex issues (Winham 1977; Zartman 1994). It is because certain agreement requires "expertise" or technical knowledge of the matters being negotiated in order to make decisions. For example, when negotiating a trade agreement, countries have to decide on the modalities of trade liberalization, which could involve setting up the rate of tariff reductions over the specified periods, or the criteria used to determine different tariff-reduction schedules among different states. Financial negotiations may involve the matters of establishing the shared standards that the members must adopt to develop regional stock markets. In the area of trade facilitation, discussions could be about choosing which principles to be adopted in order to synchronize states' custom clearances systems.

Expertise has been recognized to play a significant role in helping countries reach an agreement. By possessing more expertise, states gain themselves some degree of credibility, making others accept the validity of contents or analyses they provide. Therefore, countries sometimes embark on "technocratic strategies" to evade bargaining stalemate by helping disputants to settle their conflicts. Technocratic strategies involve "mastering the technical details of the relevant business and related laws, precedents, and institutions" (Odell 1980: 223). For example, the trade dispute between the USA and Brazil was finally settled in 1974 due to the latter's expertise. Washington previously imposed countervailing duties to Brazil's footwear exports on the ground that the latter's government tax credit program to boost such exports turned out to damage the American shoe producers. In response, the Brazilian government and shoe industry requested a US-based firm with highly trained trade personnel to conduct a study on the issues. The report found that Brazil's shoe export gained a very small market share in the USA and its tax credit program had low utilization rate of 4.8 per cent of the total export value. After the findings were released, the bilateral conflict was resolved, resulting in a rise of Brazil's shoe exports into the US market afterwards (Odell 1980). Likewise, Moon (1988) contended that the conflict between the USA and South Korea arose when the former accused the latter of subsidizing its steel exports, but Seoul counter-argued that the drop in its steel price was due to increased production efficiency. The intense negotiation between Washington and Seoul was at last settled only when Seoul sought a trade consultant for help.

Research shows that parties possessing greater expertise than their counterparts are often found to walk away from a negotiation table with more favourable agreement terms than those with less expertise (Young 1991; Tallberg 2006). For example, Tallberg's (2008) analysis of EU Council negotiations illustrated that expertise mattered in shaping outcomes more than countries' size. Small- and medium-sized countries utilized expertise to gain bargaining leverage over large-sized states.

However, one must be cautious that there exist certain boundaries to how much countries can wield their expertise power. In other words, utilizing expertise may be constrained in particular circumstances. As Quaglia (2009) argues, negotiations differ in terms of types and degrees of expertise required. Expert knowledge that translates into bargaining influence in certain negotiations might be inapplicable to other settings. It is because expert power can be effectively exercised if others are confident that one possesses special knowledge in a specific area. Thus, attempts to use expertise outside its range is unlikely to convince others that one really possesses expertise, and doing so is likely to jeopardize one's bargaining advantage.

To sum up, negotiators can exploit an informational asymmetry by making themselves experts on issues under negotiation. Such expertise enables them to evade bargaining deadlock and get more favourable outcomes than their counterparts. The hypothesis is as follows:

Hypothesis 3.2: States in the CMIM negotiations that had greater expertise on issues being negotiated were likely to close a deal with more favourable terms than those with less expertise.

The power of the chair/co-chair(s)

States can obtain bargaining leverage via the position of the chair. Owing to specific the roles and responsibilities assigned to them, chairs are able to gain bargaining leverage over non-chairing parties. Admittedly, a chairperson's power can be limited by institutional constraints which can in turn affect the extent to which he can influence outcomes (Majone 2002). For instance, Tallberg (2010) studied a chair's discretion in the European Union (EU), World Trade Organization (WTO) and United Nations (UN) conferences. He found that the chairs under a majority voting system were able to exert more influence to shape agreement terms than those under a unanimity decision-making rule. Despite such constraints imposed, chairs nevertheless have some leeway to exert their influence by resorting to informal convention such as privately consulting certain members or arranging informal meetings with particular parties to resolve conflicts between them (Odell 2005). Therefore, chairmen's actions have been confirmed to have a distributional effect on negotiation outcomes (Krasner 1983; Tallberg 2002, 2006).

Chairs' gain bargaining leverage comes from their power to set meeting agendas and manage the process of a negotiation. As one source contends, the chair "opens and concludes meetings, defines the meeting agenda, allots the right to speak . . . and summarizes results obtained [from a negotiation]" (Tallberg 2002: 22–23). For example, in the EU legislative process, chairpersons substantively shaped outcomes to their own ends by manipulating agendas and controlling the tempo of a meeting (Warntjen 2007; Aksoy 2010). Also, studies on the EU negotiations discovered that the presidency, while under certain institutional constraints, could somehow manage to use its position to obtain favourable agreement terms (Schout 1998; Kollman 2003; Schalk et al. 2007). Illustratively, in the

International Conference negotiation in 2000, the French presidency "took its own proposal as a basis for discussion and assumed that any point on which objections were not raised had been accepted" (Costa et al. 2003: 124). Moreover, the presidency was reported to rearrange the ordering of agenda issues, and put pressure on dissenting parties to agree on specific terms. Additionally, in the Non-Proliferation Treaty negotiations (1965–1968), the co-chairs – the US and the Soviet Union – took control over bargaining processes by using their drafting monopoly to advance their own interests. The co-chairs successfully shifted the meeting focus from disarmament to arm control.

In the realm of economic bargaining, Odell's (2005) analysis of the WTO rounds indicated that after the meetings were launched, the chairpersons purposefully ranked the issues on the agenda in an order that enabled them to manoeuvre the direction of the discussions. Additionally, GATT and WTO chairs affected these negotiations by "structuring the agenda through single negotiating texts, brokering agreement through bilateral talks and compromise proposals and representing the negotiating group vis-à-vis third parties" (Tallberg 2008: 6).

In other cases, chairpersons, through their power to summon meetings, ultimately alter outcomes. For instance, a study by Blavoukos and Bourantonis (2010) revealed the influence of presidency on negotiations in the UN Security Council (UNSC). The dissolution of the Soviet Union in 1991 raised the issue of which country would assume the Soviet Union's seat in the UNSC. The UK, which was the presidency in 1992, gave the Soviet Union's seat to Russia in a quick and unopposed way. Regarding the future of the USSR's seat as highly significant to itself, the British presidency preferred the matter to be resolved immediately. To achieve its goal, London first used its chair's power to convene the meeting of only Heads of States in order to ensure that no UNSC members would object to a Russian representative. Then, at the formal UNSC meeting, the British Presidency committed the UNSC to accept Russia as a successor of to the Soviet Union's seat.

In addition, a chair's bargaining influence sometimes stems from its mediation role. Chairpersons can help evade a bargaining logjam by playing a role of a mediator (Quaglia and Moxon-Browne 2006). When a dispute emerges, chairmen can intervene, resolve conflicts and shape outcomes in their direction (Wagner 2008). For example, when the countries on the UN Sea-Bed Committee in 1978 could not agree on the text of draft articles, the talk was on a brink of collapse. The committee's chair intervened by acting as the mediator. The chair took an initiative to develop a single negotiation text, which was later used as the basis for subsequent negotiations (Antrim and Sebenius 1992). Moreover, da Conceição-Heldt (2006) found that the European Commission, by assuming the role of a broker, successfully prevented the deadlock stemming from conflicts over fisheries issues and helped the involved stakeholders reach an agreement on the common fisheries policy in 1970.

To conclude, chairing parties are able to not only avoid a bargaining impasse, but also shape the final results to their advantage. In cases that two countries function as co-chairs (e.g. CMIM negotiation), both states are anticipated to gain an upper hand vis-à-vis those that do not co-chair the talk. This is formulated as a hypothesis as follows:

> **Hypothesis 4: States in the CMIM negotiations that assumed positions as co-chairs were likely to close a deal with more favourable terms than non-co-chairing states.**

Issue linkages

Most international negotiations involve discussions about more than one issue. Unsurprisingly, states often consider the matters together to create a package deal. In other words, countries usually practice "issue linkage" or the simultaneous discussion of two or more issues for joint settlement (Sebenius 1983). A common way which governments engage in issue linkages is by "trading" concessions on issues they care less about in exchange for others' reciprocal concessions on issues that are more important to them. A method of cross-linking issues to create a comprehensive agreement has been used since the Ancient Greeks (Wallace 1976). Athens created the Delian League in order to link its extended naval protection to other city states in exchange for tribute payments.

In modern times, issue linkage is found in every negotiation except those dealing with a single issue (Odell 2000). Bundling up different issues is a key factor helping states reach an agreement (Martin 1993: 779). This is because "linking together disparate issues sometimes opens up possibilities for mutually acceptable arrangements by creating opportunities for the international equivalent of logrolling and the formulation of package deals" (Sebenius 1983). Furthermore, connecting together issues is a means to prevent bargaining stalemate especially when direct side payments to particular parties are not feasible (Tollison and Willet 1979: 448).

Studies have demonstrated that issue linkage plays a crucial role in achieving an agreement in several areas ranging from security to economics (Sebenius 1983; Jensen 1988; Hopmann 1996; Lohmann 1997). For instance, Down et al. (1985) documented the use of issue linkages in the negotiation of the Washington Naval Treaty of 1922 which set a limit on the battleship construction by the three largest naval powers: the USA, the UK, and Japan. His analysis revealed that the Treaty was able to be concluded when these powers linked battleship construction limits to Pacific security and trade. Washington and London "received guarantees of an open-door policy regarding trade in China and the Pacific, and the return of Shantung province and key transportation systems to the Chinese." Japan pledged to not increase its fortifications on the Pacific Island territories taken from Germany during World War I. In return, the USA and UK gave Japan the right to take control of the territories taken from Germany. The Treaty also prevented the formation of a possible US–UK defence pact against Japan in the Pacific.

Regarding arms control negotiations, several case studies revealed that reciprocation played a major role in reaching an agreement (Bunn and Payne 1988). For instance, Jensen's (1988) analysis the Strategic Arms Limitation Talks (SALTs)[2]

(1969–1971) showed how issue linkages facilitated the conclusion of the negotiation. The Soviet Union made an offer to the USA by allowing the latter to retain foreign military bases on the condition that Washington, in return, would be more flexible on the number of Soviet missile launchers. Also, Washington later proposed to help modernize the Soviet Union's economy if the latter would soften on its SALT position.

Moreover, Da Conceição-Heldt (2006) revealed that issue linkage undergirded the making of the EU common fisheries policy (CFP). The CFP was in fact a product of deal-cutting among the members. The members diverged on how the CFP was crafted. On the one hand, France and Italy wanted to have a structural policy for the fishing industry so that they could have the Commission finance their fishing fleet upgrades. On the other hand, Belgium, Germany, Luxemburg and the Netherlands wished to have a common market organization so that they could liberalize their fish products. The final agreement was made possible when these stakeholders connected together their two matters – the structural policy and common market construction.

In economic bargaining, cross-linking issues are prevalent because economic matters are often overlapping and intertwined (Hampson and Hart 1995: 348). Trade issues may be related to monetary relations, concerns over investment and economic development. This led Sebenius (1983) to contend that with very few exceptions, no economic negotiation is completed without employing linking issues to reach package deals. For example, John Odell (2009) explained why the Doha package paradoxically included anti-dumping rules – an issue so controversial to the USA that it once refused to negotiate at any circumstances. The meeting was able to be concluded when Washington, in the last three days of the Doha talks, "traded" its anti-dumping concession for gains in other areas, namely the reduction of barriers on American farm and service exports. Similarly, in the European Economic Community Summit in 1975, Germany agreed to underwrite the British deficit in exchange for the latter's change in its position on energy cooperation with the former (Wallace 1976).

In sum, states often use issue linkage to evade stalemate and arrive at agreement details in their favour. The fifth proposition hence is as follows:

Hypothesis 5: Countries in the CMIM negotiations that were in position to employ issue linkages were likely to close a deal with more favourable terms than those that were not in position to do so.

Coalition formation

Countries have been witnessed to pursue their objectives via collective action as an alternative to do so unilaterally. Experts have long recognized coalition formation as the essence of international bargaining (Hampson and Hart 1995). Coalition refers to "two or more parties who cooperate to obtain a mutually desired outcome that satisfies the interests of the coalition rather than those of the entire group within which it is embedded" (Polzer et al. 1998: 42).

As Dupont (1996: 48) contends, "coalitions have become a key factor understanding and explaining bargaining dynamics and outcomes." For example, banding together sometimes salvages a negotiation from collapsing. Illustratively, Narlikar (2003) found that the *café au lait* group – a coalition of developed and developing countries – was able to break the WTO's Uruguay Round impasse. When the Round was on a brink of collapse, this coalition introduced its Swiss-Colombian text containing terms which ultimately resolved disagreements on agricultural issues among major disputants, namely the EU and the Cairn Groups.[3]

Beside enabling states to reach their agreement, coalitions also help their members increase the chance of getting relatively favourable agreement terms vis-à-vis their counterparts outside the groups (Dupont 1996; Zartman and Rubin 2002). It is because banding together allows states to take advantage of pooling and mobilizing their resources such as money, information and expertise, which turns out to strengthen the group's bargaining leverage and allow its members to get a larger part of the pie (Mannix 1993; Moravcsik 1993; Chasek 2005). For example, Singh (2003: 25) found that the bloc of developing countries could bargain with the West and "walk away with an agreement that did not ask them to make concessions too far beyond their domestic liberalization schedules."

Regarding trade talks, alliance building is common. Developing countries adopting this approach have been found to "flex their muscles" against the more powerful (Narlikar et al. 2004). At the General Agreement on Tariffs and Trade (GATT) negotiations, the coalitions of small states were able to resist settling on agreement terms they did not favour and make their own proposals which ultimately shaped the final details (Hamilton and Whalley 1989). Moreover, during the negotiation for the Agreement on Trade-Related Aspects of Intellectual Property Rights (TRIPS) in 2001, developing states led by Brazil Thailand and South Africa formed a counter-coalition against their more powerful counterparts, namely the USA and multinational pharmaceutical companies. The bloc's common interest was to be exempt from TRIPS penalties under particular health reasons. Illustratively, its members wanted to be permitted to produce generic medicines should a HIV/AIDS or other pandemic strike. The group at the end successfully protected their interest against the more powerful players (Sell and Odell 2003).

Regarding international banking cooperation, the practice of coalition formation has also been documented. For example, the bargaining processes of the Basle Accord agreement indicated that the Federal Reserve purposefully coalesced with the UK and later with Japan to pressure Germany to accept the deals more favourable to the former (Sebenius 1996: 333–337).

In conclusion, forming coalitions enables states to escape a bargaining deadlock and conclude agreements with outcomes in their favour. The sixth hypothesis is as follows:

Hypothesis 6: Countries in the CMIM negotiations that formed coalitions with stronger states were likely to close a deal with more favourable terms than states that did not form such coalitions.

However, uniting together is not the only way which states use to seal their deals and advance their interests. Preventing other countries from creating a coalition against oneself can also helps one conclude a negotiation with more favourable outcomes. Thus, the parallel hypothesis is as follows:

> **Hypothesis 6a: Countries in the CMIM negotiations that prevented coalition formation by other states were likely to close a deal with more favourable terms than states that did not inhibit such coalitions from creating.**

Methodology

Research design

My examination of negotiation processes takes the form of an in-depth case study. Here, a *case* refers to "an instance of a class of events or phenomena of interest to the investigator, such as a decision to devalue a currency, a trade negotiation, or an application of economic sanctions" (Odell 2004: 57).

Like other approaches, case studies contain particular constraints. First, insights gained from this method are limited as the findings from a single case offer a poor basis for generalizing (Yin 2009: 43). In other works, this approach can suffer its low external validity or the ability to apply findings across cases (Bennett 2002: 1). It is because some features or patterns are so unique to a specific case that they are unlikely to be observed in other circumstances.

Despite its limitations, we should not entirely dismiss this approach. Much can nonetheless be learned from using a case study method to explore CMIM negotiation dynamics for several reasons. First, it allows us to investigate bargaining strategies and tactics in greater detail. As Odell (2000: 22) has stated, case studies uncover "much more information about the negotiators' beliefs, tactics, context and outcomes than would be reported if these dimensions were reduced to statistical variables." While quantitative methods tend to lump individual steps in causal chains into larger data points for analysis, case studies provide opportunity for a researcher to study the dynamics of interactions in depth. In short, when one wants to tease out the details of specific cases, a case study approach permits one to examine processes more effectively.

Another benefit is that case studies helps reveal actual causal processes (Campbell 1979; George and Bennett 2005). Gerring (2004: 348) argued that "[c]ase studies, if well- constructed, allow one to peer into the box of causality to the intermediate causes lying between some cause and its purported effect." In other words, this approach allows an investigator to "connect dots" by exploring a large number of intervening variables to observe how certain causal mechanisms operate. Causal mechanisms refer to "recurrent processes linking specified initial conditions with a specific outcome" (Mayntz 2003: 4–5). Not only a case study method maps out specific chains between causes and effects, it also teases out the conditions under which such causal mechanisms function.

Because case study methods examine real-world scenarios, it eliminates a problem of artificiality which usually occurs in experimental settings. Research conducted in laboratories generally control for other factors in order to examine a relationship between independent and dependent variables. By imposing such constraints, results from experiments become "artificial" as the findings cannot be found in reality. In contrast, a case study enables one to explore how relationships unfold in actual, real-world scenarios.

To strengthen the CMIM negotiation analysis further, this book takes advantage of the fact that the CMIM talks were divided into several rounds, resulting in more data points available to validate my hypotheses. Therefore, a "within case" comparison will be conducted. This kind of comparison has been used by scholars dealing with a small number of cases, because it makes as many distinct observations as possible out of the few cases available (King et al. 1994). By exploring a case over time, one can transform what initially appear as a single case into a comparative study and examine more deeply how the independent and dependent variables relate to one another (Klotz 2008: 53). For example, this longitudinal approach can grant additional insights when there happens to be 'exogenous shocks' (e.g. economic crises, wars) that dramatically alter explanatory factors.

By applying a "within case" comparison to my analysis, I tracked *changes or shifts* in negotiators' strategies and tactics *across* the rounds (e.g. from the 2nd to the 8th Finance Ministers' Meeting) in order to add rigor to my hypothesis testing. For instance, if shifts in strategies and tactics (e.g. if Country A at the 2nd Meeting did not employ informational strategies and tactics but did so at the 3rd Meeting) are observed to alter final outcomes (e.g. Country A got more favourable deal from the 3rd Meeting than from the 2nd Meeting, ceteris paribus), then my propositions (e.g. Hypothesis 3) would be further confirmed.

Country selection

Although the CMIM negotiation involved 13 parties, this study did not include all of them due to data inaccessibility problem. Some government officials involved in the negotiations refused to participate in this research. Instead of studying all CMIM participants, I turned to focus only on the most influential players from which I could gather data. The countries included in my analysis are China, Japan, Indonesia, Malaysia, South Korea and Thailand. The details of how I selected these players are as follow.

To determine which stakeholders were the most influential in the CMIM talks, I looked at the amounts of their financial contributions to the CMIM pool recorded in the Joint Ministerial Statements (JMSs). As earlier explained, ASEAN+3 states competed over the contribution issue in order to gain as much voting power as they could. Thus, the most influential parties were the ones who could bargain to get more financial contributions (and thus obtaining greater voting power) than the others.

According to the JMS of the 13th AFMM+3 in May 2010, countries financially supplying the most to the CMIM fund were the +3 and ASEAN5 states (Indonesia,

Malaysia, the Philippines, Singapore and Thailand). Not only ASEAN5 countries contributed more to the CMIM reserve pool as compared to the other ASEAN members, one authority confirmed that they were also more influential in the negotiations than the latter.[4]

Out of the ASEAN5 states, I selected three countries: Indonesia, Malaysia and Thailand, I did not choose the Philippines for the following reasons. When the CMIM negotiations concluded in May 2009, Indonesia, Malaysia, Singapore and Thailand each made contributions of US$ 4.77 billion while the Philippines agreed to contribute US$ 3.68 billion. Moreover, Manila announced that it lacked international reserves to contribute US$ 4.77 billion as the other ASEAN5 countries did.[5] However, at the next meeting in May 2010, ASEAN5 states agreed to make contribution adjustments in the Annex 1 of the CMIM agreement, resulting to the fact that they each contributed US$ 4.552 to the CMIM. Therefore, it could be assumed that the Philippines' reserve problems in 2009 made it less influential in the CMIM talks than the other ASEAN5 nations. Hence, the country was not in my analysis. In regard to Singapore, the city-state was not selected due to a lack of direct access to data sources. Singaporean officials refused to participate in this study.

Assessing countries' bargaining influence in CMIM negotiations

How was the CMIM participants' performance evaluated? In other words, how to find out whether they gained bargaining leverage vis-à-vis the others and shape the final outcomes as they preferred? This book measures a state's bargaining influence by comparing its original goal (what it hoped for) with final outcomes (the agreement details reached at the end of the meeting). The five-point scale in Figure 2.1 depicts how well each country performed in the CMIM negotiation.

This book takes each of the participants as a central point in the analysis. Each party serves as an individual subject that achieved one of the five possibilities as seen in Figure 2.1. When a country "got *the same* as it hoped for," it means that the final outcome of a negotiation and its original goal were the same. If the final outcome exceeded a state's initial objective, then it may be said that it "got *more* or *much more* than it hoped for." If the final outcome was less than a country's initial goal, the country "got *worse* or *much worse* than it hoped for."

To gauge countries' original goal pertaining to their CMIM financial contributions and voting power, this book assesses how states weighed contribution in relation to vote. It is because these matters are actually two different sides of the same coin. According to the agreement, the more a country contributes, the more

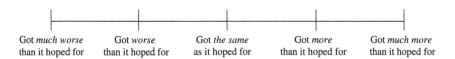

| Got *much worse* | Got *worse* | Got *the same* | Got *more* | Got *much more* |
| than it hoped for | than it hoped for | as it hoped for | than it hoped for | than it hoped for |

Figure 2.1 Five-point scale

votes it gets, and vice versa. As a result, states engaging in the CMIM talks pragmatically considered both issues at the same time.

However, when pondering these matters simultaneously, the members faced a trade-off between costs and benefits – the costs being contributions they must bear and the benefits voting power proportional to their contributions. Here, an age old maxim "you cannot have your cake and eat it too" becomes relevant. If one wants to get more votes, one must bear greater costs by contributing more. In contrast, if one chooses to reduce costs by contributing less financially, one gets fewer votes accordingly. To sum up, how a country weighed contribution in relation to vote defined its original goal for its absolute contribution amounts.

One major factor influencing states' cost-benefit calculations was their capability to contribute financially to the CMIM facility. The +3 and ASEAN differed in terms of capabilities, their objectives in the negotiations diverged. For this reason, the two group's original goals were separately analysed.

The +3

Thanks to their relatively high reserve levels, the +3 had little difficulty to make contributions to the CMIM fund. Table 2.1 reveals that CMIM contributions were minute when compared with these states' reserve holdings. For example, when the fund size in 2009 was agreed to be US\$ 120 billion, China's, Japan's and South Korea's reserve amount was about US\$ 2,453, 1,049, and 270 billion respectively. In short, the +3's capacities to contribute were not constrained by their reserve levels. Consequently, what the +3 prioritized in the CMIM talks was the number of votes they would get from the CMIM deal. Hence, these states could be assumed to focus on vote more than contribution.

There existed another reason why the +3 put more emphasis on the number of votes they would obtain than the contribution amount they could made. Owing to their ability to contribute, the +3 became the potential CMIM lenders when financial support is needed. Consequently, these parties' preference was to ensure that the CMIM facility will not give easy money to the borrowers resulting in a moral hazard. A moral hazard happens when governments, viewing that they could easily borrow from the CMIM facility during crisis times, adopt policies which increase the risks of crises in the first place. In short, the perception that the CMIM allows them to tap on extra financial resources when needed tempts governments to be less careful in their policy implementation to manage their economies.

Being in a position of potential lenders, the +3 desired to lessen the incident of a moral hazard by influencing lending decisions governed by the weighted-voting system. Having greater say in these decisions would reduce a chance of a moral hazard. Therefore, the +3 can be expected to pay much attention to their vote shares and intensely negotiate to get as many votes as they could to influence the lending decisions.

To conclude, the +3 had in mind a minimum contribution amount which would be converted into a minimum number of votes as the lowest threshold they could accept to seal the CMIM deal. If offered less than the minimum, the +3 would deny it and let the talk collapse.

It is important to emphasize that the +3 were interested in "maximizing" their contributions and votes beyond their pre-set minimum level. Driven by the desire to prevent a moral hazard, the +3 could be expected to grapple for higher contribution amount and vote shares if opportunities allowed them to do so.

ASEAN

Unlike the +3's, ASEAN states' story was different. Their capabilities to contribute to CMIM were constrained by their reserve levels. The agreed CMIM size in 2009 was US$ 120 billion, which exceeded most ASEAN countries' total reserve (Table 2.1). Consequently, these countries could be assumed to regard CMIM contributions as financial burdens and hence weigh contribution over vote. As a result, these parties had in their mind a maximum contribution amount. How much they could afford to contribute defined the highest threshold they would be able to accept. If asked to contribute more than their maximum limit, these states would be unable to afford to do so and the entire negotiation would fall apart. In short, ASEAN's original goal was the *maximum* amount they aimed to contribute.

I must highlight that it is a mistake to assert that ASEAN states, would not fight to fulfil their interests when negotiating the CMIM agreement. Despite their capability disadvantage, these countries in fact wanted to influence the decision making, but for a different reason than the +3. As the potential borrowers, ASEAN's stake was that they would require CMIM financial assistance during crisis times. Consequently, ASEAN would bargain hard to secure their pre-set maximum contribution amount which would be converted into the maximum number of votes they could get to influence the lending decisions. In short, although ASEAN countries' reserve levels limited their capabilities to contribute to CMIM fund, their need for the mechanism's assistance during the crisis times forced them to intensely negotiate for the highest amount they aimed to contribute.

Critics may claim that certain countries may set modest goals and in this way their effectiveness can increase. I counter-argue that although this practice is possible, it is highly unlikely to occur in the CMIM negotiation. When negotiators suppose the current agreement to influence their future interactions and later decision making, they tend to bargain hard to get outcomes favourable to themselves (da Conceição-Heldt 2011). Because the CMIM was set up to provide financial assistance to its members' economies in crisis times, a decision to disburse the fund to crisis economies is crucial because it fundamentally serves CMIM's purpose. Because lending decisions are determined by weighted voting, countries would scramble to get as many votes as they can. Both lending and borrowing countries alike want to influence the decisions in their favour. Hence, it would be unusual that the CMIM members were self-restraint by setting humble goals for themselves.

Table 2.1 Foreign reserves of ASEAN+3 countries (2003–2010) (in billion USD)

Country	2003	2004	2005	2006	2007	2008	2009	2010
China, PRC	416.20	622.95	831.41	1080.76	1546.36	1966.04	2452.90	2913.71
Hong Kong, China	118.39	123.57	124.28	133.21	152.69	182.53	255.84	268.74
Japan	673.55	844.67	846.90	895.32	973.30	1030.76	1048.99	1096.07
South Korea	155.47	199.20	210.55	239.15	262.53	201.54	270.44	292.14
Brunei	0.47	0.49	0.49	0.51	0.67	0.75	1.36	1.56
Cambodia	0.98	1.12	1.16	1.41	2.14	2.64	3.29	3.82
Indonesia	36.26	36.31	34.73	42.60	56.94	51.64	66.12	96.21
Laos PDR	0.26	0.27	0.31	0.46	0.71	0.87	1.01	1.10
Malaysia	44.31	66.39	70.46	82.88	101.99	92.17	96.70	106.53
Myanmar	0.65	0.77	0.89	1.38	3.28	3.92	5.51	6.05
Philippines	17.08	16.23	18.47	22.96	33.74	37.50	44.21	62.33
Singapore	96.25	112.58	116.17	136.26	162.96	174.19	187.80	231.26
Thailand	42.16	49.85	52.08	67.01	87.47	111.01	138.42	172.03
Vietnam	6.22	7.04	9.05	13.38	23.48	23.89	16.45	12.47

Source: World Bank

The elements of bargaining influence

As outlined earlier, states utilize various elements of bargaining strategies and tactics to gain bargaining leverage over the others. For the purpose of analysing the CMIM negotiation, these elements were measured as follow.

Discount rate

In the CMIM context, a country's discount rate was determined by its liquidity status. A liquidity status is a combination of reserve adequacy (how much international reserves the state has) and international borrowing capacity (how much the country can borrow abroad). Therefore, to gauge the status, an index was created by using an equal weighting of (1) the country's level of foreign-exchange reserves in months of imports and (2) its sovereign credit rating scores.

Parties with better liquidity status (i.e. high levels of reserves and borrowing capacity) may be assumed to have a lower discount rate than those with lower liquidity status (i.e. low levels of reserves and borrowing capacity). It is because higher levels of reserves and better borrowing capacity enabled countries to manage their economy in a crisis time with little assistance from the CMIM facility. As a result, these states were in little hurry to conclude the CMIM deal and could wait to settle the negotiation when they got the agreement terms they hoped for.

In contrast, countries with low liquidity (i.e. having less reserve and lower borrowing capacity) are expected to have a higher discount rate because the money needed to manage their economies during crisis times may exceed their reserve levels and their capability to borrow abroad. As a result, these countries were in more need for the CMIM as they were more likely to seek an immediate financial help from the facility should a crisis hit. Therefore, these players felt pressured to finish the CMIM agreement as soon as possible so that the facility would come into being for them to tap on its resources when a next crisis comes, even though they had to make concessions to the others. Therefore, states having a low liquidity status could be expected to walk away with agreement terms less than they initially aimed for.

Best alternative to no agreement (batna)

To determine a country's batna, this study relied on two indicators: (1) a country's past histories of exchange rate crises and (2) its experience with IMF structural adjustment programs or conditionalities. In this study, an exchange rate crisis is defined as a situation which a country's nominal effective exchange rate (NEER) drops more than 20% in a period of 6 months. States that had gone through more of these crises and had been through more painful experience with an IMF program had worse batnas than their counterparts without such conditions. The history of the crises altered these countries' mindsets as it made very crucial having new mechanisms, namely the CMIM, to give financial help. Also, because these players were put under the Fund's programmes and suffered through its conditionalities, they became disinclined to resort to the IMF's facilities again and hence had a strong incentive to pursue CMIM as an alternative to the Fund. Therefore, they could be expected to have had a strong desire to settle the CMIM negotiation although they might have to accept certain agreement terms that were less than they originally aimed for.

Conversely, countries that had experienced fewer or no exchange rate crises and did not have painful experience with an IMF programme had better batnas. Fewer previous occurrences of the crises resulted that these states did not feel as vital as the earlier group the establishment of new facilities providing liquidity assistance. Also, without being suffered from the IMF's conditionalities, these actors were less averse to the IMF than the former group, and might consider seeking the Fund's assistance in the next crisis. Therefore, these states did not have such a strong need to seek help from CMIM and could have been expected to bargain hard and reap concessions from their equivalents in the negotiations.

Informational strategies and tactics

States with better information relevant to the negotiations could use the data to their advantage, such as by developing or adjusting their strategies and tactics accordingly. Hence, these countries would have been expected to salvage the CMIM negotiation from collapsing or shape outcomes in their favour. Informational advantage can be achieved in two ways – either by knowing others' preferences or issues being negotiated. Therefore, the indicators used to measure informational advantage will be (1) knowledge about other actors' preferences and (2) knowledge about issues being negotiated (expertise). To gauge how much the country possessed these two types of knowledge, archival research and/or interviews were conducted. The first kind of knowledge was assessed by focusing on how much a country was aware of the concerns, priorities and interests of its negotiating counterparts. To gauge how much expertise the country possessed, this book looks at how well it mastered the contents of the CMIM details being discussed. The sources of such expertise can come from its own studies of particular CMIM subject matters or consultations with certain external personnel not directly related to the negotiations, or the combination of the two.

The role of chair(s)

The CMIM chairs were identified by consulting the Joint Statements of ASEAN+3 finance ministers' meetings which reported the names of the chairs. In every CMIM round, two countries served as the co-chairs of a meeting. One co-chair was from the +3 states while the other was from ASEAN countries. States that co-chaired the negotiations could be expected to gain more bargaining leverage vis-à-vis the countries that did not co-chair the talks.

Issue linkages

Issue linkages involved in international bargaining can be divided into two main types: political and economic. However, in this study, political caveats will be set aside for the following reasons. First, my interviews suggest little evidence of political linkage in the CMIM negotiation.[6] Second, it is typically difficult to get different bureaucracies especially those from different fields to work together. Security and economic departments or agencies usually have separate functions, responsibilities and standard operating procedures. Owing to these differences, issues that security bureaucrats negotiate with other countries are not usually linked to matters being negotiated by economic personnel. Therefore, in most international economic negotiations, parties do not normally merge their discussions regarding security issues with economic ones.

Another reason is that under the ASEAN+3 framework, financial matters are negotiated differently from other issues. Unlike other issues which are finalized at the summit level (i.e. ASEAN+3 Summits), decisions concerning financial elements are settled at the minister level (i.e. ASEAN+3 Finance Ministers' Meetings). Given the fact that high levels of technicalities were involved, it is unlikely that CMIM negotiation could incorporate political issues into the agreement.

A measure of the likelihood that a country might have employed issue linkages is the intensity of economic relations among bargaining parties. Statistical indicators, namely the level and degree of trade ties and foreign direct investments flows will be used to measure their economic ties. This may have been assumed that states with more intensive economic relations during the CMIM talks would have been more likely to be in a position to utilize issue linkages than countries with less rigorous ties.

Table 2.2 Metrics and indicators

Elements of Bargaining Influence	Hypotheses	Metrics and Indicators
1. Discount rate	**Hypothesis 1**: States with a lower discount rate in the CMIM negotiations were likely to close a deal with more favourable terms than countries with a higher discount rate.	Reserve adequacy (reserves in months of imports) and international borrowing capacity (sovereign credit rating).
2. attractiveness of non-agreement alternatives or best alternative to no agreement (batna)	**Hypothesis 2**: Parties in the CMIM negotiations with a more attractive batna were likely to close a deal with more favourable terms than those with a less attractive batna.	Past histories of exchange rate crises and IMF lending and experience of IMF programmes
3. Informational strategies and tactics (exploiting informational asymmetry)	**Hypothesis 3.1**: States in the CMIM negotiations that had more knowledge on other actors' preferences were likely to close a deal with more favourable terms than those that had less knowledge. **Hypothesis 3.2**: States in the CMIM negotiations that had greater expertise on issues being negotiated were likely to close a deal with more favourable terms than those with less expertise.	States' acknowledging other parties' preferences before or during the CMIM negotiations States' exercise of knowing the contents or technicalities of the issues being negotiated
4. The role of chair(s)	**Hypothesis 4**: States in the CMIM negotiations that assumed positions as co-chairs were likely to close a deal with more favourable terms than non-co-chairing states.	Names of CMIM co-chairs
5. Issue linkages	**Hypothesis 5**: Countries in the CMIM negotiations that were in position to employ issue linkages were likely to close a deal with more favourable terms than those that were not in position to do so.	For trade relations, bilateral imports and exports between countries. For financial relations, bilateral foreign direct investment flows between countries.
6. Coalition Formation	**Hypothesis 6**: Countries in the CMIM negotiations that formed coalitions with stronger states were likely to close a deal with more favourable terms than states that did not form such coalitions. **Hypothesis 6a**: Countries in the CMIM negotiations that prevented coalition formation by other states were likely to close a deal with more favourable terms than states that did not inhibit such coalitions from creating.	Nominal GDP and GDP per capita.

Coalition formation

In the CMIM negotiation, a grand bargain took place between two "camps" – the +3 countries on one hand, and ASEAN nations, on the other.[7] Within each grouping, states could have been expected to band together with their "stronger" counterparts in order to gain more bargaining influence. "Stronger" parties in the CMIM negotiation were those that possessed greater economic strength.

A country's economic strength is a function of economic size and economic wealth. To gauge the strength, an index was created by using an equal weighting of (1) GDP[8] – an indicator of economic size and (2) GDP per capita[9] – an indicator of economic wealth.

Table 2.2 summarizes the indicators used to measure the independent variables.

Data collection, data sources and method of analysis

Some data were obtained from official statements and the author's interviews with government officials and scholars from China, Japan, Indonesia, Malaysia, South Korea and Thailand. Other sources included newspaper archives, policy reports and other relevant academic papers.

Table 2.3 summarizes the data sources for each of the variables used in the analysis.

As for the method of analysis, process tracing was employed to reconstruct the making of the CMIM agreement. Process tracing is "the technique of looking for the observable implications of hypothesized causal processes within a single case" (Bennett 2008: 705). This approach can establish relationships between CMIM negotiation outcomes, members' bargaining influence and the factors contributing to it. To conduct process tracing, a researcher "examines histories, archival documents, interview transcripts and other relevant sources to see whether the causal process a theory hypothesizes or implies in a case is in fact evident in the sequence and values of the intervening variables in that case" (George and Bennett 2005: 6).

Admittedly, process-tracing method contains certain limitations. For example, it is time consuming and requires a lot of data. An investigation depends on data availability (Bennett 2008: 705). Moreover, process tracing can suffer from an "infinite regress" problem as a researcher keeps searching for steps between steps between steps in a particular event (King et al. 1994). In addition, if an examiner is not careful, he may end up undertaking biased interpretations of the obtained information.

Despite these constraints, process tracing was selected because it is appropriate to this CMIM study for the following reasons. First, the approach can identify and complete causal chains. It enables the researcher to link observations in a specific way in order to explain how bargaining processes unfold. This can in turn lessen the problem of "indeterminacy" or "an inability to choose among competing explanations for a case" (Bennett 2004: 20). Illustratively, statistical analysis can at best tell the direction of the correlation – whether X and Y correlate positively (when X's value increases, Y's also rises, and vice versa) or negatively (when X's value rises, Y's instead decreases, and vice versa). However, it cannot determine

Table 2.3 Data sources

Elements of Bargaining Influence	Metrics and Indicators	Data Sources
1. Discount rate	Reserve adequacy (reserves in months of imports). From 2003–2009.	The World Bank
	International borrowing capacity (sovereign credit rating). From 2003–2009.	Standard and Poor's; Moody's; Fitch
2. Attractiveness of non-agreement alternatives or best alternative to no agreement (batna)	Past histories of exchange rate crises. From 2004–2010.	The Bank for International Settlements, International Monetary Fund, newspaper archives; interview reports
	Past histories of IMF lending and experience of IMF programmes. From 1996–2010.	The International Monetary Fund; newspaper archives; interview reports
3. Informational strategies and tactics (exploiting informational asymmetry)	Knowing other actors' preferences	Journalistic sources (secondary sources); interview reports
	Expertise	Journalistic sources (secondary sources); interview reports
4. The role of chair/ co-chair(s)	Names of CMI and CMIM chairs. From 2004–2010.	The Joint Ministerial Statements by ASEAN+3 Finance Ministers; interview reports
5. Issue linkages	(Trade relations) Bilateral imports and exports between countries. From 2004–2010.	United Nations Commodity Trade Statistics Database
	(Finance relations) Bilateral foreign investment flows between countries. From 2004–2010.	The ASEAN Secretariat; Bank Indonesia; Bank of Japan; Bank Negara Malaysia; Department of Statistics, Malaysia; Ministry of Finance, Japan; Ministry of Knowledge Economy, South Korea; Ministry of Strategy and Finance, South Korea; United Nations Conference on Trade and Development (UNCTAD); Organisation for Economic Co-operation and Development (OECD)
6. Coalition formation	Nominal GDP and GDP per capita. From 2004–2010.	The International Monetary Fund
Outcomes	Metrics and Indicators	Data Sources
1. Country's original goal	Contribution amount a country aimed to make at the beginning of the CMIM negotiations	Newspaper archives, interview reports
2. Country's outcome	Actual contribution amount a country would contribute to the CMIM reserve pool	The Joint Ministerial Statements by ASEAN+3 Finance Ministers

whether X causes Y or the other way around. In contrast, questions such as "If X correlates with Y, did X caused Y or vice versa?" can be addressed by utilizing the process-tracing method (Bennett 2010: 209). Via its steps such as sifting through a sequence of confirming evidence to validate hypothesized mechanisms while ruling out the others, process tracing can pinpoint the direction of casual mechanisms, hence reducing the problem of indeterminancy (Bennett and Elman 2006: 459–460).

Moreover, process-tracing method can address the issue of "spuriousness." Spuriousness refers to a relationship in which two or more variables – such as X and Y – appear to be related but are in fact not causally linked. This problem happens when a third variable (Z) causes both X and Y, creating a "fake" pattern of relationship between X and Y (Bennett 2010: 352). In short, the influence of Z renders a link between X and Y spurious. If not careful, the investigator may wrongly conclude that X causes Y. However, process tracing can tackle a potential spuriousness problem as it can check whether the relationships between variables are in fact causal or not.

Using a process-tracing method may increase an opportunity for discovering additional useful factors explaining final outcomes that a researcher did not initially focus on. By tracking backwardly a sequence of events, some variables that were overlooked earlier may turn out to play a significant part in completing a causal chain. In short, this method of analysis can uncover new aspects of events which can generate new insights for the study.

Finally, not only that process tracing exposes new factors, it also reveals alternative pathways leading to final results. This method helps address the problem of equifinality, which is a situation when the same kinds of outcome occur from different sets of independent variables (George and Bennett 2005: 157). It is because the research using this method must consult a lot of data to identify and reconstruct casual chains. As he is sifting through loads of information, he may be able to map out other mechanisms/pathways explaining the same outcome variable (George and Bennett 2005: 206).

Owing to these benefits, several researchers have resorted to a process-tracing method to gain valuable insights. For example, Theda Skocpol (2007) used it explain three social revolutions – the French, Russian and Chinese. She explained these phenomena by using two independent variables: international pressure on a state and peasant rebellion. To map out causal relationships, Skocpol (2007) embarked on a process-tracing method to identify a sequence of steps between each independent variable and the outcome. Likewise, Yuen Foong Khong (1992) assessed consistency between historical analogies and chosen policy options. By employing process tracing through gathering historical records and conducting interviews, Khong was able to conclude that the Korean War analogy accounted for the US air attacks and later the deployment of large-scale ground forces during the later Vietnam War.

In the area of International Political Economy, process tracing has regularly been utilized (Martin 1993; Moravcsik 1998; Drezner 1999). For instance, Vinod Aggarwal (1985) attempted to explain certain trade outcomes that were not favourable to the USA as its relative power or a structural realist theory would have predicted. Using process tracing, Aggarwal identifies new links between the actors' decision making and their bargaining interaction that might have resulted in an outcome not anticipated by theory. Through process tracing, Drezner (1999: Chapter 8) explained the US response to curb North Korea's enthusiasm to obtain nuclear weapons in the 1990s. The author found that Washington offered economic inducements to Pyongyang as the best option given the limits of economic and military coercion (Drezner 1999: 302).

In this book, process tracing will be carried out as follows.

1. First, the original goal of each of the countries in the analysis, namely how much they aimed to contribute to the CMIM reserve fund at the beginning of the CMIM negotiations, will be identified. For the +3, their lower limit of contribution amount will be identified as their original goal. In contrast, for the ASEAN countries, their upper limit of contribution amount will be identified as their initial objective.

2. Next, comparisons between their original goal and final outcome will be conducted to see how well each country achieved its original objective. Each country's performance will be compared by using the 5-point scale outlined earlier.

3. Finally, the strategies and tactics employed by each country's negotiators will be scrutinized and the negotiation processes will be traced back in order to reveal casual links between the strategies and tactics and the state's performance. If the analysis discovers that some elements of bargaining influence listed previously were used by the negotiators to arrive at certain agreement details, the hypotheses outlined earlier will be confirmed.

Notes

1 MERCOSUR is a sub-regional trade bloc in Latin America. Its members are Argentina, Brazil, Paraguay, Uruguay and Venezuela.
2 SALTs were international agreements between the USA and the Soviet Union over disarmaments.
3 The Cairn Group was a group of agricultural exporting countries. The members were Argentina, Australia, Bolivia, Brazil, Canada, Chile, Colombia, Costa Rica, Guatemala, Indonesia, Malaysia, New Zealand, Pakistan, Paraguay, Peru, the Philippines, South Africa, Thailand and Uruguay.
4 Interview with J2.
5 Interview with T3.
6 Interview with T3.
7 Interview with I1.
8 The gross domestic product (GDP) is the market value of all final goods and services produced in one country in a given time period. GDP (denoted as Y) consists of four components: consumption (C), investment (I), government spending (G) and net exports (NX). Thus, $Y = C + I + G + NX$.
9 GDP per capita is the GDP of a country divided by its population.

3 China

China's positions regarding contribution and voting issues

In China, the process of crafting economic policies is highly insulated from domestic interest groups. Rather, the policy-making circle comprises a handful of actors, namely the Ministry of Finance (MOF), the People's Bank of China (PBC), the Ministry of Foreign Affairs (FMPRC) and a small group of scholars. Although these entities are important in furnishing the national plans, central policy-making power is often shared between the MOF and PBC. For a full picture of main entities involved in the Chinese foreign economic policy making, see Hess (2014).

In the context of ASEAN+3 financial cooperation, the Chinese representatives are generally from the MOF and PBC. It is because the finance ministry takes care of bond issuances, while the central bank manages the country's foreign-reserve holding – the elements important to East Asian financial regionalism (Elliott and Yan 2013). Regarding the CMIM, these players also played a key role in negotiating the agreement.

As far as the issues of members' financial commitments and voting power were concerned, China wanted to be the biggest CMIM contributor and voter. In other words, it aimed to financially commit to the CMIM reserve pool more than any other participants. As several observers have reckoned (Hassdorf 2011; Grimes 2011a), Beijing's preference of being the greatest CMIM contributor and voter is closely tied to its aspiration to become a regional leader. Before digging deeply into its desire for East Asian leadership, let's first explore Beijing's economic ascendance and how it has led the country to form such ambition.

China has been recognized as the world's number one factory due to its ability manufacture and assemble various commodities for export. The country has been enjoying trade surpluses with major economies such as the USA. Its current account surplus has resulted in its swelling foreign reserves, which touched around US$ 4 trillion in the first quarter of 2014 (Noble 2014), making Beijing's one of the world's largest creditor nations. Moreover, such exorbitant reserves led to the establishment of the China Investment Corporation (CIC) – the country's sovereign wealth fund (SWF) – in 2007. At the time of this writing, this SWF ranks the fifth biggest in the world (Wei 2015), with its endowment approximately US$ 653 billion (Clark 2015). In addition, the Chinese rising middle-class has opened up huge business opportunities for other states to export and sell goods to the country. Despite its recent slowdown, China's growing economic strength, large markets and increasingly integration into the global economy render it impossible to ignore the country's influence in the international community.

When exactly the notion of China's exercising its clout in the international settings originated is still debatable. Nevertheless, the first official mentioning of the term "economic diplomacy" appeared in August 2004. At the 10th Conference of Chinese Diplomatic Envoys Stationed Abroad in Beijing, China, the Chinese Premier Wen Jiabao posited that

> with the in-depth development of economic globalization and the growth of China's economic strength, economic diplomacy has increasingly become an important part of China's overall diplomacy. China will vigorously develop foreign trade, expand foreign investments, continuously explore overseas markets, further upgrade the qualities and levels of utilizing foreign investments and importing advanced technologies, and actively serve key strategies for economic development of China.
>
> (Permanent Mission of China to the UN at Geneva, 2004)

Although Beijing has never defined what "economic diplomacy" is, the preceding statement indicated that this strategy's primary goal was to protect and promote its national interests. Experts have agreed that the country's economic diplomacy not only aims at advancing its own economic interests, but also at achieving other political objectives (Men 2013). Utilizing economic tools to attain specific political or diplomatic goals is closely in line with David Baldwin's (1985) concept of "economic statecraft." In short, China's economic diplomacy can be seen as another name for its economic statecraft.

Economic statecraft is broadly defined as governments' use of economic means to influence other states' behaviour (Baldwin 1985: Chapters 2–3). It is often deployed to achieve a wider set of goals beyond purely economic ones, such as troop withdrawals and a regime change in other countries. To practice economic diplomacy, states have been witnessed to resort to a variety of tools. The instruments can take forms of inducements or sanctions,[1] or the combination of the two. Inducements can range from reducing tariff, granting import and export license, to providing foreign aids. Some examples of sanctions are trade embargo, tariff discrimination against a target, license denial, overseas asset freeze and foreign aid suspension.

China's use of economic diplomacy or statecraft has been well-documented. Illustratively, the country provided massive assistance for infrastructure development in oil-rich states, as seen in foreign aids and interest-free loans to Angola in March 2006 (Afrol News 2006). Furthermore, Beijing, through its practice of economic diplomacy was able to retaliate against the European Union (EU) countries when the latter's policies or actions clashed with the former's interests. For example, China was infuriated by the German Chancellor Angela Merkel's visit to the Tibetan Dalai Lama in 2007. In its response, Beijing cancelled high-level meetings with Berlin, including the bilateral negotiation about the intellec-tual priority rights protection, and instead turned to cut a deal worth more than US\$ 20 billion with France. Fearing of their trade disadvantage, the German cor-porations lobbied their government to restore the Sino-Germany ties. Berlin, being pressured by these businesses' demands and their society's upholding of human rights, later adopted "quiet diplomacy" by exchanging views at the closed-door meetings with the Chinese leaders on human rights matters while maintaining the bilateral relations in the public's eyes (Men 2013: 298). In addition, despite little evidence showing Beijing's utilization of the China Investment Corporation (CIC) to achieve certain political ends, it is widely suspected that this SWF "would add an additional unknown player in the financial market whose corporate governance would not be at all transparent, but would also increase the politicization of capital flows and buying spree" (Katada 2008: 411).

Thanks to the global financial crisis (GFC), China's leadership aspiration was strengthened. The great crash has improved the country's relative position in the global economy, enabling it to become one of the key drivers of growth. That the "Triad," consisting of the USA, the EU and Japan, was struggling with weak growth and economic trouble at home opened a window of opportunity for Beijing to assume a larger role in shaping international projects (You et al. 2009; Zhang 2012). As a result, China, in the post-GFC era, was in a better position to wield its influence in regional and global arenas than before. (Cohen and Chiu 2014: 11).

Regarding East Asian financial cooperation, China viewed that its participa-tion in the area could pave a way for itself to expand its power in this region. For instance, the country China exhibited its leadership stance during the AFC years, such as by refusing to devalue its currency – the renminbi (RMB) or the yuan – amidst the crisis. While Japan depreciated the yen to maintain trade com-petitiveness with ASEAN, China unilaterally maintained the yuan's value despite doing so jeopardized its commercial advantage vis-à-vis ASEAN nations. It was because by keeping the value of the RMB higher, the Chinese exports became more expensive and hence less competitive than the latter's. Moreover, the coun-try offered low-interest loans and aids to the AFC-hit economies. Additionally, at the 6th ASEAN+3 Summit in Phnom Penh, Cambodia in November 2002, Beijing unveiled the Asia Debt Reduction Plan which would reduce or cancel parts of the debts owed by Cambodia, Laos, Myanmar and Vietnam (FMPRC 2002).

China has also been active in its involvement in the ASEAN+3 financial process. For instance, the country proposed to upgrade the ASEAN+3 vice finance minis-ters' and central bank deputies' meetings to ministerial-level ones (Dent 2008: 71). Beijing's leadership was also showcased in several training programmes it offered to ASEAN+3 personnel since 2000. The courses usually concentrated on capac-ity building and technical issues, ranging from regional financial cooperation to economic reforms and development. This act could be seen as Beijing's attempt to influence the policy-making circle in the other states via educating the latter's elites (Jiang 2010).

Speaking specifically about the CMIM and its predecessor CMI, China's clout in these schemes was evident. For example, the country played a major role in setting up the CMI framework (Rana 2002: 8). Because the CMI later evolved into the CMIM, the latter automatically became the main target for Beijing to undertake its economic statecraft (Song 2013). Because the CMIM is the most advanced form of regional financial cooperation date, certain agreement details could set precedents for future mechanisms to come. Illustratively, its decision-making system could be adopted by other regional institutions in the future. Thus, China reasoned that its leadership in CMIM it was a must or a prerequisite for its realization of regional leadership in financial areas.

It is worth-highlighting that another reason why Beijing fervently took part in creating the CMIM was due to its own perception that it was able to alter regional developments more than the others in larger settings such as the IMF and G20. As one source precisely summarizes,

> In G20, China is a political minnow; in the CMIM, it looms large. Its behaviour in the G20 is more adaptive, learning the ropes from others; in the CMIM, it can afford to be more assertive and combative, for example, with respect to its relations with Japan. In the G20, it is mainly a taker of the norms and rules of the organisation dominated by the US and the G7; in the CMIM, it is in a much better position to play a greater role in shaping its rules and norms. Whilst taking a backseat relative to the developed countries in the G20, it has managed to occupy a front seat in the CMIM. In general, China's regional influence is felt more acutely by its neighbours than its influence on the global stage by non-Asian countries around the world.
>
> (Chan 2012: 205)

In short, China's relative economic clout in East Asia permitted the country to acquire larger room to manoeuvre in CMIM than wider contexts. Therefore, the CMIM serves as a suitable platform for Beijing to wield its leverage over its neighbours and establish its leadership in the region.

However, Beijing's leadership pursuit could not be attained quite easily. Its attempt to rise as a regional leader has been lessened by the efforts from Japan. Wanting also to be a leader in East Asia, the latter has long checked Beijing's clout. Tokyo has not been shy to deploy policies to ensure that Beijing will not assume the role of a regional leader by default (Stubbs 2014: 535). For example,

> Japan, the currently dominant but declining power with the strongest financial and technical capacity in the region and with the internationally accepted currency, would want to use its present currency power to lock in the existing disparity by formalizing arrangements such as the wider use of yen in the region. Meanwhile, the Chinese authorities wish to prevent Japan from locking China in at a subordinate place.
>
> (Katada 2008: 410)

Unsurprisingly, the Sino-Japanese contestation was clearly palpable. Both countries have tried to promote their own agendas as well as exhibited no reluctance to block or tank each other's proposals (Park 2013: 95). Their rivalry also spilled over into the CMIM negotiation. This regional mechanism turned out to be a prime arena in which the two states battled for regional leadership (Grimes 2011a: 84). This is because the CMIM members' financial contributions are proportionally linked to their voting power, an actor getting the greatest contribution and vote share will be able to alter the decision-making process. As a result, Beijing and Tokyo contested over the issue of "who pays more" or which would be the largest contributor and voter to the CMIM. In addition, both states competitively provided to other CMIM participants with training courses, seminars and workshops on the CMIM-related issues. (Lee 2010: 5). They were also found to intensely grapple for the seat of the AMRO's director (Chung 2013: 809).

It should be noted that China's roles in regional finance have not only been checked by Japan, but also by external players, namely the USA and IMF. History indicates that both parties were indeed influential in the development of regional financial architectures as they successfully killed the AMF idea proposed by Japan on the basis that the entity alienated Washington's and IMF's involvement. As far as CMI/CMIM is concerned, China reasoned that the facility possesses high potential to advance further and hence in the future can lessen Washington's supremacy in the region, which in turn enhancing the former's (Tso and Yeh 2013: 117). Therefore, it is no wonder why Beijing strongly opposed extending the CMIM membership to external, non-regional players (Chung 2013: 809). The Chinese attempt has so far been successful as the current CMIM membership is currently confined within East Asia. By keeping external actors out of this regional grouping, Beijing can more easily exercise its power over other regional states without little interference from the former, namely Washington.

To conclude, China's strive to become the biggest CMIM contributor and voter stemmed from its higher ambition for East Asian leadership. The CMIM was perceived as another channel where Beijing could exercise its clout or practice its economic diplomacy over its neighbours. Viewing that this regional financial safety net has potential to develop further, China aimed at securing the largest contribution and vote shares in the CMIM. Doing so was deemed as an important step for Beijing to realize its regional leadership, even though it had to fight with another tough contender – Japan – in this regard.

China's involvement in shaping the CMIM agreement details

Which aspects of the CMIM agreement did China shape the final outcomes? The following analysis reveals Beijing's influence over the following details: (1) the inclusion of Hong Kong into the CMIM; (2) the decision to multilateralize the CMI; and (3) the selection of the first AMRO's director.

Role of knowledge about others' preferences in explaining the Hong Kong inclusion

As earlier shown, China and Japan similarly wanted to be the CMIM biggest contributor and voter. The stakes were high for both of them. To Japan, the CMIM has been commonly perceived as its brainchild project due to the country's long history of involvement in regional financial cooperation. Tokyo hence saw itself taking a lead in developing the CMIM project. However, the current situations differed from the ones in the past. China has risen and is now trying to catch up with Japan by attempting to take over a leadership role in regional finance. To Beijing, the CMIM was regarded as an important venue to showcase its power to the regional states and the international community.[2] Therefore, China aimed to obtain the biggest shares in financial commitment and voting authority. As Benjamin Cohen precisely summarizes:

> The rivalry was perhaps best illustrated by the intense bargaining that took place in 2009 over the two countries' quotas in the CMIM. Tokyo was determined to gain the largest quota, reflecting its past dominance in regional finance. China, however, insisted that its own growth and size entitled it to an equal share of the total – an "equal firsts" policy.
>
> (Cohen 2010: 21)

Owing to the impact of GFC on its economy, South Korea agreed that it would not financially commit to the CMIM mechanism as equally as China and Japan (See Chapter 5 for detailed explanation). However, Seoul's concession did not better the ongoing Sino-Japanese duelling over which would acquire the greatest CMIM contribution and voting quotas. Their bilateral talk concerning this issue continued.

While both players were in the middle of bickering over the division of their contribution and vote shares, Beijing proposed to Tokyo that Hong Kong should become the member of the CMIM. The idea was thrown onto the bargaining table within little prior consultations with Japan.[3] The issue sparked another conflict between the two powers and exacerbated the situation.

Before discussing how the Hong Kong inclusion altered the negotiation dynamics and outcomes, let's first explore why China suddenly shifted gears. Why did the country abruptly push for the incorporation of the former British colony into the CMIM? In short, why did the Hong Kong inclusion issue become Beijing's objective in the CMIM negotiation?

First, Hong Kong has long been adept at dealing with financial technicalities as it is one of major financial centres in the region and the world.[4] According to Sung and Song (1991: 27–28), this past English protectorate had served as a main conduit for China's knowledge and technological transfer, as seen in the former's providing training to the Mainland's personnel ranging from after-sales-service technicians to legal consultants. As a result, Beijing needed Hong Kong's expertise to work out the CMIM details which in a large part involved financial operations.[5] Hence, incorporating Hong Kong into the CMIM mechanism was crucial as the former's financial expertise would strengthen Beijing's leverage over the crafting of the agreement details. China reasoned that the assistance from Hong Kong could enable it to be on par with Japan in its negotiation with the latter over the CMIM financial conducts.

Another reason why China was keen to have Hong Kong join the CMIM was because the former anticipated that the latter would become a key player in the process of developing the CMIM or its spinoffs (if any) in the future.[6] The former British colony was already a *de facto* participant under the ASEAN+3 financial cooperation framework. For example, in the pre-CMIM years, Hong Kong in several occasions was present at the AFDM+3 as a Chinese delegate.[7] The latter has also been very helpful in advancing regional financial initiatives. For example, Hong Kong introduced and pushed its proposal for the CMIM framework at the 10th AFMM+3 in May 2007.[8] As a result, it was no wonder why China had placed a high bet on the former British outpost to function as another actor shaping up regional financial mechanisms to come.

In addition, Beijing aimed to use Hong Kong as a regional channel to increase the use of its currency – the renminbi (RMB) or the yuan – through the network of CMIM's currency swap arrangements conducted by the latter.[9] Illustratively, once it joins CMIM, Hong Kong will be able to conclude swap contracts with other regional states, hence elevating the yuan's circulation in the international financial market. In short, bringing in Hong Kong to the CMIM was part of Beijing's "renminbi (RMB) internationalization."

What exactly is renminbi (RMB) internationalization? It is a strategy aimed at promoting the use of the Chinese currency – the renminbi (RMB) or the yuan – in international financial system. (For the history of RMB internationalization, see Box 3.1). This policy can be achieved by undertaking two kinds of approaches simultaneously (Subbachi 2010). The first path involves raising the RMB usage in international transactions (e.g. trade settlements), while the second track aims at transforming the yuan into a reserve currency, or a legal tender that foreigners want to hold.[10]

To pursue the first track, the Chinese authorities, the PBC in particular, has encouraged the Chinese firms to settle their transactions in the yuan with their foreign counterparts. One example was the experimental project conducted in July 2009, which allowed the country's export companies in Guangdong and Shanghai to conduct the RMB-denominated trade (Qiu 2012). The government has also adopted the RMB as an invoicing currency in its free trade agreements with other countries. Moreover, the Chinese central bank, the PBC, has incorporated the yuan in its bilateral currency swap packages with its equivalents around the world. The active practice of RMB internationalization was well-reflected by the fact that Beijing has increasingly engaged in the currency exchange schemes with and several foreign central banks in both developed and emerging economies (Schotter and Wildau 2014; Xinhua 2015). As for the time of this writing, "more than 20 central banks – including in Russia, the UK and Australia – have signed currency swap agreements totalling about $430 billion with China" (Talley and Wei 2015).

To implement the second approach, Beijing has boosted the circulation of the RMB-denominated bonds in its offshore markets of Hong Kong and Shanghai, and their equivalents around the world (Yu 2008). For instance, major banks such as the Hong Kong and Shanghai Banking Corporation and Bank of China were given a permission to issue bonds denominated in RMB (sometimes dubbed as "dim sum" or "panda" bonds) in Hong Kong, which is the largest offshore yuan hub. The demands of these securities have grown rapidly. When the first and second issuances took place in September 2009 and November 2011, the amount offered was merely 6 and 8 billion yuan, respectively. By August 2011, the size of the bonds proffered ballooned to 20 billion yuan or US$ 3.1 billion, and some of which were available for the private sector's purchases (*China Daily* 2011).

As seen, the relationship between the Chinese Mainland and its Special Administrative Regions (SARs) is crucial in realizing RMB internationalization. Thus, China wanted Hong Kong to participate in the CMIM as doing so could enhance the yuan usage in the region. The successful RMB "regionalization," through CMIM's swap networks via the offshore yuan market in Hong Kong, was perceived by Beijing as a vital stepping stone towards the utilization of the RMB in wider contexts (Gao and Yu 2009).

Box 3.1   The history of RMB internationalization

The idea of RMB internationalization could be traced back to the early 2000s when the Hong Kong Monetary Authority (HKMA) in November 2001 approached the PBC and raised "the idea of introducing personal renminbi business in Hong Kong" (HKMA 2014). However, the notion gained great traction in 2006 when the report prepared by the study group commissioned by PBC was released. The document titled "The Timing, Path, and Strategies of RMB Internationalization" argued that "[t]he time has come for promotion of the internationalization of the yuan . . . [which] can enhance China's international status and competitiveness significantly . . . [and] . . . increase its influence in the international economy." Moreover, China's "rise in power standing" rendered this approach "an inevitable choice" to the country (PBOC Study Group 2006).

Since then, a yuan internationalization strategy had progressively been developed as the Chinese policy makers and experts took a more active role in exploring the matter. An example was the conference in 2007 organized by the Hong Kong Monetary Authority. Because the seminar's focus was on how to advance the strategy more concretely, the earlier cases of yen and euro internationalization were examined and foreign economists were consulted to provide advice on the technicalities on realizing the RMB internationalization.[11]

The Hong Kong issue turned out to aggravate the clash between the two Northeast Asian countries during the negotiation. Admittedly, some difficulties of deciding on the incorporation of the former into CMIM involved technical aspects, which were borne out of the "one country, two systems" of the Chinese governance. Given than Hong Kong was granted a status of the SAR of China in July 1997, the question became how to apply the "one country, two systems" principle, if it was to be applied at all, to the CMIM framework. Answering this puzzle requires pondering on two major issues. The first one was whether to include Hong Kong in the CMIM. The other was that if Hong Kong were to become a member of this this regional mechanism, how would its contribution and vote share be calibrated? In other words, would Beijing's financial commitment and voting power include Hong Kong's, or be separate from the latter's?[12]

However, because of the Sino-Japanese feud, the Hong Kong membership went beyond purely technical issues. The old game of politics intervened. When China argued for Hong Kong participation in the CMIM, Tokyo quickly renounced.[13] The latter's rejection largely emerged from its suspicion that such inclusion would eventually eclipse its power in regional finance. According to Ciorciari (2011: 938), when Beijing "pushed to include both the Hong Kong Monetary Authority and the People's Bank of China as part of PRC team . . . Japan resisted, fearing a loss of relative influence."

The negotiation got stuck as both sided displayed no show any signs of backing down. The prospect of a bargaining failure was clearly lurking. Against all odds, the talk did not collapse. Inside talks between China and Japan coined the outcome.[14] The parties managed to arrive at the deal acceptable to both of them at the last minute, just before a press release of the 12th AFMM+3 in 2009.[15] Their agreement was that Hong Kong was permitted to join the CMIM but it must comply with certain "special conditions." For instance, the entity does not have power to decide on the fundamental issues.[16] Although it can vote on the executive issues (e.g. lending decisions), its votes must be conjoined with Beijing to constitute as the total Chinese vote, which is equal to the Japanese one.[17] Furthermore, Hong Kong's financial contribution amount and vote is to be combined with Beijing's, which together would equate Japan's.[18]

Looking closely, these conditions put China and Hong Kong at a disadvantage when compared to Japan. These rules not only get rid of Hong Kong's voting autonomy and hinder its voice in the decision-making process, but they also sabotage the Mainland's aim of being the biggest CMIM contributor and voter. In other words, Beijing would end up providing a lesser financial amount to the CMIM fund than Tokyo. For China which was loath to bear a smaller commitment and voting weight than Tokyo in CMIM (Chaitrong 2009), these terms could be considered as a disastrous and face-losing defeat to the country. What made Beijing swallow such arrangements?

Evidence suggests that China's knowledge about Japan's preferences accounted for the former's acquiescence regarding the Hong Kong inclusion into the CMIM. The country realized that having Hong Kong as a CMIM member would definitely stir Tokyo's nervousness because the latter aspired to be a regional leader.[19] In other words, the Hong Kong matter was sensitive to Japan as the country feared that granting the former English protectorate some voting power would turn out to undermine its own CMIM influence vis-à-vis Beijing. Also, China realized that its proposal could be seen as a big request because Hong Kong had never been an official party to the AFMM+3 system[20] (Kawai 2009a: 6). Consequently, Japan would much likely to reject Hong Kong participation. Moreover, Beijing could gauge that the involved CMIM parties, especially Japan, would not concur if Hong Kong is to vote autonomously from the Mainland. It was mainly because the entity is the Chinese SAR, and voting rights are generally given to only sovereign states, not SARs.[21] Therefore, taking into account these concerns, Beijing understood that in order for Tokyo to give a green light to Hong Kong's CMIM participation, the entity should have a low profile.[22] Consequently, Beijing was prepared for such outcomes.

China's anticipation turned out to be right. Japan swiftly responded to the Chinese request with a counter-proposal of its own. The former pushed to impose particular conditions on Hong Kong which ultimately eliminated the latter's independent voting power, through the conditions outlined previously. Tokyo was also quick to support the idea that Hong Kong's financial commitment and votes was to be combined with Beijing's to make up the total Chinese share, which will be equal to the Japan's.

What were Beijing's reactions? After calling for Hong Kong membership, China understood that it might have to appease Tokyo on some terms. For instance, one way to get the Japanese approval of Hong Kong's CMIM membership was to allow Tokyo to prevail over Beijing in the realms of financial contributions and voting power. As a result, China conceded accordingly.[23]

Although Japan's demands were teeth-clenching, they were neither entirely intolerable nor unacceptable to China. Undeniably, abiding to them required the latter to abandon its initial objective of being the "greatest contributor and voter." As the negotiation unfolded, the country seemed to have modified the meaning of this phrase. Instead of "Beijing" by itself being the sole greatest contributor and voter, the definition was later adjusted to mean "one China," or "Beijing together with Hong Kong" being the "co-biggest" contributor and voter along with Japan.

In conclusion, the Hong Kong deal was partly made possible by China's knowledge about Japan's preferences. Recognizing Tokyo's desire and interests, China was able to grasp why the latter would do anything to prevent Hong Kong from being part of the CMIM and why Tokyo set the specific rules pertaining to Hong Kong's voting power accordingly. Wanting dearly to have the previous British outpost join this regional initiative, Beijing ultimately decided to forgo its original goal of its alone making the greatest financial commitment to the CMIM by unilaterally adjusting what constitutes the "biggest contributor and voter." By doing so, Beijing could add Hong Kong into the CMIM framework and in some ways continue to claim that it is still one of the two "co-equal largest contributors and voters" in the CMIM.

Role of the co-chair in altering the decision
to multilateralize the CMI

Admittedly, the multilateralization of the CMI is not the primary focus of this book, which centres on the distribution members' financial commitments and voting power. Nevertheless, China's roles in affecting this outcome was added not only because it can shed more light on international negotiation processes, but also because the decision to transform the CMI into the CMIM was regarded as a significant step in the evolution of East Asian financial cooperation.

The question concerning which entity originally forged the idea of multilateralizing the CMI is still debatable. Some maintained that the concept was initially proposed by Japan in 2005. For instance, the report presented by the Japanese Institute for International Monetary Affairs concluded that "[i]n order to establish a stronger self-help and support system, the CMI needs to be developed as a multilateral institution" (Asami 2005: 3). Yet, different sources argued instead that the notion was initially introduced by ASEAN countries.[24] Nevertheless, other evidence points to Beijing's efforts. The Chinese Premier Wen Jiabao earlier presented the concept in 2003, at the 7th ASEAN+3 Summit in Bali, Indonesia. In his speech titled "Composing a New Chapter for East Asia Cooperation" given at this gathering, Premier Wen suggested that East Asian financial cooperation be augmented through several measures including turning CMI into a multilateralized form.

> To promote East Asian financial cooperation. The cooperation level should be elevated. To that end, I suggest the following: to build on the Chiang Mai Initiative and phase in multi-lateral currency swap arrangements on the basis of the existing bilateral ones.
>
> (Wen 2003)

Regardless of who first coined the multilateralization notion, one must not ignore the fact that China did play a crucial role in advancing forward such idea, which ultimately led to the actual multilateralization of the CMI in 2007 (Jiang 2010: 614).

Speaking about the upgrading process (i.e. turning CMI into CMIM), one could argue that the first collective effort under the ASEAN+3 framework to embark on this endeavour was officially declared in 2005. In May 2005, the finance ministers summoned at the 8th AFMM+3 in Istanbul, Turkey. Wanting to bolster the CMI's effectiveness, the officials "tasked the Deputies to study the various possible routes towards multilateralizing the CMI" (JMS, 8th AFMM+3). A year later in May 2006, the 9th AFMM+3 was held in Hyderabad, India. The meeting reached a consensus that to make progress on the multilateralization scheme, a special team must be formed to take up this task. The governments

> tasked the Deputies to set up a "new task force" to further study various possible options towards an advanced framework of the regional liquidity support

arrangement (CMI multilateralization or Post-CMI), based upon their exploration during the past year. Moreover, we instructed the Deputies to enhance the regional surveillance capacities.

(JMS, 9th AFMM)

The upgrading procedure progressed fast. Being satisfied with the results made by the new taskforce, the members reached an agreement to consolidate the bilateral swap network into a single transaction at the 10th AFMM+3 in Japan in May 2007. The Joint Statement maintains that the finance ministers

noted the substantial progress made in the activities of the new Taskforce on CMI Multilateralisation. Proceeding with a step-by-step approach, we unanimously agreed in principle that a self-managed reserve pooling arrangement governed by a single contractual agreement is an appropriate form of multilateralisation.

What accounted for this outcome? Focusing on China, the analysis discloses the role of Chinese co-chairmanship in shaping the result. Beijing's leverage came from its serving as a co-chair of the AFMM+3 in May 2007.

After the Hyderabad meeting in 2006, a consensus emerged that China and Thailand, which would co-chair the ASEAN+3 gathering in following year or 2007, were to get involved in the new taskforce and conducting a study to find a suitable approach for multilateralization.[25] In other words, these two states were assigned to contribute to the outputs of the task force in determining a modality to multilateralize the CMI.

As can be seen, since 2005 the multilateralization of the CMI had reigned as a top discussion issue among the ASEAN+3 nations (Chung 2013: 808). It is understandable why such matter constituted a chief concern among the stakeholders. The incentives to pursue a multilateralization path was mainly due to certain limitations embedded within the CMI system. Under the CMI agreement (see Diagram 1.2), the borrowing parties were required to separately negotiate with their individual lenders over whether to activate a bilateral swap arrangement and the conditions attached to the contract. If different lenders demanded dissimilar contractual terms, the negotiations could protract, delaying the activation process and disbursement of liquidity needed to manage the crisis economies. Thus, the CMI could fail to provide effective responses enabling the troubled states to weather through their financial turmoil. In sum, driven by their desire to correct the CMI's pitfalls, the participants were more or less in favour of making more efficient bilateral swap arrangements (BSAs).

Despite less dissonance about the ASEAN+3's quest for a higher efficient system of regional swap contracts, the members nevertheless diverged on the "how" question. The contentious issue was boiled down to, "how would the bilateral currency arrangements be made more efficient?"[26] This was the puzzle that Beijing and Bangkok had to figure out.

An opportunity was opened up for Beijing to exert its influence over the matter. Evidence reveals that the division of labour occurred between these two co-chairing parties. As described in Chapter 1, the process of ASEAN+3 financial cooperation encompasses several initiatives. The regional states had been advancing not only the CMI but also the other schemes such as the ABMI. Moreover, the two co-chairs were expected by the other members to furnish relevant materials to facilitate the discussions at the upcoming meeting in 2007. This meant that the preparation period was roughly one year (May 2006–2007). Therefore, Beijing and Bangkok, aiming to formulate better-quality products within this limited timeframe, decided to partition the workload between themselves. China chose to work on the CMI project.[27] Thailand, on the one hand, opted to scrutinize how to move forward the ABMI which involved the development of regional bonds markets. In short, Beijing took charge in conducting the study and writing out the paper on the subject of CMI multilateralization.

It must be emphasized that this breakdown of responsibility does not indicate that China and Thailand were ignorant of undertaking research and preparing supplementary documents for the discussions on the advancement of the CMI and the ABMI respectively. On the contrary, both countries in fact collaboratively carried out a study. Yet, due to such division of labour, Beijing took a larger part in contributing to the CMI development while Bangkok did the same to the ABMI project. Moreover, the two players provided certain inputs on these matters. Regarding the CMI case, the materials put together by China were reviewed by Thailand, which also gave its comments. To sum up, given that Bangkok concurred to have China spearhead the improvement of the CMI system, Thailand played a smaller role in carrying out the study and preparing the deliverables for this topic.

Some may wonder, why did China self-select itself to work on the advancement of the CMI system? Because it held a large amount of reserves to bail itself out of a crisis, why did the country want to build the CMIM – a regional safety net that it was unlikely to rely on?

These queries become even more perplexing if one looks back in the past. Before 2003, multilateralizing the existing CMI was not Beijing's first priority. China at one point publicly said to other Asian nations that it had some reservations about the idea.[28] Instead, the country's efforts to advance financial governance architectures were rallied towards developing the other elements of the CMI, not to multilateralize it per se.[29] For example, its policy makers were concerned about the high transaction costs involved in the entity's bilateral swaps. The discussions hence centred on how to lower such costs to facilitate the usage of this regional facility. Another issue touched on surveillance mechanisms. Questions such as "Should the CMI adopt a shallower or deeper form of surveillance?" was raised. A lighter version involved information sharing among parties, while an enhanced surveillance encompassed dialogues between members. In addition, the policy makers deliberated on the currency composition of BSAs. Questions such as "Would the future currency swaps involve a single currency or a combination of different currencies?" were explored.[30]

The sentiments shifted in 2003. The country became fonder to the notion of CMI multilateralization. One of the triggers of such change was the joint study conducted by the MOF, the PBC and some academics in 2003. This research evaluated the relationship between regional financial cooperation and other China's domestic goals. The result was positive, and turned out to ultimately shape the mindset of the country's leaders. Consequently, Beijing became more active in its engagement in this regional financial initiative (Jiang 2013: 131).

One effect of the report was that it crystallized Beijing's realization that international financial matters could affect issues at a national level. The Chinese elites reasoned that East Asian financial cooperation was crucial not only to the region but also to their country, especially in terms of long-term economic growth (Jiang 2010). Furthermore, the spill-over effects of international incidents such as the AFC in the late 1990s could jeopardize its financial security, a major component of the country's economic security. Although China was not a direct victim of the AFC, high economic interdependency among regional economies nevertheless rendered it almost impossible for any state to circumvent the "collateral damage" of a financial crisis. Because East Asia served as a main destination of the country's exports and source of its inward investment, Beijing witnessed a negative export growth in May 1998 (Yang 1998: 3). Accordingly, a "sense of crisis became deeply rooted among Chinese policymakers and scholars. Economic security, in particular financial security, has risen in the state's overall national security strategy" (Jiang 2013: 117). Thus, in the post-AFC era Beijing stepped up its effort by more actively taking part in developing regional financial architectures. Such enthusiasm was well-reflected in the proposal made by Premier Wen Jiabao at the 8th ASEAN+3 Summit in Vientiane, Laos, in November 2004,

> The Chinese side is ready to provide financial support to the joint study on ASEAN+3 financial and monetary cooperation . . . China stands ready to promote regional development through cooperation. Asia is facing both development opportunities and severe challenges . . . the task of ensuring economic and financial security has become more onerous.
>
> (Wen 2004)

As the Chinese policy makers comprehended that if other East Asian economies were to fall, the country's economy would in some ways be negatively affected, they began to search for the kinds of mechanisms which could best ride the region out transnational crises. Finding solutions to the puzzle, Beijing saw some hopes in the CMI. The MOF and PBC similarly noticed the entity's potential to help the region manage and prevent the next AFC-like turmoil.[31] Because the mechanism could function as another defence line lessening the impact of financial crisis on China's own economy as well as the others,' having CMI in place was better than nothing at all (Jiang 2010).

Nevertheless, China at the same time recognized that the separate negotiations involved in the CMI's activation process could prolong the provision of liquidity needed for crisis management. To correct such pitfall, the country advocated the multilateralization of CMI (or the CMIM),[32] reckoning that the upgraded version would provide quicker assistance to troubled economies by lumping all bilateral swap arrangements under a single contract. In other words, the idea of CMI multilateralization became the government's policy action aimed at reducing the country's vulnerability exacerbated by international financial turbulence.[33]

Another reason why Beijing finally embraced the idea of multilateralizing the CMI was because it saw this scheme as a channel to increase the adoption of renminbi (RMB), which in turn enhanced its political clout and leadership in the region (Wang 2014). A shared consensus among the elites was that the implementation of the yuan internationalization strategy must be carried out simultaneously in the two arenas – the regional and global ones. First, at the global level, the reform of international financial institutions, especially boosting China's special drawing rights in the IMF, was to be pursued.[34] To promote the use of yuan at regional level, Beijing set the CMI (and the later CMIM) as a main target.[35] In short, the mechanism serves as a regional platform for China to undertake its RMB internationalization policy.

In sum, although China might not use the CMI's bailouts as it had its own ample reserve to lean on, it nevertheless advocated the CMI because the entity could add an extra layer safeguarding to its own financial security (Katada and Sohn 2014: 146). By disbursing emergency fund to help regional states manage a crisis at home, this mechanism at the end could reduce some repercussions of international financial turmoil which would reach China afterwards. Also, if the CMI was transformed into the CMIM, the upgraded facility could be used to complement the country's implementation of its yuan internationalization, bolstering its regional influence.

As a result, according to one observer, the Chinese co-chair was very active in the preparation process of the CMI development project. Its team worked very diligently to compose background papers for the meeting.[36] The CMI research spearheaded by China turned out to significantly affect the bargaining dynamics. Not only that the recommendations provided by these papers functioned as a basis of the members' discussions, they also influenced the decision to pursue multilateralization later on. In short, "[t]he result of the joint study supported the [CMI multilateralization] proposal and became an important foundation for the governments' decision" (Jiang 2010: 613–614).

Beside wielding its influence via undertaking the CMI study and preparing discussion materials, China, taking advantage of its co-chair position, was able to settle conflicts among the participants and brought the negotiation to a close. Admittedly, finding a modality which all the participants agreed on was indeed challenging as there were several ways to realize the multilateralization of the CMI. Some examples include: whether the members' contributions were to be deposited into the centralized facility or earmarked until used; whether financial assistance was to be disbursed in a simultaneous manner (i.e. drawn from all lenders at once) or a sequential one (i.e. drawn from the first lender until exhausted, then drawn from the next one in line); and who would make lending decisions and oversee currency swap arrangements. Owing to different modalities for multilateralization, disputes arose. For instance, some countries voiced their own reservations about the direct transfer of money to the reserve pool.[37] Other players were worried that if a regional monitoring unit was created, its work could somehow conflict or constrain the functioning of the existing institutions such as the IMF.[38] While particular participants wanted to increase the de-linked portion, the others insisted on maintaining it at the current level of 20 per cent.[39] Sentiments seemed to sour as certain members, feeling that the ASEAN+3's pursuit for CMI multilateralization has encountered so much difficulties, began to think whether the region should continue on this agenda at all.[40]

Beijing, utilizing its co-chair position, jumped in and finally resolved the conflicts. Its "policymakers worked hard to get other countries to agree to multilateralising the CMI" (Jiang 2010: 614). The country led the direction of the discussions and communicated with the disagreeing states. For example, it assured some of them that the multilateralized form of the CMI would not alienate other institutions. On the contrary, the CMIM was designed to work together with the other entities at both regional and global levels.[41] As Beijing responded with detailed explanations and supported them with solid evidence from its research, the other parties found it difficult to counter-argue the former.[42] As a result, China was able to curb the clashes and convince the involved stakeholders to go down the multilateralization path.

How about the Thai co-chair? What were its parts in affecting the outcome? Evidence reveals that Thailand, as compared to China, played a lesser role in managing the discussions over the CMI development. This was partly due to the prior arrangement made between the two co-chairs. As earlier shown, in order to meet the deadline of May 2007, Beijing and Bangkok came into agreement at the initial phase over how to conduct their collaborative research. It was decided the former took a lead in the CMI multilateralization study, such as writing background papers and providing the related supplementary materials. Also, because the contents of these documents were already vetted through by Thailand during the preparation process, what presented at the ASEAN+3 gathering were more or less in accordance with Bangkok's position. As a result, the Thai co-chair let its Chinese counterpart brief the meeting about their joint products as well as manoeuvre the discussions that came after. When the clashes emerged, Bangkok lent its support to Beijing's handling of the disputes, enhancing further the latter's co-chairing leverage.

To sum up, the decision to go ahead with the multilateralization of the CMI was largely shaped by Beijing's clout as a co-chair. Owing to the prior arrangement over the responsibility breakdowns between the Chinese and Thai co-chairs, the former took charge of crafting background papers focusing on the advancement of the CMI. These deliverables were influential as their recommendations shaped the discussion dynamics and the decision making at the meeting. Also, Beijing was found to use its co-chairing power to get the other disagreeing parties on board with the multilateralization idea. Thanks to the prior agreement over their division of labour, the Thai co-chair allowed its Chinese equivalent to dominantly settle the conflicts. Bangkok instead resorted to assume a supporting role to strengthen Beijing's actions.

Role of knowledge about others' preferences and issue linkage in shaping the selection of the first director of the AMRO

Although the selection of the first director to the AMRO is not the book's main focus, it was nevertheless included for the following reasons. First, examining how China was able to grab the first year of the three-year appointment of the AMRO director sheds additional light regarding the negotiation dynamics in the ASEAN+3 context. Another reason why the selection of the first AMRO director is worth-exploring is because of a relationship between the organization and CMIM decision-making process. The AMRO is a surveillance arm of the CMIM, with the purposes of monitoring and assessing regional economies, detecting macroeconomic risks in the region, assisting the CMIM's decision making and ensuring the implementation of the CMIM's remedial actions (AMRO 2015). According to these mandates, the AMRO plays a significant role in altering the decision making of the executive-level decision-making body (ELDMB) – the main entity with a power to determine whether to disburse financial assistance to crisis economies (i.e. lending decision). It is because the organization's staffs are required to produce quarterly reports on macroeconomic situations and conduct studies to evaluate the economic vulnerabilities of the member countries. These materials were to be submitted to the ELDMB, serving as the basis for the latter to decide and vote on whether or not to approve lending.

The fact that the AMRO could impact the decision making of the ELDMB partly accounted for why several members sent in their nominees to bid for the AMRO's directorship. As mentioned in Chapter 2, all the stakeholders, both potential creditors and borrowers to the CMIM, had their own interests in affecting lending decisions. Moreover, because the AMRO was relatively new as it started its operation in 2011, "the new Director will have to put together a highly qualified team of professional staff, as well as all the hardware and software related to the AMRO office, and . . . [take part in choosing] . . . the procedures and methodologies for regional surveillance and CMIM operations" (Sussangkarn 2011b: 9). Therefore, which country hosting the AMRO during its inception years could potentially influence its institutional development in a long run (Rathus 2011). For example, certain rules and norms established by the first boss might not be overridden by the subsequent ones, which could ultimately affect the operational aspects of the AMRO, such as the approaches used to assess macroeconomic situations, the way the reports were produced, as well as other corporate cultures.

Therefore, like the areas of members' financial contribution and vote share, the decision on who would serve as the first director to this newly established regional surveillance unit was contentious. Again the two Asian nations, Beijing and Tokyo, grappled for the institution's directorship (Chung 2014: 92; Ng 2011).

Both "Japan and China felt that they should have a representative to be the Director" (Sussangkarn 2012: 81). After a selection process was conducted, the shared appointment was declared at the ASEAN+3 Finance and Central Bank Deputies' Meeting in Bail, Indonesia, on 6 April 2011. According to the press release, the members

> judged that two candidates, Mr. Benhua Wei (China) and Mr. Yoichi Nemoto (Japan), are equally qualified for the Director position through the selection process based on the meritocracy, and that it is appropriate for both candidates to contribute to the AMRO. Accordingly, they unanimously decided that Mr. Wei will assume the Director position first, and after he leaves it in one year, Mr. Nemoto will succeed the Director position for the remaining two years of the first term.
>
> (AMRO 2011)

Some observers perceived this result as a product of a deal-cutting between these two Asian countries (Chung 2013: 809). The three-year stint of the AMRO's head was partitioned between China and Japan. The Chinese Wei Benhua – the PBC's advisor and former deputy administrator of the State Administration of Foreign Exchange (SAFE) – was awarded the position in the first year, from May 2011 to May 2012. After that, he would be succeeded by the Japanese Yoichi Nemoto – a high-ranked officer from the Ministry of Finance – who would stay in the office in the following two years (May 2012–2014).

Looking closely at this deal, several puzzles appear: why was the term of the first AMRO's boss split up between China and Japan? In other words, why did not the result turn out in other ways? For instance, it could have been that one national ran the operation of the CMIM's surveillance unit in a full three-year course. Or if Beijing and Tokyo could not agree on this arrangement, why did we not witness both Mr Wei and Mr Nemoto co-heading the AMRO in these three years, as it was another way to realize a shared directorship? In addition, due to the Sino-Japanese rivalry over the matter, how did China manage to go first?

Before unlocking these enigmas, let's first examine the selection procedure of the AMRO's first director, which took place in 2010. To search for an appropriate person to fill this post, the CMIM members agreed to set up a special committee to function as an interview panel. The panel consisted of deputy-level officials from the finance ministry and central bank of the six CMIM parties.[43] These six parties consisted of the +3 nations (i.e. China, Japan and South Korea) and the other three ASEAN states. In regards to the latter, ASEAN invoked the "ASEAN Troika," which formed an ad hoc body aimed at carrying out this task of choosing the AMRO director. (For the history of the ASEAN Troika, see Box 3.2). Because this particular Troika was set up in 2010, the three ASEAN chosen to sit on this committee hence were Thailand (ASEAN chair of 2009), Vietnam (ASEAN chair of 2010) and Indonesia (ASEAN chair of 2011), respectively.[44]

Box 3.2   The history of the ASEAN Troika

The ASEAN Troika was initially borne out of security realms. Its origination can be traced back to the late 1990s. To deal with the Cambodian political mayhem in 1997, a "special foreign ministers' meeting created an ASEAN "Troika" consisting of foreign ministers of Indonesia, Thailand, and the Philippines to act for ASEAN in seeking a peaceful and democratic resolution to the situation" (Weatherbee 2015: 132). Later on, the ASEAN Troika was sometimes adopted in the context of ASEAN finance ministers' meeting (AFMM) where the three chairs (of the past, current and future years) of the ASEAN Central Bank Governors' Meeting participated in the AFMMs (Sussangkarn and Manupipatpong 2015: 126), as seen in the 16th, 17th and 18th AFMM gatherings, for example. The member states selected into this Troika are usually the ones chairing the ASEAN in those years.

To assess the candidates, the panel studied their profiles and conducted interviews with the former. The nominees were short-listed to four finalists.[45] The Thai contender named Dr Bandid Nijathaworn was the only ASEAN person able to make the cut into the final round as the others were from China, Japan and South Korea (Arnon 2011). After giving the scores to individual candidates, Beijing and Tokyo came before Dr Bandid and the Korean candidate.

While the exact explanations to why the scores turned out to be this way remained unknown, some speculated that the rankings of these finalists reflected the committee's concerns over the credibility of the CMIM. Because China and Japan were in a good position to serve as the creditors when lending is activated, having these countries head the AMRO could somehow boost market confidence of the CMIM scheme (*First Financial Daily* 2011). Also, Dr Surin Pitsuwan, a Thai diplomat and former ASEAN Secretary-General, maintained that because the combined financial contributions from Beijing and Tokyo make up more than half of the CMIM total size, these two states were judged as more suitable to run the AMRO. Doing so could further bolster the institution's legitimacy (Arnon 2011).

However, the selection procedure did not end yet. In fact, it became even more complex as the score of the Chinese contender tied with that of his Japanese counterpart. With respect to both candidates and countries, the committee suggested that Beijing and Tokyo bilaterally work out the decision concerning the first AMRO directorship and then report the result back to the group.[46]

This was when the compromise was made. After long debates, the two rivals decided to partition the three-year term into: a one-year block (May 2011–2012), which will be followed by the subsequent two-year block (May 2011–2014). Some might wonder why there was not an equal division, enabling China and Japan to each hold the directorship for one and a half years, with the first session beginning in May 2011 until November 2012 and the second from November 2012 to May 2014. One possible reason was that it was preferable to have a rotation occur in May so that the timing would synchronize with the ASEAN+3 Finance Ministers' process. Referring to Article 6 of the "AMRO Agreement," the director must report to the "Executive Committee" comprising the finance and central bank deputies from the CMIM participants. The Executive Committee is accountable to the finance and central bank ministers of the CMIM members. This reflects the chain of command of the ASEAN+3 financial cooperation. The sequence begins with the AMRO providing inputs to the deputy-level officials, who convene semi-annually at the ASEAN+3 Finance and Central Bank Deputies' Meeting (AFCDM+3). Then, the recommendations from the AFCDM+3 were to be considered at the higher ministerial-level meetings. The ASEAN+3 Finance Ministers and Central Bank Governors' Meetings (AFMGM+3) is held once a year in May and the AMRO director has participated in every AFMGM+3 since the organization's establishment in 2011. Therefore, due to the governance structure, May is a suitable month where for the handover of the institution's director to take place.

Using May as a marker of the director's rotation, the division of this stint's term was decided to be split into the one-year and two-year blocks. China and Japan then determined who got which chunk. After some extensive deliberations, a deal was ultimately strike. Mr Wei would assume the position for the first year, then leave his service immediately for the succession of Mr Nemoto later on.

What explained the arrangement? To several analysts, the result was perceived as China's victory over Japan. One source argues that the outcome was unexpected news to "the Japanese government, who were keen to have a Japanese national direct the unit" (Saputro 2011). Accordingly, why did Tokyo accept this deal anyway, instead of refusing it and let the negotiation collapse?

Evidence reveals the roles of knowledge about others' preferences and issue linkage in preventing the negotiation failure and shaping the final outcome. Mr Nemoto in several occasions exhibited great eagerness to become a director. As a result, this led to a wide speculation that he would much likely want to extend his directorship after his term ends.[47] According to one source, an outgoing AMRO director is allowed to make a request to continue his stint for another two years, which will be subjected to the approval by the Executive Committee.[48]

Taking into account such information, China opted to take up the first one year, which were pre-determinedly set to end in May 2012.[49] A reason why the country moved first could be that Beijing interpreted that the news about Mr Nemoto's intention to extend his stay as Japan's preference of holding the position in a longer period. Thus, Tokyo would much likely to deny any arrangement that crippled it from doing so and this might have foundered the talk. By promising to head the AMRO for the initial year only, China tacitly hinted to Tokyo that in return of allowing Mr Wei to assume the post first, Mr Nemoto could stay longer in office (May 2012–2014), with a prospect of extending the term for another two years. In short, that China's going first was "traded" with the Japanese candidate's longer stint. If Mr Nemoto's application to lengthen this stay was approved, he would serve as AMRO head until May 2016.

This solution brought the Sino-Japanese talks to a close. It satisfied China as the country became the first CMIM member with its national at the top of the AMRO, the main surveillance unit of this regional mechanism. Also, the arrangement enabled the country to achieve its goal of winning another race of the international organization's head, complementing its rising power in the region. According to Joel Rathus (2011), the fact that Mr Wei sat for the first year represented "China's clear transition to the East Asian leader in terms of the provision of regional public goods." For Tokyo, the settlement also made it happy because it enabled the Japanese Mr Nemoto to stay longer than his Chinese counterpart, and even request to lengthen his directorship and end his service in May 2016.

In sum, the solution was concocted via China's knowledge about Japan's interests and the former's utilization of issue linkage. Wanting to be the first country to head the AMRO, China relied on the information about Japan's preferences to offer to stay in the position for the first but terminal year. In order to obtain the Japanese approval, the deal of letting Beijing do the service first was "sweetened" by the fact that Tokyo would be able to stay in the office longer than the former. This compromise helped conclude the negotiation as it rendered these two Asian rivals walk away from the bargaining table feeling they have accomplished something.

Summary

China played an important part in affecting certain CMIM outcomes, namely the inclusion of Hong Kong into the CMIM scheme, the decision to multilateralize the CMI and the selection of the first director of the AMRO. After sifting through the bargaining dynamics, the elements underlying Beijing's leverage over these matters surfaced.

First, China utilized the knowledge about other actors' preferences to evade bargaining stalemate, close the negotiation and alter the final agreement details. As the case of Hong Kong inclusion has demonstrated, the country teased out Japan's preferences thorough its interactions with the latter. China correctly speculated that Japan wanted to make the greatest CMIM contributions to get the largest vote share, and it was concerned that Hong Kong's CMIM participation could somehow strip away its goal. Based on the information, Beijing accepted a deal that imposed some limits on the past English colony, and a term that the combined financial commitments and votes from Beijing and Hong Kong must be equated to Japan's amounts. The agreement finally circumvented a deadlock and enabled China to achieve its objective of brining in Hong Kong into the CMIM.

By acting as a co-chair, China was able to shape a decision to multilateralize the CMI. Thanks to the prior division of labour between the Chinese and Thai co-chairs in undertaking their joint research, Beijing took a lead in producing the background papers concerning the CMI development. These documents served as important foundations for the discussions and largely altered the negotiation dynamics. Also, taking advantage of its co-chairing power, Beijing intervened to settle conflicts which arose at the bargaining table. Again, because of the earlier agreed responsibility breakdown, Thailand, another co-chair at the meeting, decided to played a lesser and supportive role, which in turn boosted Beijing's authority in handling the disputes.

Regarding the selection of the first AMRO director, China's knowledge about its counterpart's preferences and usage of issue linkage were key factors helping the country circumvent negotiation failure and affect the final result. Once the director's three-year stint was partitioned into the one-year and two-year blocks to align with the ASEAN+3 Finance Ministers' process, Beijing proposed to do the service before Tokyo. The former also pledged to leave the position after the first year, clearing a way for the latter to take over. Looking deeply into the Chinese action revealed that the country used the information about the Japanese preferences to make such offer. By "trading" China's going first with Japan's ability to keep the job longer, Beijing was able to convince Tokyo to allow it to be the first CMIM member heading the AMRO.

Notes

1 Economic inducements and sanctions are sometimes regarded as positive and negative sanctions, respectively (Baldwin 1985).
2 Interview with A1.
3 Interview with J1.
4 Interview with I2.
5 Interview with J1
6 Interview with C1.
7 Interview with J4
8 Interview with I1.
9 Interview with C3.
10 Admittedly, there are some hurdles to the realization of China's RMB internationalization strategy. For example, Beijing's financial system is not fully open. The government has imposed capital controls on several occasions. Another problem concerns with shadow banking. For more details about the limitations of RMB internationalization policy, see Cohen (2012).
11 Interview with C3.
12 Interview with J3.
13 Interview with T5.
14 Interview with I1.
15 Interview with T2.
16 Interview with J3.
17 Interview with I2.
18 Interview with T2.
19 Interview with C2.
20 However, Hong Kong had informally been participated in the AFMM+3 processes (e.g. ABMI) on a regular basis as part of the Chinese delegates.
21 Interview with C1.
22 Interview with C2.
23 Interview with ASEC1.

24 Interview with T2 and T5.
25 Interview with T11.
26 Interview with T10.
27 Interview with T9.
28 Interview with T5.
29 Interview with C3.
30 Interview with C3.
31 Interview with C1.
32 Interview with C3.
33 Interview with C2.
34 Interview with C1.
35 Interview with C3.
36 Interview with ASEC1.
37 Interview with ASEC2.
38 Interview with T11.
39 Interview with T9.
40 Interview with T5.
41 Interview with I1 and T5.
42 Interview with M3.
43 Interview with J5.
44 Interview with T11.
45 Interview with M2.
46 Interview with T11.
47 Interview with ASEC2.
48 Interview with T11.
49 Interview with T11.

4 Japan

Japan's positions regarding contribution and voting issues

The Japanese positions concerning regional financial cooperation including the CMIM were mainly influenced by the inputs from the Japanese finance ministry and the country's central bank – Bank of Japan. These entities also represented Tokyo in the CMIM negotiations. Speaking about the matters of members' contribution and voting power, Japan prioritized the latter. This stance should not strike any experts as surprising. The country had ample foreign- reserve holdings to supply the CMIM pool. Thus, the issue of contributions was not seen as a problem or burden. In contrast, more emphasis was put on a vote share primarily because Japan perceived itself as a potential lender to this regional facility. The country was reported to favour granting each member votes in proportion to the member's financial contribution (Ciorciari 2011). It is because if the members' financial commitments were used to compute their voting power proportionally, those supplying the CMIM in a bigger portion would earn themselves greater influence in the decision-making processes. From the perspective of the lenders, it was quite rational for Tokyo to prefer that way.

Although how much Japan aimed to contribute was not revealed, the country aimed to put into the CMIM reserve pool more than the other countries in order to possess the greatest vote share accordingly.[1] Doing so enabled the country to wield its clout over the other regional states, as it would have a bigger say in determining whether or not to approve the provision of CMIM liquidity assistance. Therefore, Japan entered the CMIM negotiation having in mind a minimum contribution amount which would be translated into the minimum number of votes it could accept. In short, for Tokyo to seal the deal, it must at least obtain these minimums.

As far as the voting modalities were concerned, Japan initially preferred the CMIM decisions, including lending approvals, to be governed by consensus.[2] Shortly afterwards, it changed its mind, contending that a consensus-based rule could somehow undermine ASEAN+3 solidarity. Japan instead turned to favour a simple-majority voting system.[3]

However, Tokyo later shifted gears again, by abandoning its support for a simple-majority rule on the ground that the system could easily lead to a moral hazard problem.[4] In other words, a simple majority requires half of the total votes to activate lending, some governments may view that with such a low approval threshold they could easily borrow from the CMIM during crisis times. Hence, these governments may become reckless and employ policies that increase risks of crises in the first place.

Another possible reason why Japan later turned its back on a simple-majority voting system was due to the country's calculations of the future relationship between CMIM and other international organizations. Illustratively, if the CMIM's lending activation threshold is set too low or the system does not require many votes to disburse financial support, the CMIM could end up handing out "easy money" to its members. With such "easy help," the CMIM bailouts could potentially undermine the effectiveness of the policies employed by other entities. Suppose an international institution imposes an economic sanction on one of the CMIM members. If the latter can manage to get money from the CMIM, it would render the sanction ineffective. Furthermore, this situation could jeopardize the ties between East Asian countries and non-regional states. Wanting to prevent such scenario from happening, Japan pushed for the elevation of the mechanism' approval threshold and argued for a supermajority voting principle.

A careful look at Japan's stances towards CMIM contribution and votes unveiled the country's ambition to become a regional leader. This aspiration has been a main underlying force behind its active participation in regional cooperation ranging from trade to investment. Pertaining to the area of international finance, before the CMI/CMIM came into being, Tokyo had enthusiastically pushed for the advancement of regional cooperation and rolled out several initiatives, including the stillborn Asian Monetary Fund (AMF).[5] As summarized by Hook et al. (2002: 187),

> between 1997 and 2000 proposals for financial co-operation within East Asia almost came full circle. The AMF was rejected by the IMF, the US and China, only to be resurrected in various stages and different guises as the Manila Framework, New Miyazawa Initiative and then the Chiang Mai initiative. The Japanese government has clearly exercised a decisive influence in generating and pushing through this agenda.

In regard to CMIM, Japan was credited as a main locomotive behind a successful launch of the entity's predecessor, the CMI.[6] Not long before the formation of the latter, the country reportedly reminded Washington, via both official and unofficial channels, of the significance of East Asian financial cooperation. Such lobbying turned out to be fruitful as it helped prevent the American opposition. Hence, one could not deny that Tokyo's effort partly contributed to the successful inception of the CMI in 2000.

Japan's pursuit of regional leadership continued when the CMI was transformed into CMIM. To the country, this multilateralized scheme was regarded as even more essential to achieve its goal of regional supremacy because it is the most advanced initiative regarding financial cooperation in East Asia to date.

The agreement lays out decision-making procedures which could in the future be applied to other ASEAN+3 arrangements. In other words, certain details agreed in the CMIM could serve as precedents guiding and affecting the formation of the future regional institutions. Hence, by obtaining the greatest contribution and voting quota under the CMIM, Tokyo could in the future expand its power beyond this framework to other regional mechanisms to come. In sum, because Japan wanted to enhance its influence in East Asian economic cooperation, getting superior leverage in CMIM became a must.

Unfortunately, Japan's road to regional leadership is not so smooth because it is not the single one aspiring for it. As earlier stated, rising China wants to be a leader in East Asia as well.[7] Beijing can be seen as the only East Asian state which has a capacity to compete with Tokyo in the CMIM. With its reserves twice as great as the latter's, contributing to this financial safety net was not seen as a big problem for the former.[8] Combined with its passion for regional pre-eminence, China clearly stands between Japan and its goal. Therefore, it was no wonder why the Sino-Japanese rivalry persisted throughout the CMIM negotiation. According to one authority, the contestations were obvious. Both states often bargained hard and openly clashed over several issues including who would contribute most to the facility.[9]

It would be mistaken to say that the CMIM bargaining dynamics capture the whole picture of the Sino-Japanese competition over regional leadership. In fact, the battleground for their duelling has extended beyond this scheme. Let's take the area of international trade as an example. Beijing and ASEAN decided to strengthen their commercial ties and began their negotiation for the ASEAN-China Free Trade Area (ACFTA) in November 2001.[10] In its response to Beijing's move, Tokyo quickly upgraded its cooperation with its Southeast Asian neighbours through the ASEAN-Japan Comprehensive Economic Partnership Agreement (AJCEP). In short, such deal was not created in the vacuum. Rather, it was triggered by the declaration of the ACFTA negotiation. The news

> came as a major shock to Japan, since the country had considered the idea as implausible. Before the announcement, Japan was reluctant to promote an FTA with ASEAN . . . However, facing the Chinese initiative on the FTA, Japan feared that China was greatly expanding its influence over Southeast Asia, replacing Japan as a major actor in the region. This fear encouraged Japan to adopt a bolder policy. During his Southeast Asia visit in January 2002, Prime Minister Junichiro Koizumi proposed a comprehensive economic partnership with ASEAN, aiming at economic cooperation in various areas including not only trade and investment, but also science and technology, human resource development, and tourism.
>
> (Shoji 2009: 171)

As in the realm of trade, Japan's enthusiasm in advancing the CMI was largely shaped by China's increased involvement in regional financial cooperation since the 1990s. Beijing's ambition was well-reflected in Chinese Premier Zhu Rongi's statement. Just five months after the inauguration of the CMI, Zhu boldly posited

> As for the next-step financial cooperation, China is open to all ideas . . . [and] stands ready to work with other East Asian countries for the reform of the current international financial regime and the prevention and management of financial crisis.
>
> (Zhu 2000)

Seeing China as its competitor, Japan interpreted this announcement as a clear sign of the former's ambition towards regional supremacy (Yoshida 2004: 17). As a Chinese proverb goes, "One mountain cannot accommodate two tigers," Beijing's ascending clout rendered Tokyo to perceive the former as a threat to its own East Asian leadership project. China's active participation instigated worries among the Japanese policy makers as the former could potentially surpass Tokyo and become as a regional leader. Attempting to prevent this from occurring, Japan beefed up its effort to advance several regional cooperative programmes in the financial areas, where it considered itself as still reigned supreme over Beijing (Chey 2009: 641).

To sum up, Japan wished to contribute the greatest financial amount to the CMIM fund in order to obtain the biggest voting power accordingly. From the perspective of a potential lender, the country reasoned that getting a greater vote share enabled itself to influence the CMIM decisions, especially lending approvals. Doing so could reduce the probability of a moral hazard. Moreover, the country saw its CMIM involvement as part of its larger plan to attain regional dominance. However, Beijing has also aspired to be a leader in East Asia and has not been reluctant to compete against Tokyo in this regard. The Sino-Japanese rivalry hence resulted. As the CMIM negotiation unfolded, both countries were found to clash over several agreement terms, including the distribution of financial contribution and voting power among themselves.

Japan's involvement in shaping the CMIM agreement details

Which aspects of the CMIM agreement did Japan help shape the final outcomes? The analysis reveals that Tokyo was influential in determining these four issues: (1) the incorporation of Hong Kong into the CMIM framework, (2) the division of financial contributions between the +3 and ASEAN nations, (3) South Korea's financial commitment and (4) the decision to expand the CMIM fund size from US$ 80 to US$ 120 billion before the finalization of the other agreement details.

The role of issue linkage in affecting Hong Kong inclusion

Within the +3 countries, the matter of determining each of their individual financial contribution amounts was intense, especially between China and Japan. As stated earlier, these countries raced to become the biggest CMIM contributor, which would secure them the most voting power. According to Takano (2009), both parties "could not agree as to which country would contribute the greatest share. Each tried to convince the other nations that they – and not their principal economic rival in the region – should be shouldering the most financial responsibility."

The Sino-Japanese dispute became even more complicated when China began talking about bringing Hong Kong into the CMIM framework. As the previous chapter depicted, when China raised up a possibility of Hong Kong's CMIM membership, the country encountered harsh resistance from Japan. Initially, Beijing and Tokyo showed no sign of compromises. Once again, the CMIM negotiation was flirting with a potential collapse. However, the deal was finally cut, with several conditions imposed specially on Hong Kong. For example, the British former colony cannot vote on fundamental issues, but it can cast a vote on executive issues such as lending decisions. However, it must vote in a unified manner with the Mainland. In other words, Beijing's and Hong Kong's votes must always be combined and together counted as the Chinese votes. This rule hence strips away the voting independence of the previous English outpost.[11] Additionally, Hong Kong's borrowing quota is limited to only the IMF de-linked portion of the borrowing maximum (which was 20 per cent at that time and later increased to 30 per cent). This was based on a ground that the entity it is not a member of the IMF.[12]

What accounted for the settlement's terms between China and Japan? While the previous chapter studies the Chinese factors in explaining the outcome, this chapter explores how Japan played its roles in shaping the agreement. Evidence suggests that the country employed issue linkage to conclude the talk and alter the final details.

Before delving into how issue linkage was used to make possible the Hong Kong deal, let's first explore some motives behind the Japanese acceptance of the entity's inclusion. The fact that Tokyo's eventual welcome indicated to some degree that the former was interested in letting Hong Kong join the CMIM. What exactly incentivized Tokyo to be interested in this addition?

First, Japan saw that Hong Kong's economy as closely connected to China's. The former British protectorate was once a major entrepôt between China and the world during the nineteenth century, before it evolved into one of the world's financial centres after its reunification with the Mainland in 1997 (So 2004: 215, 223). Hong Kong's liberal economy is now characterized as free trade, low taxation with minimum government intervention (HKSAR 2015). The economies of Hong Kong and its Mainland were highly intertwined, as demonstrated by trade and investment figures. According to Tables 4.1 and 4.2, about 47.55 per cent of Hong Kong's exports went to China. Likewise, the Chinese imports into Hong Kong occupied about 45.22 per cent of the latter's market share. On an investment front,

Table 4.1 Hong Kong's bilateral trade relations with China and Japan (2004–2010)

Hong Kong's Export Shares		Hong Kong's Import Shares	
China	47.55	China	45.22
Japan	4.61	Japan	10.22

Source: United Nations Commodity Trade Statistics Database

Table 4.2 Hong Kong's bilateral foreign direct investment flows with China and Japan (2004–2010)

Hong Kong's Inward FDI Shares		Hong Kong's Outward FDI Shares	
China	37.08	China	49.88
Japan	1.284	Japan	N/A

approximately 37.08 per cent of the Hong Kong's total inward investment came from Beijing, and its outward investment to the latter ate up almost half of its total share, around 49.88 per cent.

Beside high economic interdependency between China and Hong Kong, the timelines of major meetings between these players, one the one hand, and between China and Japan, on the other, could also tempt Tokyo to be interested in accepting Hong Kong as a CMIM member. After receiving a SAR status, the previous English outpost continued to foster economic cooperation with Beijing. For instance, Hong Kong (together with Macao, which is another Chinese SAR) inked the Closer Economic Partnership Agreement (CEPA) with China in June 2003. The CEPA can be regarded as a landmark deal because it was the first free trade agreement (FTA) ever between Beijing and Hong Kong, and the first FTA to be implemented in the Mainland. The Ninth Supplement to the CEPA endorsed in 2012 broadened the scope of their bilateral cooperation to encompass the issues such as services liberalization, finance and investment facilitation (Xinhua 2012). To some observers, the agreement was perceived as Beijing's action to reinforce Hong Kong's position as a commercial gateway to China as well as to restore the latter's economic plight resulting from the AFC and the 2002–2003 Avian Flu epidemic (Chow 2013: 31; Sethboonsarng and Lim 2012).

As Figure 4.1 illustrates, the CEPA was finalized in 2003, before the CMIM talks were convened. That this deal between China and Hong Kong preceded the CMIM negotiation could partially account for why Japan the former two as a single bargaining counterpart in the CMIM context. One ASEAN official confirmed that Tokyo took into account the former British colony's relationship with the Mainland while negotiating with the latter over the Hong Kong membership.[13]

The overlap of the Sino-Japanese major high-level talks on the one hand, and the CMIM rounds on the other, could also underlie Tokyo's interest in letting

Hong Kong join this regional financial safety net (Figure 4.1). For instance, the China–Japan Economic Partnership Consultation was established in April 2002 as a formal venue for both sides to identify and address their economic challenges, as well as discuss the future direction of their bilateral economic ties. This process summoned the Chinese and Japanese high-ranked delegations including the deputy-level officers which exchanged their views on several issues such as trade, investment and intellectual property rights in order to ensure the continued fostering of their economic interdependency (Xia 2007: 39). The Eight Consultation was held in July 2010. In addition to these consultations, Beijing and Tokyo created the China–Japan High-Level Economic Dialogue in 2007 as another platform where their ministerial-level personnel discussed and explored ways to enhance their cooperation in several fields ranging from trade and investment to agriculture and environment. The Dialogue's first meeting was held in December 2007, followed by the second and third ones in June 2009 and August 2010, respectively (*Asahi Shimbun* 2014). The overlapping timeframes of these talks with the CMIM negotiation could to some extent entice Japan to eventually welcome the former English protectorate into the CMIM framework.

Furthermore, Japan's future projection regarding the development of East Asian financial cooperation might explain why the country was keen to accept Hong Kong into the CMIM. Owing to its financial strength as one of Asia's and the world's financial hubs, Hong Kong as the CMIM member could better support the functioning of this regional mechanism. For example, because the entity ranks eighth in the world in term of the international reserve holding, getting the previous English protectorate "on board would enlarge the supply of needed liquidity of CMIM to fulfill its mission" (Tso and Yeh 2013: 113). By leveraging on its financial expertise, Hong Kong could somehow make the swap contracts more efficient and effective.[14] Therefore, it seemed implausible to exclude the previous British colony from this regional endeavour.[15]

Moreover, Hong Kong has also actively engaged in other regional projects such as ABMI and ERPD,[16] as well as regularly participated in the Executives' Meeting of East Asia-Pacific Central Banks[17] (EMEAP).[18] It once voiced its interest in joining a proposed Asian Currency Unit (ACU), which was Tokyo's brainchild

China–Japan Economic Consultation:	2002 ------------------------------------2010
China–Japan High-Level Economic Dialogue:	2007 --------------------------------- 2010
Mainland–Hong Kong CEPA (concluded in):	2003
CMIM negotiations over contributions and votes:	2007 ----------------------------------2010

Figure 4.1 The timelines of the Mainland–Hong Kong Closer Economic Partnership Agreement (CEPA), China–Japan economic consultations and CMIM negotiations

project. Consequently, Tokyo viewed that Hong Kong could assist itself in creating an ACU in the future.[19] In sum, it was in Japan's interest to allow Hong Kong to enter the CMIM. The latter's position as Asia's financial centre and its financial expertise could further bolster the CMIM and other East Asian financial cooperation projects to come.

Although Japan was eager for the Hong Kong participation, the issue was in fact less essential to itself than to China. Unlike the latter, Japan did not need Hong Kong's expertise to develop the technical aspects of the CMIM facility.[20] Although having the previous British colony in the CMIM could help Japan attain of its objective of enhancing regional financial schemes, the CMIM without Hong Kong does not necessarily render this goal unachievable. In other words, without help from the former English outpost, Japan could manage to continue its construction of regional financial architectures on its own. Moreover, as mentioned in the previous chapter, Beijing needed Hong Kong's expertise to work out the CMIM details which mostly involved financial operations. In contrast, Japan did not.[21] Therefore, the latter was not as intensely keen as Beijing to incorporate Hong Kong into the CMIM.

Owing to their need gap, the Sino-Japanese bargaining dynamics were lopsided. Tokyo ended up gaining an upper hand in relation to Beijing. The former began pondering on how to use the Hong Kong issue as a springboard to reach its prime goal of being the biggest CMIM contributor and voter. Knowing that it was holding Hong Kong's "ticket" to the CMIM, Tokyo did not at all shy away from manipulating China.

Japan employed issue linkage as follows. The country connected its approval of Hong Kong participation to the matters of members' financial commitments and voting power. Tokyo also took a solo initiative to set up some "special conditions" to be applied on Hong Kong once it joins the CMIM. As explained in the prior chapter, these rules in fact served as the constraints on the former English colony and thwarted Beijing from becoming a single party contributing most to the CMIM fund. Furthermore, Japan signalled to China that the latter's acceptance of the "special conditions" could be "traded" with the former's approval of Hong Kong's CMIM membership.[22] In short, this arrangement was portrayed as a "take it or leave it" deal, hence putting a decision-making burden on Beijing's shoulders. Consequently, the latter gave in. The result was finally settled in the favour of Tokyo.

In conclusion, both China and Japan had their own reasons to incorporate Hong Kong into the CMIM. However, the issue of Hong Kong membership was less important to Tokyo than to Beijing. This gap was utilized by Japan to ultimately break a bargaining gridlock and shape the final deal favourable to the country. By taking advantage of the unequal need for Hong Kong inclusion between itself and China, Tokyo constructed issue linkage by connecting its approval of Hong Kong membership to the matters of CMIM contribution and vote shares. Turning the membership issue into a bargaining chip, the former forced China to accept certain conditions set specially for the former British colony and the term that Hong Kong's votes must be conjoined with Beijing's to constitute the Chinese votes. Accordingly, Japan was able to salvage the negotiation and achieve its goal of being the single biggest CMIM contributor and voter.

Role of co-chairs and informational strategies in determining the contribution proportion between +3 and ASEAN countries (the "80:20 ratio")

In May 2008, the ASEAN+3 governments convened at the 11th AFMM+3 in Madrid, Spain. This gathering marked another milestone in East Asia financial cooperation. The finance ministers worked out several important CMIM elements. Among them was 'How financial contributions to the fund were to be broken down among the members?' Japan and Vietnam served as the co-chairs of this talk.

The actual interactions reveal that the process of determining this contribution breakdown was packed with disagreements. As elaborated in Chapter 2, both +3 and ASEAN participants, despite their status of the potential lenders and borrowers respectively, were similarly keen to get as much financial contribution as they could. The reason was simple: the CMIM agreement grants larger voting power to those contributing a larger sum of money to the fund. As a result, bigger contributors have greater leverage in determining certain CMIM decisions in their favour, namely decisions to allow lending out money to the crisis economies. Therefore, all the involved players grappled to obtain as large the contribution and vote share as they possibly could. The heated contestations resulted.

Diverging states' interests were reflected by the fact that several contribution proportion between the +3 and ASEAN were tabled. Among these ratios were the ratios of 80:20, 75:25, 70:30 and 60:40.[23] A deadlock arose as particular members dearly guarded their proposed ratio and attempted to scupper the others.' Even within ASEAN, some states held dissimilar ideas about the contribution share they would get.[24] As a result, the ten ASEAN members did not create a coalition to bargain as a bloc, which could otherwise have altered the final outcome. Owing to conflicts among these stakeholders, the whole CMIM talk, once again, got stuck.

However, the ASEAN+3 governments finally managed to free themselves from the impasse. After lengthy and exhausting debates, the CMIM members at the end arrived at one of the significant outcomes pertaining members' financial contributions. According to the Joint Ministerial Statement, the participants agreed "that the proportion of the amount of contribution between the ASEAN and the +3 countries would be '20:80'" (ASEAN+3 2008). This means that the +3 (China, Japan and South Korea) together would financially contribute to cover 80 per cent of the total CMIM fund size, while the ten ASEAN states would be responsible for the remaining 20 per cent. In other word, the commitment ratio between the +3 and ASEAN was set to be 80:20.

This triggered a few important puzzles: how was the quota partitioned this way? What explained the 80:20 ratio? In short, what made the involved parties pick this proportion instead of the other options available? A main player in influencing this deal was Japan. The country played a significant role not only in resolving conflicts and concluding the talks, but also affecting the final outcome of the 80:20 split. Tokyo was among the players proposing the ratio alternatives. It not only introduced and promoted the 80:20 proportion, but also successfully convinced the other governments to agree with its idea.[25]

What exactly enabled Japan to salvage the negotiation from a potential failure as well as alter the result in the way it wanted? Part of the country's leverage stemmed from its serving as the meeting's co-chair. At this gathering, it was agreed beforehand that the task of deciding how to partition the financial commitments between the +3 and ASEAN members was to be handled by the two co-chairs, Japan and Vietnam.[26] However, the non-chairing parties were permitted to propose the ratios if they wanted. As a result, there seemed to be certain degree of authority granted to these countries to manage the process. This could also explain why few protests emerged when Japan used its co-chairing power to ultimately determine the contribution share between the Northeast and Southeast Asian participants.

A careful examination reveals some other crucial elements underlying the Japanese co-chair's bargaining influence. They were its superior data collection and transfer systems. The country was observed to obviously surpass the other CMIM members in these areas. One ASEAN negotiator maintained that Tokyo prevailed over the ASEAN members at gathering the data relating to the CMIM talks. For example, its negotiators usually came to a bargaining table with big folders containing detailed information about which persons or countries said what at which meetings.[27] Moreover, the officers in the Japanese bargaining team who were about to rotate to other departments excelled at transferring such information to their new staffs about to serve as the country's negotiators.[28] Thus, through generations the Japanese personnel were well-equipped with the information about the other CMIM parties.

What made the Japanese officers good at collecting and transmitting these data? According to one source, these skills partially emerged from the working styles, disciplines and cultures of the country's bureaucracy. The officials tend to strictly follow their organizations' procedures or code of conduct.[29] Owing to the Japanese personnel's abiding to their patterns of compiling information, the data about its counterparts were stored and transmitted in an organized and systematic way.

Specifically, how did Japan's superior data collection and transfer systems enable the country to determine the final outcome of the 80:20 proportion? Thanks to these systems, Japan was able to have available the information at hand regarding its bargaining counterparts' concerns, priorities and preferences. Such data helped Tokyo develop its own tactics and strategies deployed in the CMIM talks in several ways. For instance, the country utilized the information to predict possible scenarios including disagreements that could arise during the meetings. Japan also prepared its responses to these incidents before it actually entered the talks.[30] Moreover, if some CMIM players wavered on their stances or attempted to decline their prior offers to Japan, the latter then referred to its database of the previous meetings' details. Resorting to their information folders, the Japanese negotiators accurately pointed out who said what (or promised what) at which meeting(s). Doing so made the other CMIM participants unable to deny what they had said to or promised Tokyo in the past.[31]

Additionally, before presenting its proposed 80:20 proportion to the other members, Japan consulted its well-kept databank to gauge the figure which the former could easily agree on. Aiming to address all the involved players' concerns, the country incorporated several factors into its calibration of the financial commitment ratio between the +3 and ASEAN. Among the factors included were the members' ability to supply to the CMIM fund (i.e. their international reserve levels), and the size of their previous bilateral currency swaps.[32] The Japan's formula also had economic development and performance indicators of individual countries.[33]

The Japanese co-chair then introduced the 80:20 ratio along with the logics behind its computation and then persuaded the other stakeholders to concur with its proposal. The country's hard-working efforts turned out to be successful. The other parties, viewing that the calculation served their own interests, agreed with Tokyo's idea. Illustratively, to certain players fearing about their limited capacity to contribute, having the formula that took into account their foreign-reserve size was greeted positively.[34] Some ASEAN countries viewed that by contributing to only the 20 per cent of the total CMIM fund, they would reap more benefits from the CMIM facility than the other remaining options.[35] Constrained by their ability to contribute, these actors reasoned that by filling in the CMIM reserve pool merely 20 per cent, the ASEAN states could optimize their gains (i.e. the borrowing amount drawn from the mechanism) vis-à-vis the available alternatives. In addition, other Southeast Asian governments subscribed to Japan's suggestion on the ground that the latter's calibration took into account the size of the former's past currency swap arrangements or financial needs during the AFC. The 20 per cent quota permitted them to draw on the CMIM financial assistance sufficient to manage their economies in crisis times.[36] In short, after Tokyo proposed the 80:20 ratio and explained its calculation methods, the disputes finally subsided and the agreement was reached.[37]

It must be highlighted that Tokyo's leverage was also supported by other elements. For example, the country further exploited the information asymmetry between itself and the other CMIM parties. The Japanese during the negotiation not only teased out other states' preferences but also concealed its own. According to one source, several participants complained that Tokyo usually revealed its interests little by little as discussions proceeded.[38] In short, the country intentionally widened this data asymmetry to heighten its bargaining leverage vis-à-vis the others.

In addition, Japan's greater financial expertise further reinforced the country's informational advantage.[39] The country's proficiency was developed from its previous involvement in several international initiatives or bilateral agreements with other states, which later equipped the country's personnel with the skills useful to negotiate the CMIM agreement.[40] Tokyo's expertise was also borne out of its proactive attempts to construct East Asian financial architectures.[41] Its staffs generally were very enthusiastic in educating themselves with financial knowledge and exploring ways to advance regional financial cooperation further.

Japan's financial prowess was showcased by its behaviours at the bargaining table. This expertise explained why Tokyo played an active role in CMIM negotiation.[42] For instance, because the Japanese team did their own research on the internal procedures of CMIM operations, it was able provide advice on how the CMIM was to function.[43] Moreover, as one source described, the Japanese negotiators usually discussed the pros and cons of particular CMIM components and sometimes prepared discussion papers to stimulate the discourse.[44] By "doing the homework well," Tokyo was able to respond to the other parties' moves by to giving detailed comments on the latter's suggestions.[45]

Owing to its greater expertise, Japan's co-chairing power was enhanced. Thanks to its prevailing financial adeptness, the country gained certain credibility in the other actors' eyes. One ASEAN officer contended that Japan's arguments were often accepted as well-supported by its own research, making it difficult for the others to disagree.[46] During the times that some participants were perplexed by certain complex technical details, Tokyo had to make the former understand what the latter talked about.[47] In short, thanks to the country's expertise, the Japanese co-chair leveraged on this factor to dominate the meeting by setting agendas for discussions, controlling the direction of the talks, as well as convincing the others to go along with its idea. As a result, Tokyo was able to make its counterparts buy on to its proposed 80:20 ratio.

One might ask – What about the roles played by Vietnam, another co-chair at the meeting? Evidence indicates that Hanoi was not as good as Tokyo at wielding its co-chairing influence. The Japanese one was noticeably more assertive in managing and leading the discussions than its Vietnamese counterpart.[48] As an ASEAN official observed, the whole negotiation over the partition of the financial commitments between the +3 and ASEAN nations was by and large taken over by Tokyo, leaving Hanoi with little room to play.[49] Accordingly, the former eclipsed the latter's leverage over the determination of the contribution ratio.[50]

What accounted for Vietnam's lesser role as a co-chair? One possible reason could be that Hanoi, when compared to Tokyo, was less experienced in negotiating financial matters with other countries. Also, the former's personnel might be less equipped to discuss certain financial sophistications involved in the CMIM mechanism. These fewer experiences and lesser skills could weaken the influence of the Vietnamese co-chair during the meeting.[51]

To conclude, the contribution proportion of 80:20 was largely shaped by Japan, which served as a co-chair at that time.[52] Tokyo, via its co-chair position, was able to evade a deadlock as well as convince the others to agree on the breakdown of the contribution responsibility between the +3 and ASEAN participants the way it desired. Thanks to a consensus beforehand that the co-chairs were to take care of such division task, Japan (together with Vietnam) were granted certain authority from the other players to work on the ratio. And when Tokyo later did so, it met with few objections from the other CMIM members. Underpinning the leverage of the Japanese co-chair was the country's informational advantage over the others, partially stemming from its own prevailing data collection and transfer systems. These elements allowed its negotiation team to retrieve the information about other actors, analyse their concerns and calculate the appropriate contribution ratio that was more likely to receive positive feedback and agreement from the other stakeholders. The country also further exploited such information asymmetries by concealing its own preferences from its bargaining counterparts. Tokyo further leveraged on its greater financial expertise to strengthen its bargaining clout. In addition, without little influence from the Vietnamese counterpart, the Japanese co-chair was able to alter the discussions the way it desired. Relying on the preceding factors, Tokyo was able to conclude the negotiation over the partition of members' financial commitments as well as convince the others to adopt its proposed 80:20 ratio.

Role of knowledge about others' preferences in shaping South Korea's contribution share

Once the division of financial contributions between the +3 and ASEAN countries was settled, the +3 nations held private talks to discuss how to split up their 80 per cent contribution share among themselves. South Korea made a bold statement to China and Japan, demanding that the +3 would make equal contribution to the CMIM reserve pool. In other words, these three states were to give out the same financial amount to fulfil their 80 per cent quota. However, the idea was met with strong objections, especially from Tokyo. The reason was simple – the latter wanted to be the biggest contributor and voter to the CMIM. Having anyone else provide an equal amount of financial commitment would crush its goal. Not only that Tokyo rejected Seoul's proposal, the former also pressured the latter to contribute less than itself.[53] But the Korean continued to stick to its position. The negotiation turned into stalemate. After lengthy debates, an agreement concerning Seoul's contribution portion was reached at the ASEAN+3 gathering in Pattaya, Thailand, in April 2009 (Chung 2013). South Korea would make a lesser financial commitment to the CMIM than China and Japan.

What explained the result of this bargain? Unlike the next chapter, which will centre on the factors from South Korea's side helping to prevent the deadlock and alter the outcome, this chapter probes into the roles played by Tokyo itself. The question asked here is, what enabled Japan to successfully seal the deal with the details in its favour? The following analysis reveals that the country used the information regarding South Korea's preferences to settle their disputes and shape the outcome regarding the latter's CMIM financial commitment.

First, Japan easily compiled some information about South Korea's economy as it was not secretive. Seoul underwent two separate exchange rate crises.[54] Its currency – the won – rapidly depreciated in the two last quarters of 1997 and 2008 (see Table 4.3). Seoul in the AFC called on the IMF and was put under the Fund's programme with several conditionalities attached. (See Table 6.3 for more details about South Korea's IMF package.) Moreover, Tokyo was able to witness South Korea's clear avoidance of the IMF's assistance during the GFC years. Instead of leaning on the Fund this time, the latter entered into separate negotiations with individual governments, including Japan, to secure itself with liquidity needed to alleviate the GFC's impact on its economy.

Examining South Korea's behaviour during the AFC and GFC, especially the different course of action it undertook in these two periods, Japan correctly gauged that the former became more averse to the IMF's programme than before. In other words, the fact that Seoul chose to conduct separate bargains with each of its lenders while it otherwise could have acquired a more comprehensive package if it had gone to the IMF indicated the country's loath against the Fund.

Moreover, Japan's interactions with Seoul at the hype of GFC leaked out some information about the latter's preferences. According to one Japanese official, after the global great crash swept South Korea, their authorities appeared to be keener than in the past in advocating the completion of the CMIM. Seoul once voiced that the CMIM was very useful. The scheme would benefit itself by providing financial support should its economy undergo another round of crisis and serving as a lender of last resort when it might need.[55]

Knowing South Korea's stances allowed the Japanese to gain an upper hand in its talk with the former. It was because they revealed that the former's batna had been exacerbated by the GFC. (For the full discussion of South Korea's batna, see Chapter 5). Turning away from the Fund, Seoul planned to seek the CMIM as an alternative. After gauging its counterpart's batna, Tokyo compared it with its own batna, and realized that it prevailed over Seoul on this scale. To Japan, if its economy was to suffer, the country would not tap on the CMIM facility as it had alternative sources from which it could obtain liquidity.[56]

One possible reason why Japan was so confident in this regard was due to the status of its currency – the yen – in international monetary system or the "Currency Pyramid" (Cohen 1998). Some market forces including cross-border flows of monies gave rise to the competitions among currencies. Such rivalries led to the reconfiguration of the global monetary geography, which can be characterized by the "Currency Pyramid." The Pyramid illustrates graphically where different currencies occupy their place in the global landscape. At the apex of the Pyramid situate "Top Currencies – moneys whose scope and domain are more or less universal" (Cohen 2009: 11). The only true Top Currency nowadays is the greenback. Below the greenback, right now, sit the euro and the yen, or the "Patrician currencies – moneys whose use for various cross-border purposes, while substantial, is something less than dominant and whose popularity, while widespread, is something less than global" (Cohen 2009: 11). Therefore, the yen's supreme status vis-à-vis the other East Asian currencies could somehow assure the country that it was in a better shape than the latter in terms of managing its economy should a crisis arrive. (For a more comprehensive description of international monetary competition and the Currency Pyramid, see Cohen 1998, 2004.)

Admittedly, Tokyo wanted to advance the CMIM further, but the strength of the former's desire was not as high as Seoul. Seoul's passion to push forward the CMIM project became even more pronounced after it experienced with the GFC. As a result, their difference ultimately earned the Japanese an edge in its bargains with its Korean equivalents, as the gap opened room for the former to manipulate the outcomes of the latter's financial contributions.

Japan played it a hard way by turning South Korea's preferences against the latter. Tokyo continued to cling on its initial stance, arguing that Seoul must commit less financially to the CMIM than itself.[57] The former also refused to compromise. As the negotiation progressed, Seoul conceded. Japan was hence able to settle its disputes with South Korea and walked away with the outcomes favourable to itself.

In sum, this negotiation result was partly the product of Japan's utilizing the information about its bargaining counterpart, South Korea, namely the latter's preferences. Realizing that Seoul's worsened batna heightened the country's interest in pursuing the CMIM more than itself, Japan used this knowledge to tip the bargaining dynamics in its favour. In other words, the discrepancy in terms of the strength of the countries' desire to advance the CMIM enabled Tokyo to conclude the talk and choke down into Seoul's throat the agreement term less favourable to the latter. In short, Japan successfully forced South Korea to commit to the CMIM fund in a smaller amount than itself.

Role of knowledge about others' preferences in determining a decision to expand the CMIM size before the finalization of the other agreement details

After the CMIM members settled on how to divide financial contribution responsibilities between the +3 and ASEAN countries, the GFC struck. Against this backdrop, the ASEAN+3 governments summoned at the Special AFMM+3 in February 2009 in Phuket, Thailand. This meeting mainly deemed to speed up the CMIM process and explore how to increase the facility's effectiveness. Several matters were raised. Among them was whether to expand the CMIM reserve pool, which was US$ 80 billion at that time, or wait for a later enlargement after the other agreement details were finalized.

The Japanese Ministry of Finance was keen to adopt the enlargement option. Its officials then introduced and pushed for the expansion of the CMIM size, from US$ 80 to US$ 120 billion, for the purpose of enhancing the facility's crisis-management capability. After that, the members could move on to discuss and finalize other details of the CMIM agreements. It must be emphasized that this size change altered only the absolute amounts of members' contributions and voting power, not the ratio between the member states. In short, the distribution of financial commitments between the +3 and ASEAN would remain fixed at 80:20 as earlier agreed in 2008.[58]

However, the talks got stuck mainly because of the disagreements between Japan and some ASEAN states. Increasing the CMIM size was a big issue for the latter as they were concerned whether they had sufficient reserves to satisfy their new commitments.[59] As a result, these nations blocked Japan's proposal, arguing in favour of finalizing the other details of the CMIM first.[60] Both sides, at first, could not decide on which pathway was to be taken, or whether to increase the fund size now or later. However, the final outcome leaned towards Tokyo's position. At the Special AFMM+3, the governments agreed that the entire CMIM size "will be increased from the initially agreed level of US$ 80 billion to US$ 120 billion, the proportion of the amount of contribution between ASEAN and the Plus Three will be maintained at 20:80 respectively" (ASEAN+3 2009a).

What explained this result? Specifically, how was the impasse broken, and how was the outcome in line with what Tokyo originally wanted? These inquiries could be answered by looking at the roles of Japan's knowledge about other players' preferences. Evidence suggests that Tokyo was able to deduce information about what ASEAN wanted from the latter's claims. Being agitated by Japan's push for the expansion of the CMIM size, ASEAN counter-argued that in order to move forward the CMIM, the finalization of the agreement must be set as the first priority. Concluding all the CMIM details including the operational aspects could ensure the effective functioning of the entity during crises. In short, if all CMIM elements could be agreed upon, the regional mechanism could come into force faster and be ready to provide emergency bailouts to crisis economies.

Through its debates with the ASEAN counterparts, Japan was able to extract certain information regarding the latter's preferences. First, after GFC, some Southeast Asian states displayed more eagerness than ever to conclude the negotiation. They often stressed the importance of the successful operations of the CMIM.[61] Moreover, the claim made by ASEAN revealed along itself some reasonings, which turned out to serve as valuable information base for Tokyo. The former's call for the early commencement of the CMIM details disclosed that they were in dire need for this regional safety net. The entity could serve as an alternative venue for ASEAN countries to receive bailouts when their economies experience a financial turmoil. When compared to Tokyo, ASEAN countries were keener to use the CMIM facility should a crisis strike.[62] This was mainly due to these states' lesser capacity to finance themselves either through running down their owned reserves or borrowing abroad. These factors heightened ASEAN countries' sense of urgency. As a result, ASEAN did not want the CMIM negotiation to protract any longer. They instead wanted to finalize all the elements so that the regional mechanism could enter into force, ready for them to tap on its resources when needed. (For a full discussion concerning the roles of ASEAN's sense of urgency or discount rates, see Chapter 6).

Japan utilized the information about ASEAN parties' preferences to gain an upper hand over the latter. Seeing such data as a key to bolster its bargaining leverage, the country quickly seized the opportunity. Knowing that the ASEAN nations desired to have CMIM function in practice sooner than itself, Tokyo adopted time-buying strategies by dragging its feet in the talks.[63] One officer contended that Tokyo was intentionally reluctant to move forward the discussions if they did not go into the direction that the Japanese aimed for. Although there existed other factors which protracted the negotiation, the progress of some discussions was obstructed by Japan's deliberate delaying tactics.[64]

Also, Tokyo expressed little willingness to consider the possibility of compromises with ASEAN.[65] When the latter attempted to lobby Japan to re-negotiate the deal, the country just gave a flat no. In addition, Tokyo reportedly coerced ASEAN to soften its stance of have all agreement details settled before expanding the CMIM size. The former appeared to hint out that the development of the CMIM as a regional financial safety net could be jeopardized.[66] If ASEAN countries continued to hold their ground, the talk could simply stall. As the clock continued to tick, more pressure was mounting on the ASEAN's side. At the end, the Japanese's manipulation successfully pressed ASEAN to back down. Tokyo then steered the outcome into its favour.

To conclude, the preceding discussion has demonstrated that Japan's actions to evade a bargaining deadlock and shape the final outcome in its direction. Relying on the knowledge that ASEAN nations were in a more crucial need for the CMIM and more zealous to witness the CMIM come into force than itself, Tokyo deployed time-buying techniques to prolong the discussions and pressure ASEAN states to abandon their position of settling the other agreement terms prior to the size expansion. The latter ultimately gave in and accepted Japan's advice to raise the CMIM fund size first before moving on to finalize the other agreement details.

Summary

The analysis has disclosed the roles played by Japan in affecting several CMIM outcomes. Tokyo was found to be influential in determining the incorporation of Hong Kong into the CMIM framework, South Korea's contribution portion, the splitting of the financial commitments between the +3 and ASEAN nations, and the decision to expand the CMIM fund size before proceeding with the negotiations over other agreement terms.

In these four outcomes, different elements contributed to Japan's bargaining leverage vis-à-vis the others. In regard to the issue of Hong Kong inclusion, the country employed issue linkage to gain an upper hand in its negotiation with China. Both Beijing and Tokyo were interested in Hong Kong participation, yet for different reasons. However, the issue was less essential to Japan than to China because the former did not need the past British colony in the CMIM as much as the latter. Taking advantage of this difference, Japan strategically linked Hong Kong's CMIM membership to the matters of China's contribution and vote shares. In exchange of the Hong Kong's "ticket" into the CMIM, the former pressed China to swallow certain "Hong Kong conditions" as well as the term that the entity's votes must always be combined with Beijing's to be counted as the Chinese votes. It also pressed Beijing to accept them. China eventually gave in, turning the final outcome in Tokyo's favour.

The adoption of the 80:20 ratio reflected the Japanese co-chairing power, as the country was able to propose this option and lobby the others to agree with its idea. Tokyo's superior data collection and transfer systems underlined its co-chairing influence as they enabled it obtain informational advantage vis-à-vis other participants. Japan further exploited this data gap by concealing its own interests during the negotiation. Moreover, the country was able to leverage its financial expertise, which stemmed from its prior experience in the financial issues and negotiations. The factors were used in a combination by Tokyo to ultimately steer the final result in its direction.

The fact that South Korea ended up supplying a lesser financial amount to the CMIM than Japan reflected the latter's use of the knowledge about the former's preferences. Tokyo distilled South Korea's stances towards the CMIM from the latter's past behaviours in the two crises and its interactions with the former. For instance, South Korea's desire to circumvent the IMF was exhibited by the fact that the country during the GFC turned its back from the IMF to instead conclude bilateral liquidity deals with individual governments. This same antagonism against the Fund also drove Seoul to be more eager in pushing forward the CMIM scheme than before. Such information about South Korea was later exploited by Japan, which successfully forced the former to make a smaller financial commitment to the CMIM pool than itself.

Additionally, Japan's knowledge about ASEAN's preferences impacted the final decision to enlarge the CMIM fund size prior to finalizing the other agreement details. From the Japanese-ASEAN conflicts over which pathway to be taken, Japan was able to extract the latter's preferences and underlying concerns. Behind ASEAN's call for the completion of all the components before the CMIM size expansion was their dear wish to have the facility operate effectively in practice. Because such finalization would render the mechanism ready to supply them with some financial assistance when needed. Relying on the knowledge that ASEAN countries wanted to wrap up the negotiation sooner than itself, Tokyo twisted the former's arms by strategically protracting the discussions and threatening to undermine the talk if ASEAN refused to yield. The latter finally acquiesced, allowing Japan to pursue the course of action it initially wanted.

Table 4.3 Nominal effective exchange rates of selected ASEAN+3 countries (2004–2010)

	China		Hong Kong		Indonesia		Japan	
01–1994	73.54		101.85		451.7		74.38	
02–1994	72.9		101.12		443.47		78.21	
03–1994	72.65		100.87		435.99		79.09	
04–1994	72.65		100.89		433.66		80.79	
05–1994	72.87		100.61		431.63		80.33	
06–1994	72.62	−0.0125	100.2	−0.0162	428.39	−0.0516	81.12	0.09062
07–1994	71.54		98.82		420.2		83.81	
08–1994	72.21		98.76		421.51		82.53	
09–1994	72.28		98.11		416.37		83.06	
10–1994	72.25		97.58		414.39		82.97	
11–1994	72.56		97.71		414.58		83.61	
12–1994	73.83	0.032	98.5	−0.0032	417.07	−0.0074	82.44	−0.0163
01–1995	74.12		98.05		410.68		82.78	
02–1995	73.84		97.82		407.45		83.91	
03–1995	71.81		95.61		392.98		90.23	
04–1995	70.01		93.67		381.2		96.65	
05–1995	71.27		93.86		383.34		95.45	
06–1995	71.2	−0.0394	93.67	−0.0447	382.66	−0.0682	95.79	0.15716
07–1995	71.58		94.01		384.58		92.68	
08–1995	73.74		96.18		393.21		86.35	
09–1995	75.09		97.69		398.02		81.77	
10–1995	74.68		97.18		396.39		81.01	
11–1995	75.05		97.5		395.41		80.35	
12–1995	75.38	0.0531	97.92	0.0416	396.53	0.03107	80.82	−0.128
01–1996	76.41		98.96		401.56		78.26	
02–1996	76.51		99.03		399.73		78.32	
03–1996	76.47		99.06		395.03		78.2	
04–1996	76.88		99.43		397.35		77.43	
05–1996	77.06		99.68		398.09		78.39	
06–1996	77.65	0.0162	100.06	0.0111	400.52	−0.0026	76.66	−0.0204
07–1996	77.63		100		399.37		76.26	
08–1996	77.32		99.7		396.09		77.09	
09–1996	77.93		100.22		401.12		75.9	
10–1996	78.59		100.79		405.23		74.42	
11–1996	78.38		100.48		401.36		74.26	
12–1996	79.18	0.02	101.24	0.0124	402.37	0.00751	73.71	−0.0334
01–1997	80.49		102.41		406.59		71.79	
02–1997	82.34		104.1		413.7		69.68	
03–1997	82.71		104.62		411.29		70.27	
04–1997	83.43		105.22		412.06		68.82	
05–1997	82.31		104.38		404.43		72.8	
06–1997	81.85	0.0169	104.08	0.0163	400.84	−0.0141	75.79	0.05572
07–1997	82.89		105.46		395.76		76.34	
08–1997	84.33		107.57		372.47		75.86	
09–1997	84.78		108.4		339.9		74.51	
10–1997	85.08		109.33		285.24		74.95	
11–1997	86.65		111.08		302.76		73.13	
12–1997	91.06	0.0986	116.51	0.1048	226.25	**−0.4283**	74.13	−0.0289

Korea		Malaysia		Singapore		Thailand	
141.81		119.48		80.16		126.54	
140.89		116.18		80.49		125.81	
140.9		117.65		80.36		125.62	
140.89		118.57		81.23		125.57	
141.22		121.51		81.74		125.52	
140.91	−0.0063	122.01	0.02118	82.24	0.02595	125.29	−0.0099
138.84		119.94		81.99		123.69	
139.42		121.57		82.53		123.76	
139.18		121		82.98		123.18	
138.96		120.23		83.32		122.75	
139.61		120.21		83.88		122.81	
142.17	0.02398	121.33	0.01159	84.87	0.03513	123.81	0.00097
142.36		121.27		85.4		123.53	
141.63		120.83		84.97		123.09	
139.81		117.66		84.85		120.31	
138.2		117.81		84.18		117.68	
139.93		118.78		84.74		117.82	
139.68	−0.0188	120	−0.0105	84.44	−0.0112	117.4	−0.0496
141.31		120.26		84.73		118	
144.12		122.08		86.15		121.03	
146.15		122.92		86.35		122.96	
146.53		121.31		86.66		122.39	
146.76		121.39		87.68		122.7	
147.08	0.04083	121.76	0.01247	87.87	0.03706	123.19	0.04398
145.98		122.47		88.52		124.4	
147.49		122.79		89.16		124.69	
147.5		123.23		89.35		124.9	
148.49		125.27		89.7		125.34	
148.7		126.3		89.85		125.47	
146.16	0.00123	126.85	0.03576	90.18	0.01875	125.93	0.0123
143.35		127.12		89.62		125.86	
141.95		126.5		89.53		125.57	
142.01		126.79		90.28		126.02	
142.02		127.31		90.59		126.58	
141.27		126.04		91.05		126.26	
140.56	−0.0195	126.92	−0.0016	91.94	0.02589	126.9	0.00826
140.53		130.48		92.57		128.12	
140.97		133.21		93.32		129.89	
139.17		134.38		92.4		130.31	
138.16		133.98		92.83		130.92	
136.55		132.1		92.19		129.82	
136.37	−0.0296	130.8	0.00245	92.48	−0.001	129.37	0.00976
137.71		129.42		92.58		111.23	
139.26		123.61		92.06		105.98	
138.06		113.8		92.75		95.67	
136.1		105.25		91.59		93.54	
123.31		104.33		91.65		90.34	
87.53	**−0.3644**	97.47	**−0.2469**	92.93	0.00378	81.72	**−0.2653**

(*Continued*)

Table 4.3 Continued

	China		Hong Kong		Indonesia		Japan	
01–1998	93.67		121.17		121.17		77.41	
02–1998	92.08		118.64		123.4		78.4	
03–1998	91.91		118		116.77		75.72	
04–1998	91.82		117.48		137.59		73.28	
05–1998	92.27		118.33		115.26		72.04	
06–1998	94	0.0035	120.93	−0.002	85.19	**−0.2969**	70.62	−0.0877
07–1998	93.75		120.88		80.78		70.33	
08–1998	94.95		121.87		93.69		68.63	
09–1998	93.58		119.66		100.89		73.11	
10–1998	90.23		115.54		123.76		79.8	
11–1998	90.23		115.43		137.52		79.92	
12–1998	89.43	−0.0461	114.54	−0.0524	136.64	0.69151	81.77	0.16266
01–1999	88.97		114.39		122.22		85.1	
02–1999	90.5		115.9		121.04		83.41	
03–1999	91.97		117.41		120.83		82.25	
04–1999	92.03		117.39		124.94		82.15	
05–1999	92.29		117.37		134.83		80.37	
06–1999	92.36	0.0381	117.33	0.0257	146.79	0.20103	81.41	−0.0434
07–1999	92.31		117.2		159.01		82.3	
08–1999	90.92		116.15		143.29		86.71	
09–1999	90.12		115.9		127.86		92.25	
10–1999	89.54		115.06		139.69		92.57	
11–1999	89.75		115.27		150.52		94.14	
12–1999	89.52	−0.0302	115.19	−0.0172	146.54	−0.0784	96.29	0.16999
01–2000	89.75		115.03		144.87		93.66	
02–2000	91.28		116.43		144.14		90.7	
03–2000	91.04		116.44		143.06		93.7	
04–2000	91.23		116.62		137.73		94.87	
05–2000	93.07		118.55		130.95		93.92	
06–2000	91.84	0.0233	117.46	0.0211	124.72	−0.1391	95.07	0.01505
07–2000	92.41		118.15		118.23		93.9	
08–2000	93.18		118.86		129.68		94.38	
09–2000	93.94		119.91		128.25		96.71	
10–2000	95.05		121.2		125.2		96.16	
11–2000	95.55		121.85		120.06		96.26	
12–2000	95.52	0.0337	121.55	0.0288	118.49	0.0022	92.85	−0.0112
01–2001	95.77		121.46		118.41		88.57	
02–2001	96		121.66		116.99		89.3	
03–2001	97.8		123.42		112.32		86.37	
04–2001	99.1		124.97		104.89		85.62	
05–2001	98.97		125.06		102.69		87.17	
06–2001	99.72	0.0412	125.99	0.0373	103.42	−0.1266	87.5	−0.0121
07–2001	100.2		126.37		107.68		85.93	
08–2001	98.35		124.12		128.72		86.76	
09–2001	97.85		123.67		123.44		88.71	
10–2001	98.67		124.71		114.57		87.34	
11–2001	99.12		125.22		110.22		86.83	
12–2001	99.88	−0.0032	125.79	−0.0046	114.02	0.05888	83.54	−0.0278

Korea		Malaysia		Singapore		Thailand	
78.65		86.99		92.9		70.95	
81.27		98.19		95.14		80.97	
89.27		99.59		96.59		90.6	
95.76		99.46		97.19		94.99	
95.91		98.25		95.99		96.63	
98.03	0.24641	96.15	0.1053	95.53	0.02831	91.38	0.28795
106.18		92.47		95.05		94.22	
105.69		92.54		93		94.43	
98.84		99.9		91.91		94.38	
97.38		95.72		93.01		95.61	
101.26		95.45		92.61		100.01	
107.52	0.01262	94.68	0.0239	91.11	−0.0415	99.68	0.05795
110.91		94.54		89.45		98.19	
111.36		96		89.59		98.65	
108.98		97.41		89.22		98.91	
110.81		97.29		90.03		98.66	
112.23		97.39		90.06		100.62	
115.17	0.03841	97.28	0.02898	89.99	0.00604	100.85	0.02709
112.97		97		90.56		100.09	
110.6		95.84		90.72		96.3	
109.47		95.39		89.52		90.79	
108.4		94.61		89.9		90.98	
111.27		94.6		90.21		92.8	
115.14	0.01921	94.42	−0.0266	89.84	−0.008	93.99	−0.0609
116.06		94.58		89.88		96.34	
118		96.11		89.69		97.08	
119.16		95.98		88.92		96.3	
120.1		96.12		89.47		96.29	
121.27		97.93		90.13		95.68	
120.11	0.0349	97.01	0.02569	89.37	−0.0057	94.29	−0.0213
121.24		97.81		89.41		92.29	
122.08		98.22		90.98		91.35	
122.56		99.02		90.64		89.73	
122.38		100.21		91.11		88	
120.15		100.73		91.92		87.38	
113.91	−0.0605	100.66	0.02914	92.46	0.03411	88.69	−0.039
109.05		100.98		92.51		88.99	
111.08		101.12		92.32		90.15	
109.52		103		92.28		89.19	
107.74		104.53		91.54		87.3	
110.1		104.43		91.41		87.14	
111.2	0.01972	105.12	0.041	91.88	−0.0068	88.23	−0.0085
110.84		105.61		91.86		87.95	
110.63		103.32		93.16		87.54	
109.44		102.8		93.44		88.16	
109.66		104.05		91.02		88.32	
111.93		104.59		90.52		89.42	
111.8	0.00866	105.31	−0.0028	90.54	−0.0144	91.25	0.03752

(Continued)

Table 4.3 Continued

	China		Hong Kong		Indonesia		Japan	
01–2002	101.37		127.05		114.24		80.45	
02–2002	101.95		127.59		116.44		80.12	
03–2002	101.29		126.96		119.51		81.45	
04–2002	100.85		126.49		124.46		81.25	
05–2002	98.92		124.29		127.18		83.02	
06–2002	97.21	−0.041	122.42	−0.0364	131.31	0.14942	84.04	0.04462
07–2002	95.2		120.14		124.77		86.85	
08–2002	96.09		121.11		126.28		86.85	
09–2002	96.62		121.67		126.57		85.8	
10–2002	97.51		122.61		124.95		83.91	
11–2002	96.26		121.29		124.5		84.88	
12–2002	95.88	0.0071	120.81	0.0056	126.4	0.01306	84.12	−0.0314
01–2003	94.19		118.94		124.44		85.42	
02–2003	94.14		118.92		124.47		84.84	
03–2003	94.24		119.1		124.09		85.54	
04–2003	94.16		119.08		125.94		84.31	
05–2003	91.69		116.42		128.43		84.45	
06–2003	91.54	−0.0281	116.23	−0.0228	131.44	0.05625	83.39	−0.0238
07–2003	92.11		116.91		130.56		83.61	
08–2003	92.72		117.51		128.61		84.03	
09–2003	91.65		116.69		127.78		86.44	
10–2003	89.68		115.3		125.53		89.61	
11–2003	89.67		115.05		124.62		89.9	
12–2003	88.35	−0.0408	113.54	−0.0288	123.03	−0.0577	90.08	0.07738
01–2004	87.2		112.33		123.06		90.44	
02–2004	87.04		111.94		122.21		90.05	
03–2004	88.06		112.77		121.51		89.11	
04–2004	88.29		112.77		121.04		90.14	
05–2004	89.57		114.14		117.96		87.29	
06–2004	88.78	0.0181	113.42	0.0097	111.86	−0.091	89.03	−0.0156
07–2004	88.42		113.08		115.77		88.78	
08–2004	88.87		113.63		113.83		88.12	
09–2004	88.61		113.3		114.13		88.29	
10–2004	87.7		112.45		114.1		88.58	
11–2004	85.39		110.1		112.17		90.46	
12–2004	84.09	−0.049	108.61	−0.0395	108.36	−0.064	90.22	0.01622
01–2005	84.36		108.62		108.81		90.9	
02–2005	84.46		108.66		108.45		89.44	
03–2005	84		108.16		106.58		88.82	
04–2005	84.92		109.27		105.81		87.65	
05–2005	85.17		109.63		106.72		88.51	
06–2005	86.49	0.0252	111.49	0.0264	106.69	−0.0195	87.83	−0.0338
07–2005	88.06		112.66		105.74		85.73	
08–2005	88.5		111.5		102.6		85.8	
09–2005	88.86		112.09		100.43		85.63	
10–2005	90.18		113.5		103.19		83.31	
11–2005	91.17		114.56		104.51		81.15	
12–2005	90.79	0.031	113.9	0.011	105.96	0.00208	80.64	−0.0594

Korea		Malaysia		Singapore		Thailand	
111.13		106.58		91.49		92.3	
111.28		106.91		92.2		93.15	
110.37		106.27		91.7		93.4	
110.35		105.84		91.26		92.93	
113.59		104.07		91.18		92.47	
116.06	0.04436	102.55	−0.0378	90.66	−0.0091	92.53	0.00249
118.08		100.82		90.92		92.87	
117.16		101.58		91.43		91.41	
116.3		102.09		91.11		90.5	
114.46		102.96		90.97		89.6	
116.14		101.91		91.09		89.26	
116.14	−0.0164	101.55	0.00724	91.39	0.00517	89.08	−0.0408
117.47		100.12		91.04		88.7	
116.01		100.16		90.54		88.48	
111.4		100.25		90.09		88.72	
111.91		100.28		88.85		88.47	
112.28		98.08		89.08		87.97	
112.86	−0.0392	97.93	−0.0219	88.89	−0.0236	88.96	0.00293
114.77		98.51		88.35		89.19	
115.67		99.01		88.96		89.93	
115.82		98.05		88.5		91.48	
113.16		96.35		87.64		91.31	
111.4		96.32		88		90.84	
109.41	−0.0467	95.19	−0.0337	87.9	−0.0051	90.1	0.0102
109.07		94.17		87.73		90.51	
110.49		94		88.11		90.38	
111.77		94.95		88.31		90.57	
113.34		95.02		89.27		90.69	
112.34		96.33		88.9		89.51	
113.4	0.0397	95.81	0.01742	88.48	0.00855	88.31	−0.0243
113.02		95.48		88.19		87.68	
113.61		95.93		88.53		86.94	
114.3		95.65		89.41		86.78	
114.04		94.84		89.68		86.32	
117.46		92.84		89.33		86.37	
120.22	0.06371	91.77	−0.0389	88.91	0.00816	87.85	0.00194
122.04		91.93		89.25		89.1	
124.12		92		89.29		89.95	
125.66		91.67		89.42		89.37	
126.55		92.57		89.08		88.16	
127.9		92.76		89.27		87.59	
128.17	0.05023	93.98	0.0223	89.18	−0.0008	86.37	−0.0306
126.18		95.2		89.52		85.55	
126.57		94.96		89.74		85.84	
125.76		95.03		88.98		86.41	
125.3		95.89		89.3		87.86	
127.14		96.53		89.6		88.31	
129.02	0.02251	96.02	0.00861	90.5	0.01095	88.03	0.02899

(*Continued*)

Table 4.3 Continued

	China		Hong Kong		Indonesia		Japan	
01–2006	89.22		111.76		109.09		81.67	
02–2006	89.85		112.15		111.29		80.08	
03–2006	89.96		111.88		112.04		80.46	
04–2006	89.37		110.93		113.93		79.92	
05–2006	87.43		108.92		111.15		82.7	
06–2006	88.77	−0.005	110.05	−0.0153	107.99	−0.0101	81.28	−0.0048
07–2006	88.88		109.81		110.67		80.4	
08–2006	88.76		109.36		110.62		79.88	
09–2006	89.5		109.42		110.28		79.15	
10–2006	90.29		109.63		110.08		78.18	
11–2006	89.67		108.4		109.37		78.28	
12–2006	89.18	0.0034	107.37	−0.0222	108.77	−0.0172	77.53	−0.0357
01–2007	90.56		107.73		109.81		75.74	
02–2007	90.87		107.31		109.55		75.48	
03–2007	90.36		106.48		107.51		77.39	
04–2007	89.8		105.64		107.54		75.61	
05–2007	90.35		105.47		110.63		74.11	
06–2007	91.16	0.0066	105.9	−0.017	109.29	−0.0047	72.96	−0.0367
07–2007	90.82		104.63		106.99		72.81	
08–2007	90.89		104.72		103.6		76.36	
09–2007	90.6		104.18		103.25		76.9	
10–2007	89.64		103.11		104.07		75.25	
11–2007	89.14		101.09		100.64		77.84	
12–2007	90.39	−0.0047	101.14	−0.0334	100.3	−0.0625	77.1	0.05892
01–2008	91.17		99.76		98.25		79.76	
02–2008	91.66		99.16		99.89		79.74	
03–2008	90.62		97.08		97.57		83.41	
04–2008	91.42		96.64		97.03		81.53	
05–2008	92.79		97.65		97		80.6	
06–2008	94.21	0.0333	97.96	−0.018	97.42	−0.0084	78.57	−0.0149
07–2008	94.44		97.48		98.24		78.02	
08–2008	96.86		99.8		100.67		77.69	
09–2008	99.46		102.11		100.29		81.34	
10–2008	103.89		105.63		95.82		90.34	
11–2008	106.33		107.64		83.31		95.54	
12–2008	103.63	0.0973	105.55	0.0828	84.52	−0.1397	100.56	0.2889
01–2009	104.51		105.75		85.96		101.76	
02–2009	107.29		107.92		82.57		101.21	
03–2009	107.96		108.9		83.38		95.58	
04–2009	106		107.4		88.38		93.09	
05–2009	103.15		104.77		91.58		93.2	
06–2009	101.84	−0.0255	103.74	−0.019	92.52	0.07631	92.4	−0.092
07–2009	101.31		103.45		92.98		94.35	
08–2009	100.48		102.92		93.7		93.36	
09–2009	99.08		101.6		93.17		96.1	
10–2009	97.69		100.19		96.01		96.19	
11–2009	97.05		99.68		95.61		97.19	
12–2009	97.77	−0.0349	100.21	−0.0313	96.28	0.03549	96.93	0.02734

Korea		Malaysia		Singapore		Thailand	
132.57		94.98		91.34		89.73	
134.87		95.95		91.68		90.66	
133.94		96.38		91.9		91.5	
136.14		96.64		92.23		93.16	
135.33		96.45		92.24		91.22	
134.95	0.01795	96.12	0.012	92.49	0.01259	91.69	0.02184
135.38		95.83		92.76		92.47	
133.41		95.35		92.97		93.1	
135		95.6		92.8		93.89	
135.39		95.69		93.23		94.49	
136.5		95.57		93.55		95.52	
136.8	0.01049	97.2	0.0143	93.49	0.00787	96.51	0.04369
136.16		99.02		94.18		96.96	
135.81		99.14		94.23		97.43	
133.86		98.64		94.28		98.51	
134.91		99.55		94.16		98.48	
135.3		100.54		93.35		99.23	
135.56	−0.0044	99.47	0.00454	92.78	−0.0149	99.7	0.02826
135.57		98.55		93.23		101.27	
132.86		97.43		93.07		99.6	
132.37		96.97		93.02		98.43	
133.01		98.5		94.8		97.55	
130.12		97.51		94.8		96.67	
128.8	−0.0499	98.64	0.00091	94.93	0.01823	97.63	−0.0359
125.51		99.59		95.19		97.77	
124.34		100.18		95.77		98.76	
116.5		99.17		95.75		99.94	
115.48		99.62		96.95		99.36	
110.76		98.75		97.81		98.57	
111.27	−0.1135	97.74	−0.0186	98.03	0.02984	95.73	−0.0209
112.33		97.42		98.05		94.27	
111.07		97.03		96.7		95.35	
103.59		95.45		96.9		95.57	
90.33		96.05		96.77		97.61	
86.85		96.11		97.12		97.21	
87.78	**−0.2186**	95.34	−0.0214	97.44	−0.0062	95.29	0.01082
88.52		94.96		96.61		95.77	
84.69		95.13		96.9		96.68	
84.69		94.81		96.76		96.44	
91.31		95.14		96.82		95.95	
95.18		95.19		97.25		96.09	
94.06	0.06258	94.56	−0.0042	97.04	0.00445	96.54	0.00804
93.55		93.38		96.92		96.26	
94.65		93.61		96.82		95.8	
95.67		93.18		97.13		94.96	
97.8		94.43		97.47		94.86	
98.24		94.33		97.65		94.69	
98.75	0.05559	94.21	0.00889	97.61	0.00712	95.39	−0.009

(*Continued*)

Table 4.3 Continued

	China		Hong Kong		Indonesia		Japan	
01–2010	98.24		100.24		99.01		95.38	
02–2010	99.62		101.32		98.56		97.73	
03–2010	99.34		101		99.99		96.82	
04–2010	99.47		100.74		101.55		93.56	
05–2010	102.01		102.42		101.41		96.94	
06–2010	103.15	0.05	103.08	0.0283	102.35	0.03373	99.07	0.03869
07–2010	101.58		101.29		101.57		101.53	
08–2010	100.15		100.19		101.24		103.41	
09–2010	99.84		99.01		99.98		103.58	
10–2010	97.98		96.48		98.01		104.53	
11–2010	98.76		96.91		98.26		103.89	
12–2010	99.85	−0.017	97.31	−0.0393	98.06	−0.0346	103.57	0.02009

Note. Boldface indicates an exchange rate crisis, which is a situation in which a country's nominal effective exchange rate (NEER) drops more than 20 percent in a period of six months.

Korea		Malaysia		Singapore		Thailand	
101.43		95.4		97.6		96.27	
100.77		95.22		97.52		96.82	
102.34		97.57		97.94		98.37	
104.53		101.11		98.92		99.2	
101.63		101.35		99.89		100.45	
97.86	−0.0352	101.54	0.06436	100.29	0.02756	100.66	0.0456
96.89		101.66		100.18		99.14	
98.01		102.27		100.67		99.76	
98.75		102.77		101.3		101.75	
99.7		100.39		101.38		102.13	
99.4		100.22		102.07		102.72	
98.69	0.01858	100.49	−0.0115	102.25	0.02066	102.74	0.03631

Notes

1 Interview with ASEC1.
2 Interview with J2.
3 Interview with J3.
4 Interview with J3.
5 Interview with C2.
6 Interview with T5.
7 Interview with T1.
8 Interview with J3.
9 Interview with T2.
10 As a result of the negotiations, China and ten ASEAN member states signed the Framework Agreement on China-ASEAN Comprehensive Economic Cooperation at the 6th China-ASEAN Summit in November 2002.
11 Interview with T2.
12 Interview with T2.
13 Interview with T2.
14 Interview with J3
15 Interview with J4.
16 Interview with I1.
17 EMEAP is an organization of central banks and monetary authorities (in the East Asia and Pacific region. The members are Reserve Bank of Australia, People's Bank of China, Hong Kong Monetary Authority, Bank Indonesia, Bank of Japan, Bank of Korea, Bank Negara Malaysia, Reserve Bank of New Zealand, Bangko Sentral ng Pilipinas, Monetary Authority of Singapore and Bank of Thailand. EMEAP's goal was to enhance the cooperation among these central banks.
18 Interview with T6, 16 February 2011.
19 Interview with J4.
20 Interview with J1.
21 Interview with J1.
22 Interview with P1.
23 Interview with T2 and I1.
24 Interview with T13.
25 Interview with ASEC 2.
26 Interview with T4.
27 Interview with T2
28 Interview with T2.
29 Interview with A1.
30 Interview with J1.
31 Interview with T2.
32 Interview with T4.
33 Interview with M3.
34 Interview with T12.
35 Interview with I1.
36 Interview with T4.
37 Interview with J2.
38 Interview with T2
39 Interview with M2.
40 Interview with M3 and M4.

41 Interview with C2.
42 Interview with SK1.
43 Interview with M3.
44 Interview with ASEC1.
45 Interview with T3.
46 Interview with T3.
47 Interview with C2.
48 Interview with T12.
49 Interview with I1.
50 Interview with I1.
51 Vietnam co-chaired the CMIM negotiation again at the 13th AFMM+3 in May 2010. This time, Vietnam co-chaired the meeting with China. It was reported that Vietnam was significantly more active during the discussions than when co-chairing with Japan (interview with ASEC1).
52 Interview with T2.
53 Interview with T2.
54 In this study, an exchange rate crisis is defined as a situation which a country's nominal effective exchange rate (NEER) drops more than 20 per cent in a period of 6 months.
55 Interview with J4.
56 Interview with I1.
57 Interview with T5.
58 Interview with T3.
59 Interview with T11.
60 Interview with J5.
61 Interview with T13.
62 Interview with I2.
63 Interview with M1.
64 Interview with M1.
65 Interview with T4.
66 Interview with P1.

5   South Korea

South Korea's positions regarding contribution and voting issues

For South Korea, major agencies responsible for crafting the country's financial policies are the Ministry of Finance and Bank of Korea. In regards to the making of the CMIM agreement, these entities work together and serve as the main negotiators representing South Korea.

In regards to positions concerning CMIM contributions and voting power, South Korea's story was different from that of China and Japan. Like the latter, when the CMI was initiated, Seoul realized from the beginning that it would assume a role of a lender. However, South Korea was regarded by the two powers as a lesser player among the +3 countries.

Thus, the CMIM negotiations could be viewed as consisting of three tiers. The top tier contains potential lenders – China and Japan. Potential borrowers – ASEAN states – descended to the lowest tier.[1] South Korea's place seemed to occupy the middle. It is because Seoul's overall economic power was not as much as China's and Japan's. According to the Economic Strength Index (Table 5.1), the former's score figured at 9.78 while Beijing (including Hong Kong) and Japan's score was 27.31 and 33.11, respectively. This is also in line with what the involved negotiator observed. Regarding CMIM negotiation, two layers emerged within the internal interactions among the +3 countries, with China and Japan presided above and South Korea a bit below.[2]

The actual CMIM negotiation dynamics reflected the logics mentioned earlier. Seeing itself as one of the potential lenders, South Korea's goal was to have as much influence in the decision making of the CMIM as possible. Unsurprisingly, the country at first set a goal of matching its financial commitments to CMIM with China and Japan, as some part of the contributions determine voting power. It once bargained hard for equal sharing among the +3 countries.[3] However, China and Japan strongly refused Seoul's idea as they wanted the latter to instead give out a smaller portion than themselves.[4] Owing to the GFC and its aftermaths, South Korea eventually acquiesced and agreed to supply the CMIM with lesser amount than Beijing and Tokyo.

Table 5.1 Economic Strength Index of ASEAN+3 countries (2004–2010)

Country	GDP	Shares (in percentages) of Each Country's GDP of ASEAN+3 Countries	GDP per Capita	Shares (in percentages) of Each Country's GDP per Capita of ASEAN+3 Countries	Economic Strength Index
China, PRC	3683.49	34.034	2777.87	1.664	17.85
Hong Kong, China	198.62	1.835	28515.96	17.082	9.46
Japan	4752.91	43.914	37229.22	22.302	33.11
South Korea	905.55	8.367	18681.01	11.191	9.78
Brunei	11.33	0.105	28982.40	17.362	8.73
Cambodia	8.76	0.081	626.90	0.376	0.23
Laos PDR	4.31	0.040	698.55	0.418	0.23
Indonesia	442.26	4.086	1945.56	1.165	2.63
Malaysia	180.00	1.663	6595.93	3.951	2.81
Myanmar	23.83	0.220	405.79	0.243	0.23
Philippines	137.70	1.272	1538.84	0.922	1.10
Singapore	165.17	1.526	34347.38	20.575	11.05
Thailand	235.27	2.174	3726.50	2.232	2.20
Vietnam	73.92	0.683	862.84	0.517	0.60
Total	10823.12	100	166934.76	100	100

Note: Economic Strength Index is an equal weight of percentages of each country's GDP and GDP per capita of ASEAN+3 countries

Source: International Monetary Fund, World Economic Outlook Database, April 2011

Being pressured to make a smaller contribution did not prevent Seoul from pursuing its objective to having as much as say in CMIM as possible. The country's approach to achieve this goal shifted from focusing on the issue of financial contribution amount alone to, another important aspect of CMIM – the on decision-making procedures. This was because Seoul was concerned about a potential moral hazard problem.[5] In other words, Seoul wanted to have a say in disbursing CMIM funds via the decision-making process in order to avoid giving easy money to potential borrowers.

In regards to decision making, South Korea wanted lending decisions to be governed by supermajority rather than simple majority.[6] The supermajority rule dictates that in order to activate lending or disbursement of financial support to the borrowing countries, more than half of the votes are required.

Why did it prefer a supermajority voting system? We may consider possible scenarios to better understand why Seoul wanted so. Suppose the CMIM were governed by simple majority. A crisis occurs and either Japan or China cuts deals with ASEAN countries. Japan (or China) could combine its votes with those of ASEAN states in decisions to disburse CMIM funds to swap-requesting countries.

Consequently, Seoul, also a potential lender, would be left out from lending decisions in practice.

In contrast, if the CMIM lending decisions were to require a supermajority,
South Korea's chance of itself being bypassed in the determination to give CMIM
financial support would be reduced. Even better, a supermajority could be tailored
in certain ways to increase Seoul's decision-making power. For example, supermajority could be designed in a way that it always requires South Korea's vote
to give the green light to activate swap requests and disburse financial assistance.
In other words, Seoul could become a pivotal player to cast its "decisive" votes
under this decision-making rule – a veto player, in effect.

Therefore, it was quite reasonable for South Korea to prefer supermajority to a
simple majority in order to enhance its leverage in lending decisions. In short, it
was the country's interest to gain more decision-making power through this form
of voting system.

South Korea's involvement in shaping
the CMIM agreement details

There existed several CMIM components that reflected much of South Korea's
influence. Seoul was found to shape the following CMIM elements: (1) South
Korea' financial commitment; (2) the breakdown of contribution amounts among
the +3 nations; (3) the drafting process of the CMIM agreement; and (4) the 2/3
supermajority voting principle.

Roles of discount rate and best alternative to no agreement (batna)
in shaping South Korea's financial contribution to CMIM

As mentioned earlier, the +3 could to some extent be regarded as potential CMIM
lenders. They strongly wanted to have as much votes as possible to determine the
lending decisions based on weighted voting. Hence, the distributions of financial
commitment among the +3 became inevitably contentious. Unlike the previous
chapter which focused on Japan's roles in shaping South Korea's contribution portion, this chapter highlights the factors from the latter's side which made possible
such deal. The following analysis below reveals that the country's discount rate
and batna played a significant part in its decision to yield to China's and Japan's
demands.

South Korea's discount rate could be gauged by looking at the country's
liquidity status (see Table 5.2). At the first glance, it seemed like Seoul did
well on this aspect. Seoul's liquidity status prevailed over most ASEAN states
Seoul's international liquidity score stood at 8.89, which was higher than those
of ASEAN countries except Singapore. In other words South Korea possessed a
lower discount rate than the other ASEAN countries. In short, based on its higher
reserves and better borrowing capacity than most ASEAN countries, South Korea
could be expected to possess for more bargaining leverage in CMIM talks than
the former.

However, when comparing South Korea's discount rate with that of Japan and China, the picture looked different. Seoul's international liquidity score was inferior to China's (13.43) and Japan's (14.65). Beijing's and Tokyo's score was, respectively, about 1.51 and 1.65 times higher than South Korea's. This suggests that when compared to China and Japan, Seoul had a higher discount rate which put it under a disadvantaged bargaining position than the former. Hence, the preceding comparisons show that South Korea's discount rate might allow it to have an upper hand when negotiating with ASEAN. However, when it came head-to-head with China and Japan, Seoul's relative leverage vis-à-vis the latter was eclipsed. With a higher discount rate than Beijing's and Tokyo's, Seoul's eventually acquiesced to the latter's pressure in regards to the breakdown of financial contributions among the +3.

Table 5.2 International Liquidity Index of ASEAN+3 countries (2003–2009)

Country	Reserve Adequacy (Total Reserves in Months of Imports)	Shares (in percentages) of Each Country's Reserves of ASEAN+3 Countries	International Borrowing Capacity (Sovereign Credit Rating)[7]	Shares (in percentages) of Each Country's International Borrowing Capacity of ASEAN+3 Countries	International Liquidity Index
China, PRC	15.86	17.703	12.00	9.148	13.43
Hong Kong, China	4.43	4.944	14.68	11.190	8.07
Japan	16.00	17.863	15.00	11.435	14.65
South Korea	7.29	8.134	12.64	9.638	8.89
Brunei	2.29	2.552	17.00 [c]	12.959	7.76
Cambodia	3.71	4.147	4.00 [a]	3.049	3.60
Indonesia	5.14	5.742	5.14	3.921	4.83
Laos PDR	5.71	6.380	1.00 [b]	0.762	3.57
Malaysia	6.14	6.858	11.00	8.386	7.62
Myanmar	3.57	3.987	1.00 [b]	0.762	2.37
Philippines	5.29	5.901	5.86	4.465	5.18
Singapore	5.29	5.901	17.00	12.959	9.43
Thailand	5.86	6.539	9.57	7.296	6.92
Vietnam	3.00	3.349	5.29	4.029	3.69
Total	89.57	100	131.18	100	100

Sources: World Bank Statistics (for reserve adequacy data); Standard & Poor's, Moody's and Fitch (for international borrowing capacity data)

[a]Cambodia's available datum is "4" in 2007; I applied "4" to all other years. [b]Myanmar and Laos PDR have no available data. I assigned the lowest credit rating or "1" to them, assuming that they have absolutely no creditworthiness and any loans to them would be regarded as too risky. [c]Owing to its oil wealth, I assigned to Brunei the highest credit score or "17." One reason might be that the country is not rated because it has never borrowed internationally.

Furthermore, South Korea's batna were worse off than that of China and Japan. Table 4.3 indicates that, unlike the latter, South Korea had endured exchange rate crises during the period of 1994–2010. During AFC, the country's nominal effective exchange rate (NEER) plummeted by 36.45% from July to December 1997. GFC brought Seoul another drop in its exchange rate by 21.86% from July to December 2008. Therefore, from these figures, Seoul could be expected to walk away with less favourable agreement terms than the other two powers. Now, let us turn to examine how the actual events shaped Seoul's bargaining leverage and negotiation outcomes.

The interactions of Seoul's heightened discount rate and worsened batna turned out to determine the party's withdrawal from its previous position after the GFC. The crisis hit South Korea hard. Business confidence plummeted, resulting in a capital flight from the Korean financial market. The country witnessed a sharp drop in its currency, the won, in the late 2008 (Table 4.3). The abruptness and severity of the crisis resulted in a problem of international illiquidity.[8] Being in a dire need for financial rescue to help weather through the GFC storm, the country ended up seeking money from other governments, such as through swap arrangements with the US Federal Reserve (US$ 30 billion) and other central banks in late 2008 (Bank of Korea 2008). In short, the crisis of 2008 unfortunately threw one of the East Asia's vibrant economies to the borrowing side. Seoul found itself asking for money from others instead of the other way around (see Box 5.1).

Box 5.1 South Korea in the global financial crisis

After the collapse of the Lehman Brothers in September 2008, South Korea encountered its own financial market turmoil. The repercussions from the US financial market hit Asia's fourth biggest economy hard. Panic set in and foreign investors began pulling out capital from the market. A credit crunch resulted, as reflected by depleting foreign currency supply, even though the economy was not directly exposed to sub-prime mortgage-related securities. This financial market unrest, coupled with export decline due to contracted demands in the developed markets, namely the USA and EU, plummeted South Korea's economy into a recession. Its GDP growth experienced a drop of 5.1% in the fourth quarter of 2008. The won depreciated against major currencies. By the end of November 2008, the Korean won's value fell about 25.4 per cent in dollar terms (Kim 2009). Bank of Korea also witnessed the depletion of its foreign reserves, shrinking from US$ 264 billion in March to about US$ 200 billion in December 2008 (Bank of Korea 2008).

To curb the ongoing market's anxiety over its depleting reserves, South Korea concluded a bilateral currency swap contract with US Federal Reserve in October 2008 to secure US$ 30 billion (*Korea Times* 2008). Between

December 2008 to January 2009, the two parties concluded additional five swap deals totalling US$ 16.3 billion (Bank of Korea n.d.). In addition, Seoul in December 2008 concluded swap contracts with Bank of Japan and the People's Bank of China, for US$ 20 and US$ 26 billion respectively (*China Post* 2008). The government successfully contained further currency speculation and stabilized the market. Market confidence restored and the won recovered.

One might wonder, why did the bulk of the Korean's liquidity assistance come from the USA? Several reasons can be warranted. First, there was an ideational factor at play here. Although the Bank of Korea's reserve holding figured around US$ 200 billion, its officers were anxious about dollar shortage in the banking system, which led South Korea to conclude a swap agreement with the US Federal Reserve (Grimes 2011b). Another reason why South Korea resorted to Washington for financial rescue was because of the former's strategic calculation. The bilateral currency deal was linked to the fact that Seoul had "special security relationship with the USA and . . . [its attempt] to forge a free trade agreement with the latter, which was passed by the US Congress in October 2011 and by the South Korea Parliament a month later" (Chan 2012: 204).

In regards to CMIM negotiation, when GFC occurred the +3 countries were at the middle of discussing how to break down the contributions to the mechanism's reserve pool among themselves. The GFC did alter the bargaining dynamics among these states, especially due to the fact that it negatively impacted South Korea's bargaining leverage. Owing to the crisis, Seoul's liquidity status was jeopardized. The country experienced a substantive decrease of its reserves during the 2007–2008 period, plunging from US$ 262.5 billion to US$ 201.5 billion or about 23 per cent drop (Table 3.1). Such reserve depletion not only undermined the country's ability to supply to the CMIM pool.[9] South Korea's lesser liquidity capacity diminished a likelihood that it would take up contribution amounts as equal as China's and Japan's. Seoul found it more difficult than before to cling on to its previous demand of equal financial commitments to CMIM pool among the +3. This highlighted the "hidden hierarchy" of this regional financial facility, in which only Beijing and Tokyo served as its most likely lenders while Seoul's status wavered between the lender and borrower (Huotari 2012: 20).

Let's go back to the 1990s to comprehend the full picture of how GFC shaped South Korea's batna, pressing it to rush to conclude the CMIM talks. GFC brought back the memory of the country's AFC experience of 1997–98. The Korean authorities at that time resorted to the IMF for financial rescue (see Box 5.1). Although South Korea's IMF package was less harsh when compared with the ones ASEAN countries received (see Box 5.2), it did inflict some suffering to the country. The plight led Seoul to become a persistent advocate of East Asian financial cooperation, even after the AMF turned out to be a stillborn (Lee 2010). Moreover, South Korea's past IMF experience account for its later aversion from going to the Fund amidst GFC. This policy move reflected that the country's AFC experience was still vivid justifying the country's avoidance from using the Fund's service (Sohn 2012). Sussangkarn (2011a: 12) posits that,

> Given the experience with the IMF in the aftermath of the 1997/98 crisis, it would likely have been political suicide for Korea's government to take the country into another IMF program, even though during the sub-prime crisis IMF conditionality had become much more loose under the new so-called "Flexible Credit Line (FCL)," introduced in March 2009, for countries it regarded as having strong fundamentals and sound macroeconomic policy track records.

Some may wonder, why did Seoul not resort to the CMI for help, which could have granted the country with a maximum of US$ 23.5 billion? Evidence reveals that the country's non-utilization of CMI stemmed from its IMF aversion. To borrow the maximum amount meant that Seoul eventually had to abide to the Fund's conditionalities as the CMI agreement linked borrowing beyond 20% of total CMI commitment with the IMF programme. Thus, going to the CMI to draw the preceding amount of US$ 23.5 billion was equal to going directly to the IMF (Kawai 2010). As one official contends, the Korean politicians avoided the Fund due to the latter's negative image in the country.[10] To Seoul, leaning again on the IMF's help potentially brought about the loss of market confidence which would further exacerbate its economy (Grimes 2011b). "Using CMI would have required IMF involvement, which would have been economically disruptive and politically unpalatable, and so the Korean government consciously avoided working through CMI" (Grimes 2014).

However, if the government chose to evade the IMF stigma by borrowing from the CMI less than the 20% of entire commitment, the scale of financial assistance the mechanism released, which would be US$ 3.7 billion – would be too small to help stabilize its economy. In addition, unlike the later CMIM, the earlier CMI agreement required Seoul to conduct separate bilateral negotiations with each of its individual lenders to secure additional liquidity which could be time consuming. Therefore, to alleviate its dollar shortage, South Korea bypassed the Fund and instead signed bilateral swap arrangements with other governments.[11] However, these deals were not concluded at the same time. The country had to negotiate each contract separately with each of its lending counterparts.

It must be emphasized that South Korea's non-use of the CMI did not mean that the country completely neglected in this regional scheme. On the contrary, its GFC experience heightened Seoul's interest in advancing the CMI further. The logics went as follow. The GFC worsened South Korea's batna. The global event solidified its aversion of the IMF borne out of the AFC in the late 1990s, as seen its bypassing of the Fund. This same aversion acted as a drive behind Seoul's preference to pursue CMI/CMIM. The country saw that if CMI/CMIM was to be enhanced, it could somehow serve as an alternative to the IMF.[12] Moreover, the separate negotiations between South Korea and its lenders during the GFC years heightened its discount rate. The nature of the bargains tempted Seoul to be even more enthusiastic in advancing the CMIM than before. It is because CMIM facility would make all swap contracts "multilateral" in which all lenders could collectively activate the swap arrangements, enabling liquidity assistance to be disbursed quickly in time to help manage economic turmoil. It should be noted that although the members had earlier agreed to launch the CMIM since the 10th AFMM+3 in May 2007, the project was at best a work-in-progress as several component of the facility had yet been worked out. Tempted by the global crisis' impacts on its economy, South Korea felt that making the CMIM function in practice was an urgent issue. Hence, the country became very keen than ever to conclude the CMIM negotiation as soon as possible so that the entity would enter into force which allowed it to tap on the resources available.

It is worth-highlighting that Seoul's self-perception also played a significant role in shaping the country's approach in its talks with Beijing and Tokyo. Inflicted by the GFC, the former viewed itself as having less bargaining leverage than the latter which not suffer as much as itself. As one source contends, there existed a shared view among the Korean politicians and elites that the country's market strength was very frail, although the other nations viewed otherwise.[13] Driven by this perception, Seoul became more convinced that it could no longer be able to flex its muscles against the two regional giants, especially during the negotiation to determine the breakdown of financial contributions among the +3.

Therefore, the softening of South Korea's demand was observed as the CMIM talks unfolded. According to one authority, South Korea was not as staunch as before in insisting that it must at least give to the CMIM fund as much as China and Japan did.[14] Seoul's discount rate and batna made it became less capable to resisting China's and Japan's influence. The latter then gained a bigger say on how the 80% share would be split among the +3.[15] These countries' ongoing attempt to pressure South Korea to contribute less than themselves began to bear fruits. The result was in China's and Japan's favour as both achieved their goal of making Seoul supply to the CMIM fund less than themselves.

To conclude, the combination of its most recent liquidity shortage due to GFC, laborious negotiations with the lenders that came afterward, and its persistent avoidance of IMF programme heightened Seoul's discount rate and worsened its batna. These factors in turn accounted for the division of CMIM financial contributions among the +3, specifically explaining why South Korea finally agreed to make a smaller commitment to the CMIM reserve pool than China and Japan. The crisis experience aroused Seoul to pursue CMIM to circumvent IMF as a lender. This desire to conclude the CMIM negotiation as soon as possible coupled with its reduced ability to contribute, Seoul later backed down from its previous position in favour of equal sharing among the +3 and accepted to supply the CMIM with a lesser financial amount than Beijing and Tokyo.

Box 5.2　South Korea's IMF experience

During the Asian financial crisis (AFC), market confidence in South Korea faltered and the panic set in. In late October 1997, the value of the Korean won sank quickly as investors sold the stocks. A month later Seoul found itself consulting with the IMF. On 4 December 1997, the Fund approved a three-year stand-by arrangement of about US$ 21 billion. With help from other entities, namely the World Bank, Asian Development Bank and the USA, the IMF rescue package totalled US$ 57 billion (BBC News 1997).

The Korean programme primarily targeted restoring market confidence and stabilizing financial markets. As a result, it emphasized macroeconomic policies and financial sector reform. The country's macroeconomic policies were designed to stabilize its currency (the won) and rebuild reserves. Thus, the policies involved increasing the interest rates on foreign-exchange advances from the Bank of Korea to commercial banks. Minimum levels were set on both net foreign-exchange reserves and net domestic assets.

Once the won was steady, the government turned to adopt an expansionary fiscal policy to avoid the impact of recession. Social safety nets were enhanced. For example, the government directly supported public works programs. The unemployment insurance system was also expanded.

In regard to financial sector reform, much effort was geared towards restoring financial system stability via suspending the operations of nonviable financial institutions and recapitalizing commercial banks. For instance, 14 out of 30 merchant banks were closed while the remained were subject to suspension unless they submitted rehabilitation schemes (Nanto 1998). The authorities also adjusted financial sector regulations and supervision to be consistent with international standards.

The country's situation improved after its embraced the IMF programme. Market confidence was restored and foreign-exchange reserves rebuilt. The Korean government then stopped drawing from the IMF. It also finished repaying to the IMF about nine months ahead of schedule.

Box 5.3　IMF program comparison: South Korea, Indonesia and Thailand

When compared the Korean programme with those of Indonesia and Thailand (Table 6.3), Seoul's package appeared to be the least strict. Although these countries adopted similar measures regarding monetary and exchange rate policies (e.g. imposing floors on net international reserves (NIR) and ceilings on net domestic assets (NDA) as quantitative performance criteria[16]), the Korean package contained fewer quantitative performance criteria regarding fiscal austerity. Also, the government was not required to include formal performance criteria concerning external sector policy.

Role of knowledge about other actors' preferences in determining CMIM financial contribution breakdown among the +3 countries (the 2:2:1 ratio)

As just demonstrated, Seoul's sense of urgency (i.e. discount rate) and batna explained why the country ended up supplying the CMIM fund with a smaller portion than Beijing and Tokyo. However, they did not shed light on why the CMIM financial contribution proportion among China (plus Hong Kong), Japan and South Korea arrived at 2:2:1. Unlike the previous chapter, which used the issue of Hong Kong itself as a centre of analysis, this chapter focuses on South Korea's coordinating role in shaping this outcome. This was revealed that South Korea's use of informational advantages accounted for the contribution ratio among the +3. In short, to learn more on this bargaining detail, we must turn to the role of information strategies and tactics in shaping the outcome.

Speaking about how the +3's share was split, several options were examined. Among them were 34%:34%:12%, 33%:33%:14% and 32%:32%:16%.[17] Translated into ratios, they were 2.83:2.83:1, 2.35:2.35:1 and 2:2:1, respectively. Out of these alternatives, the ratio of 2:2:1 was finally selected. In other words, China and Japan would each commit US$ 38.40 billion (now raised to US$ 76.80 billion after the total CMIM size was doubled) while South Korea would put in half this amount, which was US$ 19.20 billion (now increased to US$ 38.40 billion).

A careful examination showed that this outcome was not reached easily. Beijing and Tokyo found themselves on the opposite side of South Korea. As Lee (2009) contends, "At first, China and Japan both tried to convince South Korea to provide less than half of the amount they would provide, but South Korea held its ground and got its share of US$ 19.4 billion."

This leads to a puzzle. We have learned from the preceding that South Korea's discount rate and batna lessened its bargaining influence vis-à-vis China and Japan. Crippled by these disadvantages, how did the country manage to fight back and resist the latter from pressing itself to contribute less than half of their amounts? In other words, how did Seoul negotiate and convince its two neighbours to adopt the 2:2:1 ratio instead of choosing the other available options?

Although China and Japan similarly wanted the Korean portion to be smaller than theirs, these parties diverged on how to divide up the financial commitment share among themselves. Beijing and Tokyo once again clashed with each other. According to Rathus (2009):

> . . . the CMIM has faced difficulty in reaching a decision about contribution levels. This problem was political; boiling down a simple question of whether China would succeed in persuading Japan to accept an 'equal firsts' solution, or whether Japan would succeed in making its case that it should to be the largest single contributor.
>
> (Rathus 2009)

This Sino-Japanese dispute intensified when both states fiercely fought over which factors would be used to determine their individual financial contributions.[18] Each side proposed different factors to be incorporated into the formula calculating their share. Japan wanted to use GDP as a main factor. In other words, some parts of members' financial commitment and voting power would proportionally be determined by their GDP. China abruptly rebuffed Japan's calculation method. One possible reason behind the country's rejection was that Japan's GDP during the CMIM negotiation was greater than Beijing's (see Table 5.2). If the contribution share was largely determined by GDP, the latter would end up supplying the CMIM in a smaller portion than Tokyo. Beijing then suggested using the levels of foreign-exchange reserves as a major factor for the computation. Unsurprisingly, Tokyo quickly refused its rival's idea, on the similar account.[19] Having international reserve amounts as a main factor would make Tokyo's contribution share less than that of Beijing, due to the latter's larger reserve holding. The Sino-Japanese contestation swung the negotiation to the verge of a deadlock. Neither Beijing nor Tokyo exhibited any sign of backing down.

The deal was finally concluded when Seoul stepped in and provided a helping hand. With the intervention by South Korea, the +3 states could finally settle their dispute, merely in the matter of hours before the Joint Ministerial Statement of the 12th AFMM+3 was released. Much credit was given to Seoul, which

> . . . rose to the role of a go-between and proposed the strong alternative solution that the two warring parties contribute equally while she, Korea, shoulder the burden of a 16-percent contribution to the US$ 120-billion pool. Finally, the three parties arrived at a consensus to adopt the Korean suggestion, so amply demonstrating how Korea executed a delicate, successful balancing act in reconciling her powerful Northeast Asian neighbors.
>
> (The Korea Trade-Investment Promotion Agency (KOTRA), 2010)

What explained this outcome? As the negotiation unfolded, South Korea's knowledge about other actors' preferences was found to play a key role in making the agreement possible. As an observer recalled, South Korea was able to extract information about China's and Japan's interests from their interactions including bilateral quarrels between the latter. First, Seoul learned that Beijing and Tokyo shared a similar interest in incorporating Hong Kong into the CMIM, but for different reasons.[20] Also, both parties took the issue of prestige seriously. Either one would lose face if its rival ended up financially putting into the CMIM pool more than itself.[21] For these two rivals, such deal would be deemed detrimental and unacceptable. Moreover, the Sino-Japanese dispute revealed their different preferences over the factors used to compute their financial commitments. What remained to be solved as how to calculate Hong Kong's contribution and vote share as well as make China and Japan equally provide to the CMIM fund. In short, the issue concerned with how to devise a formula which at the end gave out equal contributions between China and Japan.

Seoul was not shy to show that it was up for this task. About a year before the 2009 Bali meeting, it convened trilateral informal talks with Beijing and Japan.[22] At these meetings, South Korea assumed the roles of a "middle-man" role to resolve the conflict between Beijing and Tokyo.[23] In short, Seoul acted as an information broker which

. . . enjoys the trust of the [conflicting] parties [and hence] can enhance the flow of information by only passing on information that, in his judgement, will not hurt the other party. [A]cting as a selective conduit of information . . . [enables a broker to] . . . reduce the expected or feared cost of disclosing information.

(Lax and Sebenius 1986: 172)

How did South Korea concoct its formula and how did the latter helped reach the agreement? First, the country welcomed the factors proffered by China and Japan. Instead of choosing which one of the elements to be included into the formula, Seoul suggested that the calculations for the division of their individual financial contribution and voting power be relied on three main components: (1) the country's GDP, (2) its foreign-exchange reserves and (3) its total import and export values.[24] After calibrations, the proportion between China's (plus Hong Kong's), Japan's and South Korea's commitments was set at 2:2:1. Using this formula, Beijing (together with Hong Kong) and Tokyo would put in an equal amount to the CMIM, while Seoul's portion would be half of the former's

This carefully crafted solution in the end settled the Sino-Japanese conflict simply because it saved their face (Sussangkarn 2011a: 212). Out of this deal, Beijing and Tokyo saw that they more or less gained something. Seeing Hong Kong as part of itself, the fact that the combined contribution portion of Beijing and Hong Kong equated Japan's allowed China to say that it attained a major achievement. The deal marked the first time the in the history the country equalled Tokyo in terms of contribution and voting power in an international organization (Dolan 2009). As Eichengreen (2009) argued,

In previous regional agreements, like capital subscriptions to the Asian Development Bank, China had always been treated as a second-rate power and asked to contribute less . . . That China is now acknowledged as a co-equal means that it will not stand in the way of further cooperation.

For the Japanese, they were satisfied with the result as well. The calculation made Tokyo rise as a single member that supplies the largest amount to CMIM, which was what it initially aimed to get from the CMIM negotiation. As Grimes (2011a: 96) maintains, "The face-saving compromise between Japan and China – i.e., creating equal shares but assigning a share of China's commitment to Hong Kong in order to allow Japan to retain its nominal role as the largest contributor." In this sense, Japan's prestige was ultimately upheld.

Not only that the formula permitted China and Japan to supply the CMIM fund, it also granted South Korea to commit half the amount of the former. The Sino-Japan contestation over which gave the greater amount to the CMIM enabled Seoul to slip in the third factor – total import and export values – into the formula. Consequently, the contribution proportion among China, Japan and South Korea turned out to be 2:2:1. Seoul ended up being better off with this ratio than the other options pondered at the negotiation, namely 2.83:2.83:1 and 2.35:2.35:1.

In conclusion, one could argue that without help from South Korea, the CMIM negotiation could have broken down, or the contribution and vote share among the +3 might not have been finalized as soon as they were. Using the information about China's and Japan's preferences gathered from their clashes over their individual commitments, the country devised the solutions to prevent negotiation failure. Moreover, by taking advantage of the ongoing Sino-Japanese rivalry, Seoul was able to determine how to divide the +3' contribution share in its favour. As Beijing and Tokyo agreed to adopt the 2:2:1 ratio calculated by Seoul, the latter was able achieve its own goal of resisting the former's demand of pressuring it to give to CMIM less than half of their amounts.

We learned that South Korea's bargaining leverage emerged from its acquisition of knowledge. This echoes an old adage of "knowledge is power." We have so far discussed how Seoul utilized information about the preferences of its counterparts to evade deadlock and steer the outcomes into its direction. Now, Let us turn to explore another kind of knowledge South Korea used to shape the final result – knowledge about the contents of issues being negotiated, or expertise.

Role of expertise in shaping the writing process of the CMIM legal text

Observers hailed when the Joint Ministerial Statement of the 11th AFMM+3 in May 2008 announced that the CMIM members settled on the key elements of the agreement. They regarded this result as a big step towards the deepening of East Asian financial cooperation. However, this was too soon to give an outright celebration. The CMIM was yet a finished product, hinting that technical discussions on the other CMIM components were required for a comprehensive agreement. The ASEAN+3 governments were "committed to further accelerate [their] work in order to reach consensus on all of the elements which include concrete conditions eligible for borrowing and contents of covenants specified in borrowing agreements" (ASEAN+3 2008).

The process of developing the CMIM agreement began after the 11th AFMM+3. South Korea and Thailand, being co-chairs at that time, were responsible for taking care of the procedure.[25] This writing phase could be broken down into several steps. First, the ministerial-level meetings (AFMM+3) provided a broad mandate regarding the drafting of the text. A bulk of work was carried out by the ASEAN+3 officials at the working-group level. These officers communicated several times among themselves to exchange their comments on the drafts. Some comments were later used to revise the text. Once the final draft was completed, it was sent upward for approval at the deputy-ministerial-level (AFDM+3) and ministerial-level meetings (AFMM+3).[26]

Critics might argue that the drafting process carries a great risk of negotiation collapse. Because particular CMIM functions involved a lot of technicalities issues, namely as borrowing terms, LIBOR rates, borrowing renewals and steps of activating financial support, the members could have clashed among themselves over specific terms to put in the final CMIM document. The critics' claim was more or less in line with the accounts given by the involved negotiator. When it came to technicalities, different parties had different ideas of doing things.[27] They diverged on how they operate such matters. As a result, their conflicts could have spiralled into a bargaining deadlock.

Fortunately, the impasse did not happen. The outcome did not turn out to be as speculated. A year and a half later, in November 2009, the CMIM agreement was completed. This period spanned about five meetings between the officials at the working-group level. The final legal document was officially endorsed by the ASEAN+3 finance ministers and central bank governors in December 2009.[28]

Admittedly, there emerged some conflicts among the ASEAN+3 states at the drafting phase. However, according to one officer, most disagreements over the development of the 70-page legal text involved terminology changes. For instance, particular parties requested for some alterations of certain wordings so that their own staff at different departments or units could share the same understandings of how the CMIM was to be operated.[29]

Some may ask, why did the disputes merely involve minor adjustments over language and word choice rather than major clashes over which technical modalities or approaches over the specifics of financial operations which could have stalled the whole writing procedure? What accounted for fewer clashes regarding the latter matter? According to one ASEAN authority, Seoul, by exercising its expertise, was able to play a dominant role in writing the CMIM treaty.[30]

Where did South Korea hone its technical knowledge and skills from? As far as the source of expertise was concerned, the country reportedly hired international financial and legal specialists to assist itself during the development phase of the CMIM agreement. Why did the other members allow Seoul to bring in the expert team? One reason was because there was consensus among the CMIM players that Thailand and South Korea, acting as the co-chairs during that time, were to take charge of composing the legal text.[31] Thus, Seoul's being proactive in putting together the writing team was justified. Another reason involved the credentials of these experts and the fact that they were internationally recognized. By resorting to these professionals, Seoul was able to boost the credibility of its drafting team in the eyes of other CMIM participants.[32] Consequently, the likelihood of the latter's protesting during the development of the legal text dwindled.

How did the country utilize such expertise to bolster South Korea's influence? These financial personnel and lawyers played a major role in undertaking the legal scrapping of the CMIM document.[33] They assisted the country by fine-tuning the language of the text. In short, by seeking experts, Seoul was about to bolster its ability to compose the 70-paged treaty.

These professionals not only helped refined the language, they also gave advice on how to arrive at certain CMIM aspects which were highly technical (e.g. borrowing renewals). These experts were assigned to carry out studies and produce discussion papers and materials supplementing their work. The findings and papers were distributed to the other CMIM participants during the writing phase.

Using these discussion papers advanced the development of the legal document in the following ways. First, the reports were used to check in advance whether the involved parties understood the concepts incorporated into the legal document in a similar way. With several financial technicalities involved in the operations of the CMIM mechanism, the official text possessed several jargons. Because the reports were given to the other CMIM members as the drafting went on, Seoul was able to be notified about disagreements over the definitions of particular terminology. When such conflicts emerged, Seoul acknowledged them at the early stage and settled them before they escalated and undermined the writing progress. Illustratively, in cases that the stakeholders diverged on certain vocabulary to be incorporated into the CMIM text, they could debate and find ways to arrive at agreed meanings of such terminology before the drafting proceeded further.

Moreover, South Korea used the experts' reports to solicit opinions and comments pertaining to the CMIM technicalities from the non-drafting states.[34] The latter often responded in some ways after reading the discussion papers. Their remarks enabled Seoul to learn about their concerns or sensitivities over certain technical aspects of the CMIM facility. After receiving these inputs, South Korea went back and edited the text.[35] Because there existed different ways to compose a language to convey similar meanings, Seoul, by taking into account the preferences of its counterparts, was able to adjust some words or rephrase some parts of the document which had potential to trigger strong negative reactions or oppositions from the other CMIM parties.

Doing so turned out to facilitate the text development. Suppose the Korean had chosen to go "solo" in developing the legal document without seeking or considering any inputs from the other CMIM participants. When the former presented its final draft, it could have met with fierce protests by the latter. The ASEAN+3 states could somehow have managed to resolve their clashes, by requiring Seoul to conduct a major "face-lift" to its draft. This would have wasted time and other resources, delayed the finalization of the CMIM legal document and the date which the mechanism entered into force. Hence, South Korea's taking into account its equivalents' concerns when composing the treaty to some extent helped smooth out the writing process.

In sum, the discussion papers gave South Korea an opportunity to check for conflicts and misunderstandings regarding terminology used in the treaty. This enabled the disputes to be sorted out at the early stage, rather than intensified to block the progress or founder the negotiation. Moreover, the reports were used to extract others' sensitivities and concerns over the CMIM technicalities. This knowledge about other actors' preferences was later utilized by Seoul to revise the text's language to ameliorate disagreements which could otherwise have prolonged or stalled the writing process.

One may wonder, what were Thailand's roles in crafting the CMIM text? Compared to the team from Thailand (another co-chair), the Korean officials were reportedly more active than the former.[36] Bangkok left the drafting task in Seoul's hand and let the latter take a lead. The country instead resorted to play a supporting role, namely by reviewing the text earlier drafted by South Korea and helping the latter distribute the document to the other ASEAN+3 governments for their comments.[37] Bangkok's assuming a lesser role might be explained by the fact that

South Korea had hired qualified experts to draft the CMIM treaty, bolstering the trustworthiness of the Korean writing team in the former's eye.

In conclusion, South Korea's consultations with certain specialists with credentials suitable for the drafting the CMIM legal document facilitated the progress. Because it was serving as a co-chair at that time, Seoul was able to seek the experts with little opposition or legitimacy. Some major reasons why there existed no protests from the other states over Seoul's selection included the fact that the former shared a consensus that the co-chairs was to be in charge of the writing phase, and that the recruits were internationally recognized professionals. By calling on these experts, Seoul enhanced the credibility of its drafting team, and lessened conflicts which might have arisen during the drafting process. Without Seoul doing so, clashes over technical details could have escalated and foundered the entire negotiation.

Role of co-chairs and non-alliance in affecting the two-thirds (2/3) supermajority voting system

When the Special AFMM+3 and 12th AFMM+3 were convened in 2009, the ASEAN+3 governments discussed how the decision making were to be governed. South Korea, together with Thailand, served as the co-chairs of the meetings. As mentioned in the previous chapter, some CMIM members doubted whether the lending decisions should be governed by consensus. Relying on unanimity could potentially delay the disbursement of financial assistance, jeopardizing the main objective of CMIM. Therefore, a consensus-based rule was eventually dropped. After it was later agreed that lending decisions were to be determined by weighted voting, the participants moved to ponder over which type of voting principle to be adopted: simple majority or a supermajority. As Henning (2009: 6) contended:

> There appears to be broad support among members for the principle of weighted voting, where each country wields votes in rough proportion to its contribution to the fund, and for taking decisions by a supermajority rather than by simple majority or unanimity.

Once the parties decided to use a supermajority voting system, their discussions turned to focus on one matter: what fraction or percentage of votes would be regarded as a supermajority? Specifically, what is the minimum number of votes required to approve or reject the disbursement of CMIM financial assistance to the borrowers? Finally, the members agreed to adopt the two-thirds (2/3) supermajority rule.

The road towards this voting principle was quite bumpy. Distrusts among the participants loomed large as they were concerned over the possibility that their counterparts would veto their decision to activate lending. As a result, different countries proffered dissimilar voting rules which if implemented would best serve their interests. For instance, ASEAN pushed for the principle of "one man, one vote," meaning that each individual member, regardless of their contribution amounts, would cast only one vote.[38] The governments also suggested using a "double majority" voting, which posits that the number of votes and the number of countries must both be more than half of the total in order to determine executive issues such as lending decisions. This principle would at the end gain ASEAN an upper hand in the decision-making process

Unsurprisingly, these ideas were strongly rejected by the +3 nations. The latter feared that ASEAN countries would gang up against themselves by voting as a bloc. Illustratively, if all ASEAN states join their votes together, their votes would be counted as ten, which would be higher than the combined votes from the +3 (which would be three). In other words, by relying on such "head count," the chance that the voting power of the three Northeast Asian countries was outnumbered by that of the ASEAN countries would be very high (Ciorciari 2011). Accordingly, the +3 could not accept this outcome as it could ultimately hijack their veto authority and influence over lending decisions.

Beside the disagreement between ASEAN and the +3, internal rifts inside the latter grouping were no less intense. Grappling for regional leadership, Beijing and Tokyo were worried about its rival's obtaining a veto power which would undermine its own clout in determining CMIM decisions.[39] Accordingly, both states quarrelled over which would get more voting power than the other.

All of the preceding disputes could be understood by exploring how the power was dispersed at the talks concerning the CMIM voting system. For this particular matter, tri-polarity characterized the power distribution among the parties, with ASEAN states, China, Japan occupying each corner of a triangle (Figure 5.1), which was created from the data from Table 5.2, graphically demonstrates the economic strength of the CMIM members. The score of China (together with Hong Kong), Japan and 10 ASEAN countries read 27.35, 33.11 and 29.81, respectively. These three entities had roughly equal economic clout. This partly explained why they ended up bargaining hard to prevent each other from obtaining a veto authority in CMIM lending decisions. Neither Sino-Japan, Sino-ASEAN, nor Japan-ASEAN coalitions emerged during the talks.[40]

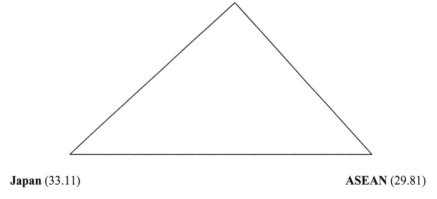

Figure 5.1 Tri-polarity at the discussions about voting principles

Source: Author's illustration

As the disputing members did not appear to yield to one another, the negotiation approached a gridlock. However, the Korean co-chair was able to resolve the clashes and being the negotiation to a close. The agreement was settled only two days before the 12th AFMM+3 in 2009 was commenced.[42]

What did the Korean co-chair do to salvage the talks? It adopted a backward calculation with the starting point being that no single member has veto power.[43] That no single player possesses a veto authority means that neither ASEAN nor the +3 nations could on its own block a collective decision made by the others.[44] To prevent such veto power from happening, Seoul assigned China, Japan and ten ASEAN countries an equal number of votes, which constituted 28.41% of the total votes (see Table 1.3). In addition, lending decisions were to be governed by a two-thirds (2/3) supermajority rule, meaning that at least 66.67 per cent votes is required to approve decisions to provide CMIM financial support to the borrowers.[45] The outcome was precisely described by Injoo Sohn (2012: 590):

> Under the CMIM, the threshold for approval – more than two-thirds of the total votes is needed to approve some key decisions – was set high enough that neither Japan nor China alone is able to block disbursement. China, Japan and ASEAN have acquired an approximately 28 per cent voting share each, with South Korea receiving a 14 per cent voting share, making it almost impossible for big countries to act alone or to block decisions made by a majority of other countries.

Not only that the 66.67 per cent threshold removed a chance of a veto authority by a single player, it also prevented a veto emerging from potential bilateral alliances formed by the two out of the three parties. In other, the 2/3 supermajority rendered impossible the ability of China-ASEAN, Japan-ASEAN and China–Japan coalitions to overturn the CMIM decisions. Even though they did coalesce, their votes would top at 56.82 per cent, which would be insufficient to invoke a veto. These solutions turned out to ameliorate China's, Japan's and ASEAN's anxiety over the possibility of the other's nullifying its veto in the decision-making process. Therefore, all members ultimately agreed to accept what Seoul proposed.

In sum, South Korea assumed a role of a mediator and took control over the management of the issues under dispute. By choosing not to side with either Beijing, Tokyo, or ASEAN, Seoul was able to reign supreme as a neutral co-chair and resolve their trilateral conflicts.

One might ask, why did South Korea choose to remain a middle player instead of banding with either China, Japan, or ASEAN, which would have strengthened its bargaining leverage? Let's take a look at the figures to grasp why staying out of the trilateral conflict at the end enhanced Seoul's influence. According to Economic Strength Index (Table 5.2), South Korea's strength (9.78%) was much lower than that of either China (plus Hong Kong) or Japan, which were 27.31% and 33.11% respectively. Seoul's score fared better than that of individual ASEAN states except Singapore, but the former's clout fared less than that of all ten ASEAN economies combined (29.81%).

What do these figures suggest? They indicate that, if South Korea were to form an alliance with either China, Japan or ASEAN, it could significantly boost its economic power and bargaining leverage vis-à-vis its counterparts. Illustratively, if Seoul banded together with Beijing (and Hong Kong), their combined economic strengthen would read 37.09, overcoming that of Japan, and all 10 ASEAN combined. Alternatively, South Korea could unite with Japan and increase their combined clout to 42.89, which would be greater than that of China (plus Hong Kong), and of all 10 ASEAN combined. Or, Seoul could choose to gang up against Beijing and Tokyo by forming a coalition with all ten ASEAN states because their combined economic strengthen would rise to 39.59, above that of the two other Northeast Asian states. In sum, South Korea had three options which it could coalesce to boost its bargaining power. Looking at these scenarios alone, the country could be expected to band together either China (plus Hong Kong), Japan, or ten ASEAN states.

Why did South Korea's actual course of action diverge from what is expected? In other words, why did the country refuse to form such alliances? It was because by not joining the coalitions, the country was able to acquire greater leverage than the banding-together option. As mentioned earlier, Seoul was interested in seeing the CMIM facility come into being. By being non-partisan, it was in a better position to act as the co-chair taking up a mediating role in settle the trilateral clash and helped the conflicting players reach their agreement. In short, neutrality strengthened Seoul's co-chairing authority, creating trust from the disputants.[46] By being as an honest broker, the Korean's influence in reconciling the conflicts was bolstered, raising a probability of concluding an agreement. Moreover, impartially helped the country "sell" more easily its ideas. Acting neutral facilitated South Korea's effort to lobby the others to buy on to its suggestions on the voting system.[47]

Looking closely, the adoption of the two-thirds (2/3) supermajority principle bears a paradox. The system, on the one hand, abolishes a veto authority by a single member. On the other hand, it ultimately grants South Korea a decisive vote in lending decisions. Based on the principle, the approval of CMIM financial disbursements requires at least 66.67 out of 100 votes (Figure 5.2). This means that China (including Hong Kong)'s votes combined with all ASEAN's votes, adds up to only 56.82 votes, which cannot determine the decision to lend out money (Scenario 1). Neither can Japan and all ASEAN together when they together cast their votes, which will total 56.82 votes (Scenario 2). Also, in a case that China and Japan give "no" votes to the lending decisions but the ten ASEAN countries vote "yes" (Scenario 3), the former cannot trigger the disbursement of the fund. Therefore, to pass the 66.67 per cent approval threshold, the Korean votes (14.77 votes) must be counted (Scenarios 1a, 2a and 3a). In short, to get the lending approved, the other parties must convince South Korea to vote in the same direction as they do. Therefore, the adoption of this 2/3 supermajority rule allows Seoul to have a final say in lending decisions. It simply gears the country with the ability to cast an "up or down" vote for these matters.

Scenario 1: ASEAN + China (HK)[48] = 28.41 + 28.41 = 56.82

Scenario 2: ASEAN + Japan = 28.41 + 28.41 = 56.82

Scenario 3: Japan + China (HK) = 28.41 + 28.41 = 56.82

Scenario 1a: ASEAN + China (HK) + **S. Korea** = 56.82 + **14.77** = 71.59 → Lending approved

Scenario 2a: ASEAN + Japan + **S. Korea** = 56.82 + **14.77** = 71.59 → Lending approved

Scenario 3a: Japan + China (HK) + **S. Korea** = 56.82 + **14.77** = 71.59 → Lending approved

Note: To approve CMIM lending, at least 66.67% of votes must be in favour of lending.

Figure 5.2 The combinations of votes to approve CMIM lending decisions

To sum up, the two-thirds (2/3) supermajority rule which prevented China, Japan and ASEAN states from single-handedly wielding a veto power. This principle also rendered bilateral deal-cutting among these stakeholders unfeasible as their combined votes will land at 56.82 %, which is less than 66.67% threshold needed to approve lending. As a result, that the trilateral disputes were settled and the agreement was salvaged.

Paradoxically, this principle made South Korea rise above the other parties as it gives the country an actual veto power despite the fact that it has a smaller number of votes amounts than Beijing, Tokyo and ASEAN. Although Seoul's financial commitment was half of Beijing's and Tokyo's, "this should not matter too much in practice as South Korea is likely to hold the swing vote between China and Japan on many important issues." (Sussangkarn 2011a: 212).

Some may wonder, how about Thailand which served as another co-chair? What were its roles in altering the outcome? Evidence reveals that the Thai co-chair was not as influential as its Korean equivalent. One ASEAN official assessed that Bangkok did not act as a co-mediator together with Seoul. In regards to voting issues, the former's task turned to focus on cranking out the exact number of votes for each individual CMIM member.[49] A possible explanation for Thailand's lesser roles could be that the country feared that the others might suspect of its neutrality should it intervene and manage the clashes. This was because Thailand is an ASEAN member state and ASEAN was among the disputing parties in the discussions about the voting system. Thus, Bangkok decided not to play a mediating role and let the Korean take up the task.

In conclusion, South Korea took advantage of the ongoing disputes among China, Japan and ASEAN to step in and resolve the conflicts. Being neutral not only bolstered the former's co-chair position to reconcile clashes, but also enabled it to conclude the negotiation in its favour. With the adoption of the two-thirds (2/3) supermajority rule, Seoul successfully reached its goal of getting a determining vote in lending decisions. As one source summarizes:

> [South Korea] . . . has played the roles of both diplomat and honest broker by allotting the contribution ratios equitably to ensure no party became a

dominant voting power. By doing so, Korea is able to award the casting vote in any decision-making when a difference of opinion among the members arises.

(The Korea Trade-Investment Promotion Agency (KOTRA) 2010)

Summary

South Korea played a significant role in shaping the following CMIM details: (1) its own financial contribution; (2) the breakdown of contributions among the +3 countries; (3) the drafting of the CMIM treaty; and (4) the adoption of the 2/3 supermajority system governing the CMIM lending decisions.

Several factors underlined South Korea's influence on these matters. The 2008 global financial crisis heightened its discount rate more than China's and Japan's. As a result, the country retreated from its initial preference, which was to shoulder an equal financial commitment to those of Beijing and Tokyo. Moreover, the GFC inflicted Seoul with less attractive batna than its two neighbours. This factor also accounted for the fact that the former softened its earlier demand and ended up giving less to the CMIM reserve pool than the latter.

Knowing other players' preferences enabled South Korea to break the bargaining impasse and reached certain CMIM terms in its favour. For instance, Seoul was able to move the CMIM process forward by reconciling conflicts between Beijing and Tokyo over Hong Kong participation. Taking into account Beijing's and Tokyo's preferences allowed Seoul to advance its idea of using the third factors to calibrate the financial commitments for individual +3 states. With the third factor incorporated, the calculation formula was tweaked in a way that it increases Seoul's portion to be half of that of China and Japan.

Moreover, South Korea exercised its expertise in the process of drafting the CMIM agreement. The country hired qualified financial and legal professionals to compose the legal document. Via the credibility of these experts, Seoul successfully reduced clashes over agreement details which might otherwise have arisen during the drafting process. Moreover, the experts' reports were used to solicit the information about the other parties' preferences, especially their sensitivities or concerns over specific financial technicalities of the CMIM. Utilizing such information boosted Seoul's ability to draft the legal agreement which the involved stakeholders could agree upon. In short, South Korea's expertise lessened potential conflicts that might have delayed the writing process of the CMIM text.

Additionally, South Korea significantly affected the two-thirds (2/3) supermajority voting rule governing lending decisions. The Korean co-chair proposed this principle and convinced the other states to go along with its idea. A main element undergirding Seoul's success was its adoption of a non-partisan position. By being neutral and refusing to side with any of the players in the trilateral disputes among China, Japan and ASEAN, the country gained co-chairing credibility in the latter's eyes, which in turn strengthened its ability to function as a mediator and settle the conflicts.

The two-thirds (2/3) supermajority system which effectively prevented veto emerged from a single party and bilateral coalitions formed by the two out of three players – China, Japan and ASEAN, paradoxically turned out to grant South Korea a veto power in effect. This voting principle was crafted in a way that it requires Seoul's vote to determining the decision to lend out the CMIM liquidity to crisis economies.

Notes

1 Interview with ASEC2.
2 Interview with I1.
3 Interview with T2.
4 Interview with T2.
5 Interview with SK1.
6 Interview with SK2.
7 A sovereign credit rating refers to a long-term foreign currency rating. It is because the CMIM is purposed to provide finance for deficiencies of foreign exchange. Therefore, the proper indicator would be long-term foreign currency rating.
8 Interview with T7, 29 September 2010.
9 Interview with T7.
10 Interview with T6.
11 Interview with C3.
12 Interview with J4.
13 Interview with J1.
14 Interview with J3.
15 Interview with J3.
16 Performance criteria are the conditionalities (or economic policies that members intend to follow) of the IMF-supported program. Performance criteria directly govern the disbursements of the IMF loans. In other words, if performance criteria are not met, disbursement will be interrupted.
17 Interview with J4.
18 Interview with SK1.
19 Interview with SK1.
20 Interviews with J1, J3.
21 Interview with J4.
22 Interview with SK1.
23 Interview with A1.
24 Interview with SK1.
25 Interview with T3.
26 Interview with T3.
27 Interview with M1.
28 Interview with T9, 30 September 2011.
29 Interview with T3.
30 Interview with ASEC1.
31 Interview with T3.
32 Interview with M3.
33 Interview with T3.
34 Interview with ASEC1.

35 Interview with T3.
36 Interview with T3.
37 Interview with T3.
38 Interview with T2.
39 Interview with SK2.
40 Interview with ASEC1.
41 The figures in parentheses indicate the country's economic strength.
42 Interview with ASEC1.
43 Interview with T3.
44 Interview with T2.
45 Interview with J3.
46 Interview with T4.
47 Interview with SK2.
48 HK represents Hong Kong.
49 Interview with I1.

6 Indonesia, Malaysia and Thailand

Indonesia's, Malaysia's and Thailand's positions regarding contribution and voting issues under the CMIM framework

As earlier mentioned in Chapter 2, ASEAN countries in general can be regarded as the potential borrowers to the CMIM. However, the following will show that this status did not entirely cripple these states from bargaining with the other parties and getting the interests addressed. Before exploring the roles played by the ASEAN participants in shaping the CMIM outcomes, let's first examine their stances towards the issues of members' financial commitments and votes.

Similarly, the key players in shaping Indonesia's, Malaysia's and Thailand's positions regarding the CMIM and negotiating the agreement were their finance ministries and central banks. For Jakarta, the main bodies were its Ministry of Finance and Bank Indonesia (Bank Sentral Republik Indonesia). For Kuala Lumpur, the entities were its Ministry of Finance and Bank Negara Malaysia. The division of labour was divided between these two bodies. While the central bank was mostly involved in shaping the technical elements of the CMIM mechanisms, the finance ministry worked the domestic internal processes by getting approvals from the Malaysian Parliament to proceed with the CMIM.[1] For Thailand, Bank of Thailand and the country's finance ministry were responsible to negotiate the CMIM agreement. The ministry took a lead of the negotiation team while the former supplemented the latter with its financial technical expertise.[2]

Among the ASEAN participants, there was a consensus that the +3 countries would assume a role of lenders to the CMIM.[3] As far as the members' financial contributions were concerned, Indonesia, Malaysia and Thailand viewed the matter as their financial burden. For Jakarta, the considerations of its individual commitment were much influenced by its ability to provide the money. According to one source, the country was concerned more about how much it would financially supply the CMIM reserve pool than the number of votes it would get.

Indonesia factored in its foreign-exchange reserves when calculating its preferred commitment.[4] At the time of deciding how much it would provide to the CMIM mechanism, the country's reserves figured around US$ 46 billion. From this figure, Jakarta then set its CMIM maximum contribution to be 10% of its reserve level, equivalent to around US$ 4.6 billion. In addition, one official viewed that US$ 5 billion was too big a number to put in.[5]

Likewise, Malaysia worried about its ability to commit to the CMIM reserve pool. Even though the amount it aimed to give were confidential, one authority contended that Kuala Lumpur had an upper contribution limit, which was figured out from its reserves level.[6] The country also planned not to supply more that its predetermined amount.[7]

As for Thailand, its approach to the CMIM stemmed from the fact that it perceived itself as being on the borrowing side of the CMIM facility. When engaging in the CMIM talks, Bangkok also looked at worst-case scenarios – how much money it would need in the time of a crisis and its total past bilateral swap arrangement (BSA) amounts.[8] The country viewed CMIM commitment as its financial burden. In calculating Bangkok's appropriate contribution amount, the officials first took into consideration the country's foreign-reserve level. This factor significantly defined Thailand's upper contribution limit prior to CMIM negotiations. The maximum Bangkok preferred to put into this regional facility was set at US$ 5 billion, which was approved by the Thai Parliament.[9]

ASEAN's roles in affecting the CMIM agreement details

The ASEAN participants in the CMIM were found to help affect the following bargaining outcomes: (1) the decision to increase the size of the CMIM prior to the actual finalization of the other components; (2) the breakdown of financial commitments between ASEAN5 and CLMVB; and (3) the decision to adjust the Philippines' contribution portion.

Roles of discount rate in explaining ASEAN's concessions to Japan over the CMIM size expansion

From Chapter 4, we already learned about Japan's influence over the decision to enlarge the size of the CMIM fund prior to the complete finalization of other agreement details. This chapter turns to explore what shaped the outcome from a different angle, focusing instead on ASEAN countries. What were these states' roles in affecting this bargaining result? Disparities in terms of discount rates between Japan and ASEAN states shed additional light on this puzzle. A noticeable difference persisted when their discount rates were compared. According to the International Liquidity Index (Table 5.2), Japan's score landed at 14.65, which was higher than those of the ten ASEAN members. The figure of Indonesia, Malaysia and Thailand – the three ASEAN countries examined in this study – read 4.83, 7.62 and 6.92, respectively. Putting them in comparison, Tokyo's liquidity score was 3.03, 1.92 and 2.12 times higher than Indonesia's, Malaysia's and Thailand's, respectively.

These figures suggested that Japan had a superior liquidity status (i.e. lower discount rate) than ASEAN. Hence, the former could be expected to walk away from the CMIM negotiation with more favourable outcomes than the latter. It is because a lower discount rate permitted Tokyo to allow the current talk to collapse and wait for a subsequent negotiation round where it could manage to achieve better agreement terms. On the contrary, ASEAN countries' lower liquidity status left them with a higher discount rate, resulting that they exhibited a stronger preference to conclude the current negotiation instead of letting it falter. These parties could be expected to have less bargaining leverage than Japan in the CMIM context. In other words, Indonesia, Malaysia and Thailand could be expected to walk away with less favourable outcomes than Tokyo.

Actual CMIM bargaining dynamics confirmed that the disparities in these participants' discount rate not only altered their positions, but also determined the decision to expand the CMIM size before concluding other agreement terms. Let's first delve into how the discount rate affected each side's stance.

With higher reserves, Japan was in a better position to bail out itself than ASEAN should a crisis hit. By holding excess reserves, Tokyo had no need to request financial assistance from the CMIM mechanism.[10] As one official recalled, Japan once declared at a bargaining table that it would not seek the CMIM's rescue during crisis times as it had domestic sources to turn to.[11] It should be noted that beside usurping its owned resources to finance its economy, the country can secure additional liquidity elsewhere by borrowing abroad. In a case that Tokyo opts for the latter choice, its ability to borrow internationally would still prevail over ASEAN's, thanks to the former's higher credit rating. Therefore, Japan's capability to bail itself out of a crisis – either by tapping on its owned assets or borrowing from others – granted the country with a lower discount rate. Tokyo hence was in no rush to close the CMIM deal, especially when the agreement terms do not allow it to attain the objective of increasing the CMIM size. In sum, due to its lower sense of urgency, Tokyo continued to advocate the expansion option, proposing that the CMIM size should be raised from US$ 80 to US$ 120 billion.

ASEAN's story was the opposite of Japan's. With its limited reserves and ability to borrow money internationally, ASEAN as whole possessed a higher discount rate than Japan. Therefore, these Southeast Asian nations had a greater need for the CMIM financial facility in a time of crisis. In other words, the regional arrangement became more important to these states than Tokyo. Consequently, the ASEAN participants were more concerned about developing the details of the CMIM agreement and hence pushed for the finalization of all CMIM details than merely increasing the size of the pool. It was because if these terms were to be finalized, the CMIM agreement would be signed and the mechanism would come into force ready to disburse liquidity assistance to their economies should the next crisis hit.

ASEAN's higher discount rate and sense of urgency also accounted for why some of these states, such as Malaysia and Vietnam, clearly opposed Japan's idea of increasing the size of the CMIM. They claimed that ASEAN+3 countries should first finalize all details of the CMIM agreement. After all elements including voting system, members' individual contributions were settled, ASEAN+3 could start to discuss a possible expansion of the CMIM size.[12]

Owing to their conflicting stances, Tokyo and ASEAN clashed with one another. Each side wanted to CMIM talks to proceed the way they desired. ASEAN countries at first strongly held their ground. However, ASEAN's limited reserves undermined their bargaining influence vis-à-vis Japan.[13] With a lower sense of urgency, Tokyo clung to its positions and insisted to re-negotiate until the details were crafted in the way it wanted, even if it would require subsequent meetings. As a result, certain ASEAN governments complained about the rigidity of Japanese negotiators as the latter were considerably firm on their agendas.[14]

As the disputes dragged on, increasing pressure mounted on the side of the ASEAN countries. Owing to their higher sense of urgency, these parties viewed that if they still cling onto their position and failed to convince Japan, the CMIM talks could falter, resulting that East Asia could lose this regional financial safety net altogether. In other words, the last thing the ASEAN participants wanted was to see the CMIM morph into another stillborn project like the AMF. Wrapping up the negotiation and salvage the entity with particular terms less preferable to themselves was hence better than no CMIM at all. Consequently, ASEAN countries decided to yield to Tokyo's demand. The result was that the members in 2009 agreed to raise the CMIM size from US$ 80 to US$ 120 billion prior to the finalization of the other details. To conclude, inflicted by their higher discount rates, ASEAN states possessed less bargaining leverage than Japan. As a result, the former were unable to maintain their stance and eventually gave in to Tokyo's idea about enlarging the CMIM size before finalizing all agreement terms.

Beside the discount rate, it is worth-exploring other elements affecting the bargaining dynamics between Japan and ASEAN. The first one was the Japanese greater financial expertise than the latter. Although some ASEAN states, namely Thailand and Malaysia, were active in voicing their opinions at the bargaining table, the degree to which ASEAN influenced the outcomes was far less than Tokyo.[15] According to one authority, Indonesia's, Malaysia's and Thailand's financial expertise appeared to fare less than the latter.[16] Their lesser adeptness primarily stemmed from the fact that the three nations honed less experience in handing financial matters through its previous participation and cooperation in this area in both regional and global levels than the Tokyo.[17] Although this research cannot directly connect the expertise disparity between Tokyo and ASEAN to the final result of the CMIM size expansion, the gap did alter their bargaining dynamics in favour of the former. Owing to Tokyo's greater proficiency, ASEAN countries generally found it difficult to convince the former to go along with their ideas.[18]

Japan-ASEAN economic ties also affected their CMIM interactions. However, economic relations between Japan and Indonesia, Malaysia and Thailand, at the time the CMIM agreement was being negotiated, were unequal. In other words, there existed an asymmetric dependence on trade, with Japan having an upper hand over the trio.

Regarding bilateral commercial ties, Tokyo relied much less on the ASEAN trio. Among the countries under this study, Japan was the number one trade partner of Malaysia and Thailand, in terms of imports and exports (see Table 6.1). As for Indonesia, Tokyo stood as the former's number one export partner, and Number Two in terms of imports, behind China. On the contrary, number one and number two trade partner, from the players being examined here, were China and South Korea respectively. On the contrary, Japan's number one and two trade partners were China and South Korea, in both import and export accounts. Approximately 15.90 and 7.84 per cent of Japan's exports went to Beijing and Seoul, while Tokyo's imports from the latter constituted about 20.77 and 4.33 per cent of its total imports.

The following statistics indicated that their uneven trade relations between Japan and the ASEAN trio were obvious. About 19.33 per cent of Jakarta's total exports went to Japan, but this equated to about 4.14 per cent of Tokyo's import share. Malaysia's exports to Japan made up about 9.81% of the former's total exports. Nevertheless, this figure constituted only 2.97 per cent of the Japanese total imports. About 11.75 per cent of Thailand's exports went to Japan consumed, but it occupied a minute 2.93 per cent of the latter's market share.

Likewise, Indonesia received about 11.13 per cent of its imports from Japan, but this amount constituted merely 1.56 per cent of the Japanese exports to the world. Around 13.32% of Malaysia's imports came from Japan, but the latter's exports to Kula Lumpur figured about 2.16 per cent of its total. As for Bangkok's total imports, approximately 20.48 per cent came from Japan. However, this amount cut into only a much smaller 3.80 per cent of Tokyo's entire export market.

On the investment front (Table 6.2), Japan was the number one investor into Indonesia, Malaysia and Thailand, but not the other way around. When compared with inward FDI flows to these ASEAN economies from China, Tokyo's clout in this aspect was clearly dominant. For instance, the latter's inward investment shares into Indonesia and Thailand were 4.55 and 22 times greater than those of Beijing. Investment from Japan gulped up around 18.91, 17.97 and 36.40 per cent of Indonesia's, Malaysia's and Thailand's total inward FDI, respectively. However, these figures were tiny when pitched against Japan's entire portfolio. The shares of Indonesia, Malaysia and Thailand stood minutely at 1.07, 1.34 and 2.98 per cent of Tokyo's total outward investment. In addition, 0.50 and 2.22 per cent of Malaysia's and Thailand's total investment went into Japan. Tokyo received 0.66 and 0.05 per cent of its total inward FDI from Kuala Lumpur and Bangkok, respectively.

To sum up, Indonesia, Malaysia and Thailand relied more on Tokyo in the areas of trade and investment than the opposite. (Figure 6.1 depicts their uneven economic relationships.) Therefore, the unequal interdependence could alter the interactions between Japan and ASEAN and render the former to walk away from the CMIM negotiations with more favourable terms than the latter.

Table 6.1 Bilateral trade relations (2004–2010)

Shares (in percentages) in the Country's Trade of Its Total Trade Values, by Partner

China's Export Shares		China's Import Shares	
Hong Kong SAR	14.71	Hong Kong SAR	1.25
Japan	8.85	Japan	13.88
South Korea	4.65	South Korea	10.54
Indonesia	1.17	Indonesia	1.33
Malaysia	1.48	Malaysia	3.16
Thailand	1.08	Thailand	2.31

Japan's Export Shares		Japan's Import Shares	
China	15.90	China	20.77
Hong Kong SAR	5.61	Hong Kong SAR	0.25
South Korea	7.84	South Korea	4.33
Indonesia	1.56	Indonesia	4.14
Malaysia	2.16	Malaysia	2.97
Thailand	3.80	Thailand	2.93

South Korea's Export Shares		South Korea's Import Shares	
China	22.44	China	16.38
Japan	7.11	Japan	16.16
Indonesia	1.70	Indonesia	2.87
Malaysia	1.46	Malaysia	2.33
Thailand	1.29	Thailand	1.02

Indonesia's Export Shares		Indonesia's Import Shares	
China	8.69	China	12.44
Japan	19.33	Japan	11.13
South Korea	7.28	South Korea	5.03
Malaysia	4.88	Malaysia	6.10
Thailand	2.74	Thailand	5.30

Malaysia's Export Shares		Malaysia's Import Shares	
China	9.32	China	12.36
Japan	9.81	Japan	13.32
South Korea	3.75	South Korea	5.00
Indonesia	2.79	Indonesia	4.54
Thailand	5.11	Thailand	5.67

Thailand's Export Shares		Thailand's Import Shares	
China	9.51	China	11.36
Japan	11.75	Japan	20.48
South Korea	1.95	South Korea	3.92
Indonesia	3.31	Indonesia	2.84
Malaysia	5.27	Malaysia	6.10

Source: United Nations Commodity Trade Statistics Database

Table 6.2 Bilateral FDI flows (2004–2010)

	Shares (in percentages) in Each Country's Total FDI, by Partner		
China's Inward FDI Shares		*China's Outward FDI Shares*	
Hong Kong SAR	36.89	Hong Kong SAR	50.69
Japan	5.31	Japan	0.24
Korea	4.54	Korea	0.15
Indonesia	0.14	Indonesia	0.34
Malaysia	0.43	Malaysia	0.12
Thailand	0.13	Thailand	0.38
Japan's Inward FDI Shares		*Japan's Outward FDI Shares*	
China	3.71	China	11.59
Hong Kong SAR	3.45	Hong Kong SAR	2.40
Korea	2.28	Korea	2.15
Indonesia	0.08	Indonesia	1.07
Malaysia	0.66	Malaysia	1.34
Thailand	0.05	Thailand	2.98
Korea's Inward FDI Shares		*Korea's Outward FDI Shares*	
China	2.49	China	20.07
Japan	23.94	Japan	2.02
Indonesia	4.66	Indonesia	1.97
Malaysia	0.01	Malaysia	2.11
Thailand	0.03	Thailand	0.41
Indonesia's Inward FDI Shares		*Indonesia's Outward FDI Shares*	
China	4.16	China	N/A
Japan	18.91	Japan	N/A
Korea	3.28	Korea	N/A
Malaysia	4.88	Malaysia	N/A
Thailand	0.51	Thailand	N/A
Malaysia's Inward FDI Shares		*Malaysia's Outward FDI Shares*	
China	0.03	China	1.53
Japan	17.97	Japan	0.50
Korea	4.89	Korea	0.18
Indonesia	-0.09	Indonesia	13.87
Thailand	0.48	Thailand	4.19
Thailand's Inward FDI Shares		*Thailand's Outward FDI Shares*	
China	1.57	China	7.17
Japan	34.60	Japan	2.22
Korea	1.15	Korea	0.11
Indonesia	0.02	Indonesia	0.74
Malaysia	2.49	Malaysia	6.17

Sources: ASEAN Secretariat; Bank Indonesia; Bank of Japan; Bank Negara Malaysia; Department of Statistics, Malaysia; Ministry of Finance, Japan; Ministry of Knowledge Economy, South Korea; Ministry of Strategy and Finance, South Korea; United Nations Conference on Trade and Development (UNCTAD); The Organisation for Economic Co-operation and Development (OECD)

Notes: Negative signs indicate net decreases in liabilities (inward FDI); N/A indicates unavailable data

Indonesia's, Malaysia's and Thailand's Exports to Japan

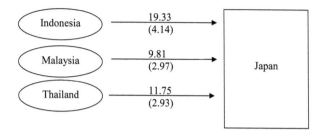

Indonesia's, Malaysia's and Thailand's Imports from Japan

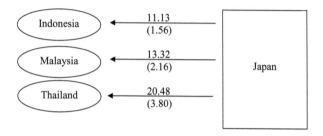

Indonesia's, Malaysia's and Thailand's outward investment into Japan

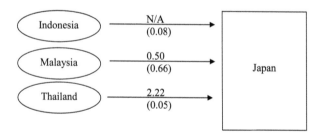

Indonesia's, Malaysia's and Thailand's inward investment from Japan

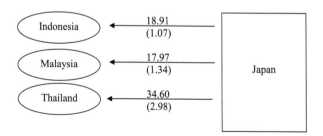

Figure 6.1 Bilateral trade and investment patterns of Japan–Indonesia, Japan–Malaysia and Japan–Thailand

In addition, the timelines of certain bilateral partnership agreements between Japan and individual ASEAN nations on the one hand, and the CMIM talks on the other, overlapped. As the CMIM talks advanced, ASEAN countries were at some stages of concluding economic partnership agreements (EPAs) (Figure 6.2). For instance, ASEAN-Japan Comprehensive Economic Partnership (AJCEP) began in 2003 and was concluded in 2008. Japan–Indonesia Economic Partnership Agreement (JIEPA) was initiated in 2005 and concluded in 2007. Moreover, Japan–Malaysia Economic Partnership Agreement (JMEPA) started in 2003 and was concluded in December 2005. In addition, Japan–Thailand Economic Partnership Agreement (JTEPA) was initiated in 2003 and concluded in 2007. These EPAs were more or less comprehensive, covering various areas of cooperation such as trade in goods and services, investment and government procurement. In regard to investment, although none of Indonesia, Malaysia and Thailand has bilateral investment treaties with Japan, each of them incorporated the investment chapters in their EPAs with Tokyo.

These pending bilateral deals and the CMIM negotiation interacted. As one authority observed, ASEAN states' ongoing EPA deals with Japan and the CMIM talks were sometimes considered as going hand-in-hand.[19] The parties considered their EPA relationship when engaging their CMIM talks.

Admittedly, even though this study could not exactly determine whether the economic interactions between Japan and ASEAN did alter the decision to expand the CMIM size before starting to bargain over the other elements of the agreement, one cannot ignore the fact that Japan's involvement with ASEAN in terms of trade and investment were highly important to the latter's economies. It could also be argued that due to the lop-sided economic ties and Tokyo's ongoing EPA negotiations with Indonesia, Malaysia and Thailand could at least serve as supporting factors influencing the outcome. In short, this could partly explain why

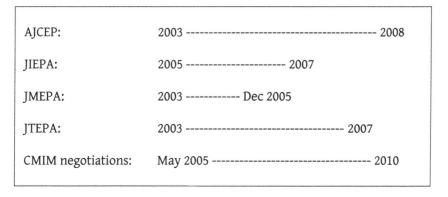

Figure 6.2 The timelines of economic partnership agreements among Japan and ASEAN countries and CMIM negotiations

these ASEAN countries eventually yielded to Japan and allowed it to go ahead with its course of action.

Role of best alternative to no agreement (batna) in the division of contribution amounts between ASEAN5 and CLMVB

Indonesia, Malaysia and Thailand similarly suffered from an exchange rate crisis from July to December 1997. From Table 4.3, Indonesia's, Malaysia's and Thailand's exchange rate during this period plummeted by 42.83%, 24.69% and 26.53%, respectively.

Although these countries suffered an exchange rate crisis, their experiences differed in terms of magnitude and length. In terms of severity, Indonesia suffered the most in the AFC out of the countries examined in this study. When compared to situations in Malaysia and Thailand, Indonesia witnessed the largest currency depreciation as its NEER tanked by 42.83%. Moreover, Jakarta endured a crisis longer than the other two countries. While Malaysia and Thailand experienced upward rebounds of their NEERs after December 1997, Indonesia's exchange rate further declined by 29.69%, reflecting that the crisis persisted in the country. In short, exchange rate crises in Malaysia and Thailand began in July 1997 and ended in December 1997, covering a period of 6 months. However, Indonesia's crisis lasted for 12 months, starting in July 1997 and ending in June 1998.

In addition, the three ASEAN states took a different course of action in crisis management, resulting in their divergent AFC experiences. While Indonesia and Thailand went under the IMF programme, Malaysia adopted unorthodox policies to cope with the crisis. Boxes 6.1 and 6.2 summarize and compare the experiences of Indonesia, Malaysia and Thailand in detail.

Box 6.1   AFC experience comparisons: Indonesia, Thailand and Malaysia

Indonesia

Indonesia was a prime case of a country's catching the contagion originated in Thailand. In July 1997, the floating of the Thai baht put a downward pressure on the value of the Indonesian rupiah. Bank Indonesia responded with contractionary monetary policies, namely raising the interest rates of its certificates (Sertifikat Bank Indonesia or SBIs). However, these measures undercut economic growth. Moreover, weaknesses in the financial sector and a high level of short-term private sector external debts led markets to doubt the authorities' ability to continue the currency peg. Two additional attacks hit Jakarta on 12 and 13 August 1997. On 14 August, the government decided to float the rupiah, but doing so did not better the situation. The rupiah continued to depreciate. As pressures mounted, Indonesia called the IMF.

The Fund approved on 30 October 1997 a three-year stand-by arrangement for US$ 40 billion, in which US$ 10 billion came from the IMF, US$ 8 billion from the Asian Development Bank, US$ 5 billion from Japan and US$ 3 billion from the USA. In July 1998, the Fund decided to increase its financing under the stand-by credit by US$ 1.3 billion, totalling the package to about US$ 11 billion.

This initial IMF rescue package seemed to better the situations as the rupiah appreciated briefly. However, markets lost confidence again when Bank Indonesia closed down 16 insolvent banks in November 1997. The country's domestic politics partly led to the delays of its IMF programme implementation. After the resignation of President Suharto on 21 May 1998, the rupiah in June 1998 depreciated by about 62.35 per cent in relation to its end-1997 value.

In August 1998, a new Indonesian government consulted the Fund. The outcome was a new extended fund facility20 which replaced the former stand-by arrangement. The new package involved strict control on base money to break inflation, banking sector reform, deregulation and privatization as well as improved governance. Although these measures helped improve market sentiment, the Fund was not satisfied with the progress. Lags in programme implementation, especially in the areas of banking and corporate restructuring, were evident. The Bank Bali scandal21 in August 1999 further revealed weaknesses in governance. These led to the suspension of the IMF assistance in September 1999.

Indonesia underwent another election and a new government assumed office in October 1999. The new administration arranged with the Fund a new three-year extended fund facility for about US$ 5 billion in February 2000. The programme was crafted to enhance bank restructuring efforts which included restructuring state banks, improving supervision of the banking system and deepening bond and equity markets.

The programme eventually led to economic recovery. GDP data showed a small positive growth in 1999 with inflation remaining flat after June. Interest rates were brought back to pre-crisis levels.

Thailand

Thailand suffered from the AFC when its currency – the baht – came increasingly under speculative attacks after it reached its lowest value in eight years. The attack instigated a further decline of the baht, and market sentiment soured. At first, Bank of Thailand responded by curbing foreign currency trading and enlarging the exchange rate band. However, its reserves soon ran dry. Thailand decided to float the baht on 2 July 1997.

When freeing the bath did not appear to help alleviate the crisis, Bangkok sought help from the IMF on 28 July. On 20 August 1997, the IMF approved financial support to Thailand. The size of the stand-by arrangement was about US$ 4 billion. Expiring on 19 June 2000, the arrangement covered a period of 34 months.

Thailand's IMF programme put a significant emphasis on financial sector restructuring. Several efforts were made to reorganize the sector. For example, the Thai government took over bankrupt financial firms, and privatized the weakest financial institutions. The authorities restructured corporate debts and recapitalized the banking system. Additionally, the bankruptcy act was reformed and foreign investment restrictions were loosened.

Monetary policy aimed at supporting exchange rate stability as well as enhancing an economic recovery. The measures thus involved setting minimum levels of net international reserves (NIR) and net domestic assets (NDA) of the Bank of Thailand. As for fiscal policy, the government controlled its overall balance by reducing the public sector's borrowing and increasing a value-added tax (VAT). The authorities also provided social safety net programmes to protect the Thais who were affected by the AFC.

Thailand's economy returned to a positive growth in late 1998. The baht began to stabilize, and foreign-exchange reserves reached a satisfactory level. The government then announced in September 1999 that it would make no further IMF drawings.

Malaysia

For Malaysia, its AFC symptoms resembles those of its neighbours, which included a loss of market confidence, substantial capital outflows, depletion of foreign-exchange reserves and currency depreciation. Unlike Indonesia and Thailand, Malaysia's macroeconomic conditions during the crisis were stronger, especially in the areas of inflation and savings. The performance of its banking and corporate sectors were better than those of the other two.

Instead of going to the Fund as Jakarta and Bangkok did, Malaysia responded with its own measures. The government first attempted to alleviate the problem via domestic interest rate reduction and credit expansion. However, these policies turned out to be less effective. The cut in interest rates heightened the offshore ringgit speculation. The economy continued to plunge. Kuala Lumpur hence imposed capital controls, which were somehow regarded as unconventional and controversial at that time (Kaplan and Rodrik 2001; Athukorala 2008), on 1 September 1998. The capital controls targeted the offshore ringgit market in Singapore in order to curb the downward pressure on interest rates. In addition, the country returned to a fixed exchange rate to the US dollar, at about 3.80 Ringgit to 1 Dollar. Bank Negara Malaysia loosened banking sector regulations and injected liquidity into the financial system (Haggard 2000: 74). The government underwent financial and corporate restructuring. Eventually, market confidence was restored. Malaysia was able to get through the AFC and also avoid the IMF's recourse.

Box 6.2   The IMF programmes of Indonesia and Thailand

In general, the IMF usually assists countries in several areas such as enhancing the Fund's surveillance over its members; policies, giving technical assistance to boost the operation of financial markets, and providing policy recommendations and financial assistance during crises (Nanto 1998). Owing to particular conditionalities imposed, Indonesia's and Thailand's IMF-supported packages to some degree differed from each other. In regard to social sector policies, for example, Jakarta eliminated the subsidies on foodstuffs except rice, introduced public work projects in rural and urban areas, and rolled out measures enhancing health care and education. As for Thailand, the government provided safety nets for the unemployed such as increasing the severance payment 10 months for labourers with more than 10 years of service and giving cash support to laid-off workers of bankrupt companies (Lane et al. 1999: 75).

Despite certain differences, the IMF's programmes of Indonesia and Thailand can nevertheless be compared. Table 6.3 reveals that Indonesia's one was less strict than Thailand's. Illustratively, in regard to fiscal austerity, Jakarta's and Bangkok's packages were equally strict. Both countries put a cap on their overall government balance. Indonesia's fiscal policy focused on raising the prices of utilities. In contrast, Thailand's fiscal austerity dealt with increasing a value-added tax (VAT) and limiting net credits to the public sector. As for external sector policy, Thailand's IMF package was more demanding. Indonesia did allow contracting and guaranteeing new debts and used a quantitative number as a ceiling. In contrast, Bangkok set a firmer ceiling on any expansion of public debt. The public sector was not allowed to contract or guarantee any new short-term debts at all. In these aspects, its package was more stringent than Indonesia's.

Table 6.3 IMF program comparisons

	Monetary and Exchange Rate Policies			Fiscal Policy		External Sector Policy	
	Floor net international reserve (NIR) of a central bank	Ceiling for net domestic assets (NDAs) of a central bank	Ceiling on base money	Floor overall central government balance	Other performance criteria	Ceiling on contracting and guaranteeing of new external debts	Ceiling on the stocks of short-term debt outstanding
South Korea (Stand-by Arrangement)	Yes	Yes	–	–	–	–	–
Indonesia (Stand-by Arrangement)	Yes	–	Yes	Yes	Increase electricity price by 30%	Yes	Yes
Indonesia (Extended Fund Facility 1)	Yes	Yes	–	Yes	–	Yes	Yes
Indonesia (Extended Fund Facility 2)	Yes	Yes	–	Yes	–	Yes	Yes

Thailand (Stand-by Arrangement)	Yes	Yes	–	Yes	–	Limit banking system net credit to public sector	Increase value-added tax (VAT) from 7% to 10%	Yes	The public sector will not contract or guarantee any new short-term debts (except guaranteed associated with financial restructuring programs, forward contracts, swaps and other future market contracts).

Sources: For South Korea, Letter of Intent and Memorandum on the Economic Program, 3 December 1997; Letter of Intent, 24 December 1997. For Indonesia, Letter of Intent and Memorandum of Economic And Financial Policies, 31 October 1997; 15 January 1998; 10 April 1998; 24 June 1998; 29 July 1998; 11 September 1998; 19 October 1998; 13 November 1998; 16 March 1999; 14 May 1999; 22 July 1999; 20 January 2000; 17 May 2000; 31 July 2000; 7 September 2000; 27 August 2001; 13 December 2001; 9 April 2002; Letter of Intent, 11 June 2002; 20 November 2002; Letter of Intent and Memorandum of Economic and Financial Policies, 18 March 2003; Letter of Intent, 11 June 2003; 16 September 2003; 10 December 2003. For Thailand, Letter of Intent and Memorandum of Economic Policies, 14 August 1997; 25 November 1997; 24 February 1998; 26 May 1998; 25 August 1998; 1 December 1998; 23 March 1999; 21 September 1999.

Despite having different AFC experiences and deploying dissimilar policy responses, these three states seemed to share more or less IMF grievances and were not satisfied with the IMF conditionalities imposed during the AFC.[22] This partly emerged from the fact that the certain measures were regarded as wrong-headed and unable to fix to the problems on the ground (Ito 2007). For instance, Thailand's fiscal austerity spearheaded by the Fund in the early stage of AFC was implemented even though fiscal spending and budget deficits did not cause the crisis. Also, the Indonesia government were told to undertake reforms in certain areas such as rice distributions, which were unrelated to the capital account issues (Kawai 2009b). Therefore, it is no wonder why "Thailand, and Indonesia – which had recently graduated from IMF programmes – were not eager to return to the Fund and became more sympathetic to Malaysia's push for looser CMI linkage with it" (Ciociari 2011: 934).

Jakarta felt grave pains while implementing its IMF-guided policies. Accordingly, it preferred getting money from other sources rather than going for another round with the Fund. One authority contended that had the CMIM been still-born, Indonesia would have asked for individual BSAs from the +3 countries as it did during the AFC.[23] Going to the IMF for bailouts would be the country's last choice.

Like Indonesia, Thailand's IMF experience shaped the country's approach towards the CMIM. The country's suffered from the IMF programmes and regarded its conditionalities as stringent.[24] Wanting to avoid going under the Fund in the future, Bangkok viewed regional mechanisms, namely CMIM, as alternatives or even substitutes to the Fund. This preference reflected by Thailand's active involvement in the CMI/CMIM development.[25] Beside its IMF aversion, Bangkok's CMIM enthusiasm was propelled by a consensus among the Thai policy makers that the country would be a potential beneficiary should the CMIM come into being.[26]

One might assert that Thailand was not actually keen to advance the CMIM scheme. An argument goes that Bangkok exhibited some reluctance to advance this regional financial safety net because it signed onto the CMIM agreement in June 2010, six months after the other participants did in December 2009. This is a mistaken assertion. Bangkok's late signing stemmed from its domestic processes which were at that time obstructed by the country's political turmoil of 2008–2010.[27] Because the CMIM agreement would significantly impact the country's economy, the Thai Constitution required it to be approved by the Parliament before the country inked the document. According to Section 190 of the 2007 Constitution of the Kingdom of Thailand,

> A treaty which provides for a change in the Thai territories or the Thai external territories that Thailand has sovereign right or jurisdiction over such territories under any treaty or an international law or requires the enactment of an Act for its implementation or affects immensely to economic or social security of the country or results in the binding of trade, investment budget of the country significantly must be approved by the National Assembly. In

such case, the National Assembly must complete its consideration within sixty days as from the date of receipt of such matter.

Although the political unrest eventually led to the dissolution of the Thai Parliament in May 2011, it should be emphasized that the prolonged turmoil since 2008 caused delays in domestic ratification process prior to the Parliament's demise itself.[28] The introduction of the CMIM text to the Thai Parliament was postponed to May 2010.[29] The National Assembly later approved the treaty. In sum, it was certain internal political procedures caused by domestic political chaos that accounted for the Thailand's late ratification and signing of the CMIM agreement, not the country's inherent unwillingness to make progress in the CMIM development.

As far as Malaysia's case is concerned, although the country did not have direct interactions with the IMF during AFC, Kuala Lumpur felt the agonies of its neighbours, which ultimately nevertheless its perception of the Fund. In short, Malaysia had "learned from the others" about the IMF programme, which in turn shaped its own experience regarding the Fund.

Observations about the others' predicament led to the country's aversion of the institution's assistance. As one source noted, seeing how much the other ASEAN countries, namely Indonesia and Thailand, suffered through their IMF packages, Malaysia did not want to go down the same path should another financial crisis strike.[30]

Consequently, one Malaysian authority argued that if the country were to be hit by a crisis, it would first seek financial support from elsewhere, such as the CMIM facility. If the liquidity assistance from the CMIM was insufficient to help Kuala Lumpur cope with the crisis, it would ask for additional resources from individual countries, in the form of bilateral currency swap arrangements.[31] Going to the IMF would be the country's last resort – only when it could not get any financial help elsewhere.[32]

Kuala Lumpur's IMF abhorrence explained why it had been seriously committed to developing the CMIM. The country viewed the facility as a mechanism for crisis management by ameliorating the impact of a crisis as well as functioning as a lender of last resort.[33] Moreover, it believed that the facility had potential to boost market confidence in the country and region.[34]

In sum, these experiences altered shape Indonesia's, Malaysia's and Thailand's batnas and preferences regarding the CMIM. Because the trio had all suffered from an exchange rate crisis in the late 1997, and in some ways shared their dissatisfaction with the Fund's assistance during the AFC. These plights ignited a strong incentive for the trio to desperately seek alternative financial facilities, namely the CMIM, with fewer constraints than the IMF (Katada and Sohn 2014: 141). In other words, having turned their backs against the IMF, Indonesia's, Malaysia's and Thailand's batnas were worsened because they had to find other bailout options beside the Fund. Consequently, these states could all be expected to push hard on advancing the CMIM project. When facing with a dilemma between letting the CMIM negotiation collapse on the one hand, and salvaging the talks even though they might had to make unilateral concessions to their equivalents and walk away with certain outcomes less favourable to themselves, these parties would be expected to opt for the latter.

The actual negotiation to partition the CMIM financial commitments among ASEAN countries, or particularly between ASEAN5 and CLMVB, revealed the influence of batnas in shaping the final outcome. In other words, Indonesia's, Malaysia's and Thailand's need for the CMIM altered the decision about how to divide up the 20% share among the ASEAN participants.

According to one source, it took a few meetings for the Southeast Asian nations to work out their individual contributions to the CMIM pool.[35] Conflicts arose when ASEAN5 states attempted to adopt the equal-sharing principle, meaning that CLMVB had to put into the CMIM facility at the same level as the former.[36] Like ASEAN5, CLMVB regarded the contribution issue as their financial burden and declined to shoulder equal commitments.[37] Instead, the latter's response was to insist on supplying to the reserve pool a smaller portion.[38,39] At first, both sides resisted on their demands and the talks reached a deadlock. After intense debates, the agreement was finally reached. CLMVB were to be responsible for 5% of all ASEAN's share while ASEAN5 would cover the remaining 15%.[40]

Had the ASEAN states not been able to agree on their individual contribution, the CMIM talks might have broken down. How did the ASEAN members arrive at this particular outcome? How were the ASEAN parties able to settle their disputes and reach such agreement? This result could be explained by the unilateral concessions made by ASEAN5. The latter finally offered to provide the CMIM reserve pool less than CLMVB.

Why did ASEAN5 give up their position of equal contribution and yield to CLMVB's demand? The difference in terms of batnas between ASEAN5 on the one hand, and CLMVB on the other, ultimately determined the final outcome. The former's experience of the AFC and with the Fund worsened the batnas of ASEAN 5. This was especially so in the cases of Indonesia, Malaysia and Thailand. These nations were eager to seal the CMIM negotiation rather than letting it collapse.

In contrast, CLMVB ended up having better batnas and thus were less enthusiastic than ASEAN5 to conclude the CMIM deal. Several reasons can justify this phenomenon. First, CLMVB reasoned that their economies were less advanced than ASEAN5, rendering them less exposed or less vulnerable to market fluctuations and external crises.[41] In short, if another crisis were to strike, these parties knew they would have suffered less than ASEAN5, making their batnas fare better than the latter. Another explanation might be that some CLMVB countries at that time prioritized certain domestic issues over international cooperative projects, and allocated more of their resources to address their domestic interests. As a result, these states were not fond of making financial commitments as equally as ASEAN5.[42]

Owing to their worsened batnas, ASEAN5 felt that they could not afford to let the CMIM fail. Driven by their previous crisis experience and IMF avoidance,

Indonesia, Malaysia and Thailand – together with the other two ASEAN5 – at the end acquiesced and decided to bear more burden than CLMVB in supplying the CMIM facility. These states allowed CLMVB to decide first on how much they would provide.[43] As the negotiation unfolded, the latter gave out only 5% of the share, while ASEAN5 filled in the remainder by splitting it up equally among themselves.[44]

The preceding interactions reflected that despite their limited ability to financially supply to the CMIM fund, CLMVB were in some occasions were able to hold their ground and bargain with more powerful members. Another example was the negotiations over their purchasing multiples, which are numbers used to multiply with the members' contributions to determine the maximum borrowing amount. According to Table 2.1, each of the CLMVB states get the multiple of 5, while individual ASEAN5 countries secured a lower multiple of 2.5. Some scholars argue that the CMIM aims to provide more assistance to smaller contributors in order to help them ride out their crises. For example, the multiples were calculated by taking into account, "a different likelihood of and vulnerability to a liquidity crisis among the participating members, borrowing quotas are set as multiples of contributions in an inverse relationship to their size – that is, the ASEAN members making smaller contributions have higher purchasing multiples" (Cho 2014: 101–102). Nevertheless, it should be emphasized that beside the good will, the agreement concerning the CLMVB's multiples was partly made possible by these countries' active involvement in determining the outcome.[45]

In conclusion, Indonesia's, Malaysia's and Thailand's experiences with an exchange rate crisis and with the Fund worsened their batnas. They saw CMIM as an alternative to the Fund. Accordingly, the trio had an incentive to continue making progress on the CMIM process. When disputes emerged as CLMVB were reluctant to bear equal financial commitments as ASEAN5 and the talks got stuck, ASEAN5 played a key role in preventing the negotiation from faltering by conceding to supply CMIM pool in a larger portion than CLMVB.

Roles of co-chairs in determining the Philippines' contribution adjustment

Against the backdrop of the GFC, a common position shared by the ASEAN+3 governments was that the CMIM development should be accelerated. As a result, these participants convened at the Special AFMM+3 in February 2009. Thailand and South Korea co-chaired the meeting. Among the topics discussed was the division of the ASEAN's contribution share, which amounted to the 20 per cent of the total CMIM fund. As previously noted, it was agreed that the CLMVB would financially supply the 5 per cent of this share. The rest 15 per cent would be taken up by ASEAN5 countries. The latter earlier subscribed to shoulder equal responsibility among themselves. Given that this remaining 15 per cent portion was equivalent to US$ 22.76 billion, meaning that each of them would put out US$ 4.552 billion.

However, the Philippines was not able to give out the preceding amount. Owing to certain economic hardship such as rising debt and deficit problems, the country's reserve dwindled to less than US$ 45 billion.[46] Manila was loath to give US$ 4.552 billion as it initially pledged, reasoning that the figure exceeded 10 per cent of its total reserve holding. As a result, Manila declared at the time the 12th AFMM+3 was about to complete that it could no longer put in US$ 4.552 billion.[47] Nevertheless, one authority argued that the Philippines showed some ASEAN's spirit when it also promised to later commit US 4.552 billion as soon as its reserve increased beyond US$ 45 billion.[48] In short, Manila declared it could abide to the equal-sharing principle once it had a capability to do so.

These alterations led to a clash among the ASEAN participants. Not everyone welcomed the Philippines' proposal. Thailand and Malaysia agreed and even said that they would cover the Philippines' reduced portion by increasing their own contribution amounts temporarily. However, Singapore protested.[49] The country reasoned that ASEAN must equally share the responsibility.[50]

It would be gravely mistaken to claim that this particular protest from Singapore reflected the country's reluctance to advance the CMIM process. Likewise, it would be false to assert that Singapore's call for the equal-sharing principle was driven by its own attempt to tank this regional mechanism. In fact, the involved negotiators observed that the city-state has been active in developing the CMIM, especially in the area of setting up and operating the ASEAN+3 Macroeconomic Office (AMRO), a surveillance arm of the CMIM.[51] Singapore has housed the AMRO headquarter since 2011. It also played a large part in calculating the budget for running this entity for the first few years of its inception.[52]

Because consensus usually governs the decision-making process of ASEAN, every member state possessed a veto authority. Hence, Singapore's objection against the Philippines' exemption from the equal-contribution/equal-sharing principle stalled the agreement.[53] The negotiation was unable to proceed as the city-state did not show any sign of backing down on its positions. The talk about the Philippines' commitment reached a gridlock. At the end, the CMIM participants managed to reach their agreement. As seen in the Joint Ministerial Statement of the 12th AFMM+3 in May 2009, the Philippines was required to give out less than the other ASEAN5. Manila would supply to the CMIM reserve pool US$ 3.68 billion while the other ASEAN5 nations each would put in a bit more amount of US$ 4.77 billion. Later on the Philippines showed that it kept its words. In February 2010, the country announced to the working-group-level meeting that it could store US$ 4.552 billion as its reserves had reached US$ 45.59 billion.[54] Accordingly, at the 13th AFMM+3 in May 2010, ASEAN5 adjusted their commitments to make them each contribute US$ 4.552 billion, totalling US$ 22.76 billion of the ASEAN5's share.

What explained this outcome? Evidence unveils that a pivotal role played by the Thai co-chair. As ASEAN officers recalled, Bangkok presided over the internal ASEAN talks by controlling the direction of the discussions, targeting specific discussion items on the meeting's agenda and presenting certain solutions which were beneficial to all stakeholders.[55] Moreover, Bangkok intervened before Singapore's opposition would have scupper the negotiation. Mr Korn Chatikavanij, utilizing his position of a co-chair, summoned the city-state at separate meetings and successfully lobbied the latter. In the private gatherings, Mr Korn emphasized that the Philippines' contribution reduction was merely temporary. ASEAN now must be flexible by having the Philippines put into the CMIM fund less and the remaining ASEAN5 countries did more at this point. Doing so helped reach a goal of moving the CMIM process forward, which would yield benefits to all the involved parties.[56] Singapore, making little effort to fight back, eventually acquiesced.

One may wonder, what enabled the Thai co-chair to successfully convince the city-state to go along with its request? Why did Singapore, at the bilateral talks with the Thai co-chair, soldier on and persuade the latter to uphold to the equal-sharing principle? One reason was that Bangkok stressed that its actions served ASEAN's interest, not its own.[57] In other words, if the negotiation was to collapse because of conflicts over the Philippines' contribution problem, it would be detrimental to all ASEAN countries as there would be no regional liquidity safety net available for use in the next crisis. Another possible factor might be that because the Thai co-chair's stance was shared by Malaysia and the Philippines, implying that Bangkok's move had the backing of Kuala Lumpur and Manila. Indonesia, however, did not voice its opinion about this matter.[58] Even if Jakarta did side with Singapore, the two countries would constitute a smaller alliance than that formed by the former three. The chance of winning over the latter would be slim. Consequently, the city-state backed down.

Additionally, the success of the Thai co-chair's lobbying hinged on the fact that there was no interference by the +3 countries, including South Korea which served as the other co-chair at the meeting. This was primarily due to the exclusive nature of the issue being negotiated – or "issue exclusiveness." After the +3 and ASEAN agreed on the contribution proportion – the +3 would supply 80 per cent to the CMIM reserve pool while ASEAN would cover the rest 20 per cent – each grouping were responsible in working out the commitment amount for each of their member. That meant the +3 (China, Japan, South Korea) would talk among themselves to determine their individual contribution, and so did the ten ASEAN countries. Consequently, the +3 regarded the Philippines' contribution issue as ASEAN's internal affair which were to be solely dealt with by the organization.[59] As a result, the +3 refused to intervene.

What made the +3 governments respect the exclusive nature of Manila's contribution and see the issue as ASEAN's internal matter? In other words, why did the former adopt a hands-off approach? The answer could be found in the agreed rules and procedures regional states together devised to manage their interactions. Under the ASEAN+3 process, "[a]t the start of every negotiation, ASEAN and +3 officials segregate and meet in separate rooms to coordinate positions before assembling as a whole" (Pempel 2008: 175). This process gave an opportunity for ASEAN to utilize the so-called ASEAN Caucus during the CMIM talks. A caucus refers to a coalition of players united to safeguard their shared interests and advance their common positions in larger settings. In short, ASEAN Caucus can be regarded as a form of coalition formation. See Box 6.3 for more information about the ASEAN Caucus.

Box 6.3   ASEAN Caucus

The Association of Southeast Asian Nations (ASEAN) has reached out and forged cooperation with non-ASEAN countries to tackle various cross-border matters. To boost its engagement with the outside world, the organization has adopted an outward-looking approach. As reflected in the "Vision 2020" coined in 1997, the member states envisioned ASEAN as "playing a pivotal role in the international fora, and advancing ASEAN's common interests [as well as] having an intensified relationship with its Dialogue Partners and other regional organisations based on equal partnership and mutual respect" (ASEAN 1997).

Several mechanisms have been established to help ASEAN achieve these objectives. One prominent example is the use of the "ASEAN Caucus" in international negotiations. The ASEAN Caucus was originated in 1989, within the context of the Asia-Pacific Economic Cooperation (APEC). T Assembled in Kuching, Malaysia, the leaders to deliver the "Kuching Consensus" which posited that regarding ASEAN's participation in APEC,

"ASEAN's identity and cohesion should be preserved, and its cooperative relations with dialogue partners and third countries should not be diluted in any enhanced APEC." (Feinberg 2003: 33). The ASEAN Caucus, which was held before the APEC Ministerial Meetings, was found to help the member countries consolidate their votes and increase their influence in shaping the APEC's agendas (Ganesan 2006).[60]

The practice of the ASEAN Caucus was also adopted in other international arenas. For instance, the mechanism was used to find the organization's common positions in its negotiation of ASEAN-China Free Trade Agreement (FTA) and China-Hong Kong FTA.[61] Moreover, the member countries have resorted to the Caucus since the Uruguay Round of the World Trade Organization (WTO). Doing so strengthened ASEAN's voice in the global stage as "ASEAN was perceived as an influential sub-group within the G-77 group of developing countries." (Desker 2001: 8).

Under the CMIM setting, ASEAN nations in several occasions resorted to ASEAN Caucus by holding their own meeting not only about 1–2 hours prior to but also one hour afterwards.[62] During the Caucus, the ASEAN states usually had an informal discussion among themselves to develop shared views and positions and solve misunderstandings among themselves.[63]

It must be highlighted that the Caucus was not the only mechanism which ASEAN countries have utilized to find their shared positions regarding the CMIM. Beside the former, the governments hold the ASEAN Finance Ministers' Meetings (AFMMs) every year. The AFMM serves as a forum for exchanging ideas and views regarding ASEAN and ASEAN+3 issues. During these talks, the finance ministers sometimes discussed the CMIM elements and find ASEAN's common positions before they entered into a discussion with the +3 nations.[64]

Resorting to the Caucus yields some benefits to ASEAN participants. First, this apparatus provides a channel for them to gather comments and opinions, as well as arrive at a common ground to be posted to the +3.[65] Illustratively, after they came up with their joint responses at their private Caucus discussions, ASEAN participants went back into the formal CMIM meetings.[66]

ASEAN parties also use the Caucus as a mechanism for conflict resolution. Mediation was seldom adopted in ASEAN interactions. Instead, these nations often rely on consensus or use peer pressure to settle their disputes.[67] As a result, ASEAN Caucus was sometimes called upon in the middle of the meetings, such as during an intermittent coffee break, to convince disagreeing parties to go with the majority of their ASEAN peers.[68]

As the previous chapters have demonstrated, the +3 did have much say in the shaping of the CMIM agreement details. However, it is gravely mistaken to argue that ASEAN's roles in advancing regional financial cooperation in this area were totally negligible. Beside some individual ASEAN states which to some extent did "have a say in the further development of financial regionalism, either owing to capacities in international finance (Singapore) or economic relevance and regional weight (Indonesia)" (Huotari 2012: 24). The Caucus provided the ten member states a channel which they could bargain as bloc against the +3. Although the former are considered potential borrowers to CMIM, they were recognized by the latter to have some say in shaping the agreement results.[69] From ASEAN's perspective, if they had not negotiated collectively, they might have ended up getting far less favourable terms than the finalized ones. In other words, if the ASEAN bloc had not been formed, a chance that the +3 states cut deals with individual ASEAN countries would have heightened, further weakening the other ASEAN states' bargaining leverage. Additionally, the Caucus mechanism allows the Southeast Asian states to take advantage of rivalries among their North-eastern neighbours. "Some ASEAN officials involved in the process privately express the view that a degree of Sino-Japanese tension is desirable because it enables smaller members to gain leverage and punch above their weights" (Rowley 2008). Let's take a look at the combined ASEAN's economic weight to see more clearly how forming a coalition allowed ASEAN to flex its muscles against the +3. According to Table 5.1, each individual ASEAN member does not score as much as China, Japan and South Korea in terms of economic weight. However, if the ten ASEAN states banded together, their combined weights would be 29.81%, which is actually more than China's (27.31%) and South Korea's (9.76%) but a bit less than Japan's (33.11%). Thus, staying put as a bloc was a response by these smaller players to ensure that "a regional institution where no sole power can dominate" (Lee 2010: 7). To sum up, via banding together, ASEAN could somehow resist or counter the greater power's demands.

Unlike the ASEAN countries, the +3 countries did not usually discussed CMIM matters prior to the talks. As one source noticed, the +3 states often expressed their different opinions and made diverging comments on several issues at the CMIM meetings.[70] Thus, coalition formation did not exist among the +3 nations.

Not only that ASEAN Caucus benefited ASEAN, it also provided certain gains to the +3. Ciorciari (2011) maintained that the latter was in favour of ASEAN's style of diplomacy in the CMIM process. For instance, the Northeast Asian nations saw the Caucus as a mechanism rendering the negotiation more speedy and convenient.[71] Thanks to the practice of ASEAN Caucus, the +3 could circumvent conducting separate bargains with individual ASEAN members, but instead wait for the ASEAN to reach its common positions and negotiate from that point onwards.[72] As the +3 nations saw the Caucus as one of the main locomotives advancing the CMIM talks, they left the decision of particular matters, such as the Philippines' commitment, at ASEAN's discretion.[73] This also explained why the South Korean co-chair chose not to weigh in.

As a result, the existence of the ASEAN Caucus enhanced the Thai co-chair's handling of Manila's contribution reduction. Bangkok had room to manoeuvre independent from the external influence by the +3. Accordingly, Thailand was able to press Singapore to eventually accept the Philippines' decreased portion.[74]

In sum, the issue of the Philippines' contribution was shaped largely by the Thai co-chair's taking advantage of the "issue exclusiveness" – or the nature that this matter was widely perceived to fall within ASEAN's realms. The fact that Manila's matter was recognized by all involved stakeholders as exclusive to ASEAN enabled Bangkok to wield its supreme authority over the issue without the +3's interference. Thailand ultimately persuaded Singapore to accept the Philippines' proposal to temporarily decrease the latter's financial commitment to the CMIM pool.

Some conditions under which Thailand's exercise of "issue exclusiveness" was successful can be identified. First, the country's success leaned on the fact that the +3 nations accepted the practice of ASEAN Caucus in the CMIM process, leading to their decision to adopt a hands-off approach. Such acceptance resulted that the latter did not form a counter-coalition against Bangkok in regards to the Philippines' reduced contribution, which could have undermined Thailand's effort to convince Singapore. This element also helped Bangkok define its sphere of influence over Manila's financial commitment and manage the matter by itself. Furthermore, within ASEAN grouping, there was no ASEAN country opposing Thailand's use of its co-chair power to press Singapore. Should there be any internal protests against Bangkok's handling, the latter might not have been able to persuade the latter to go along with the group's position.

Summary

Several factors accounted for Indonesia's, Malaysia's and Thailand's bargaining leverage and roles in affecting the outcomes of the CMIM negotiation. These states' higher discount rates, as compared with Japan, were reflected in their urgency to finalize all CMIM details before discussing a possible increase of the size of the CMIM. However, their higher discount rates prevented the ASEAN trio from convincing Japan to go along with their idea. Although I cannot connect economic relations which Indonesia, Malaysia and Thailand had with Japan to this particular outcome, their ongoing EPA deals which overlapped the CMIM negotiation could play at least a supporting role in explaining why these ASEAN states got less favourable terms than Tokyo.

Also, Indonesia's, Malaysia's and Thailand's experiences with past exchange rate crises and the IMF worsened batnas, and shaped the decision about how to split the 20% contribution share among ten ASEAN countries. The gap between ASEAN5's batna and that of CLMVB explained why the former conceded to supply more to the CMIM pool than did CLMVB.

The case of the Philippines' contribution reflected Thailand's co-chairing clout. Thanks to the acceptance of the practice of ASEAN Caucus in the CMIM context, Bangkok was able to resort to the notion of "issue exclusiveness" when dealing with Manila's reduced portion. Without the +3's intervention, the Thai co-chair reigned supreme in managing the matter. It then successfully persuaded Singapore to the Philippines' temporary reduced commitment.

Notes

1 Interview with M4.
2 Interview with T13.
3 Interview with P1.
4 Interview with I2.
5 Interview with I1.
6 Interview with M3.
7 Interview with M3.
8 Interviews with T10 and T13.
9 Interview with T3.
10 Interview with ASEC2.
11 Interview with I1.
12 Interview with J5.
13 Interview with P1.
14 Interview with T2.
15 Interviews with T2 and ASEC1.
16 Interview with M3.
17 Interview with M4.
18 Interview with T2.
19 Interview with J1.
20 The amount of the available fund under the extended fund facility and its duration were identical to those remaining under the stand-by arrangement credit that it replaced. However, the repayment period of the extended fund facility was substantially longer than that of the stand-by arrangement. Disbursements under the former were repayable over a period of 4.5 to 10 years. In contrast, the repayment period for financing under the stand-by arrangement was over 3.25 to 5 years.
21 The scandal involved the transfer of US$ 80 million owed to Bank Bali under a government guarantee programme on interbank debts to a private firm as a fee for helping collecting the guarantee. It was revealed that the firm was actually run by Setya Novanto,

a leading member of Indonesia's ruling Golkar party. This led to a claim that the money was siphoned to support the election campaign activities of the party itself.

22 Interview with T6.
23 Interview with I2.
24 Interview with T5.
25 Interview with T6.
26 Interview with T12.
27 Interview with T3.
28 Interview with T13.
29 Interview with T3.
30 Interview with M4.
31 Interview M1.
32 Interview M1.
33 Interview with M3.
34 Interview with M4.
35 Interview with ASEC1.
36 Interview with T1.
37 Interview with T3.
38 Interview with I1.
39 Vietnam was reported to make a heroic stance as it proposed to shoulder the CMIM contribution as equal to all ASEAN states. (Interview with P1.)
40 Interview with ASEC1.
41 Interview with M1.
42 Interview with T2.
43 Interview with T2.
44 Interview with M3.
45 Interview with M3.
46 Interview with P1.
47 Interview with T3.
48 Interview with I1.
49 Interview T2.
50 Interview with T2.
51 Interview with J3.
52 Interview with SK3.
53 Interview T2.
54 Interview T2.
55 Interviews with M2 and T4.
56 Interview T2.
57 Interview with T4.
58 Interview with T2.
59 Interview with M2.
60 The ASEAN Caucus within APEC meetings was eventually neglected and ceased to exist in 1993. However, the use of the Caucus in other negotiation fora continues.
61 Interview with T14.
62 Interview with I2.
63 Interview with I2.
64 Interview with M3.
65 Interview with T10.
66 Interview with I1.

67 In rare occasions, a deviation from consensus – the so-called ASEAN-X formula – was adopted to resolve conflicts. However, my interview results did not show any use of the ASEAN-X formula during the CMIM negotiations.
68 Interview with T11.
69 Interview with C1.
70 Interview with T13.
71 Interview with M3.
72 Interview with J2.
73 Interview with I1.
74 Interview with M3. Despite certain differences, the IMF's programmes of Indonesia and Thailand can nevertheless be compared. Table 6.3 reveals that Indonesia's one was less strict than Thailand's. Illustratively, in regard to fiscal austerity, Jakarta's and Bangkok's packages were equally strict. Both countries put a cap on their overall government balance. Indonesia's fiscal policy focused on raising the prices of utilities. In contrast, Thailand's fiscal austerity dealt with increasing a value-added tax (VAT) and limiting net credits to the public sector. As for external sector policy, Thailand's IMF package was more demanding. Indonesia did allow contracting and guaranteeing new debts and used a quantitative number as a ceiling. In contrast, Bangkok set a firmer ceiling on any expansion of public debt. The public sector was not allowed to contract or guarantee any new short-term debts at all. In these aspects, its package was more stringent than Indonesia's.

7   Conclusions

As many practitioners would argue, international cooperation is not a natural thing. Rather, it is a matter needed to be worked on. Owing to inherent tensions between states' desires to reap gains which stem from cooperation on the one hand, and their temptations to protect or promote their domestic interests on the other, certain amount of effort is needed to foster and sustain collaboration. Otherwise, domestic interests usually take over.

To achieve successful cooperation, parties are required to engage in some kinds of negotiations. States must somehow bargain to resolve conflicts or settle on the agreed terms. They also have to discuss, for example, when their collaboration will begin or resume, and what sorts of measures to be taken to realize such cooperation.

However, every negotiation bears the risk of collapse. Even among the likeminded countries which commonly want to achieve cooperation, they often diverge how to pursue collaboration. It is because different stakeholders have dissimilar priorities and diverging ideas of doing things. Consequently, a negotiation becomes entangled in a morass of competing interests and positions among the parties. States usually clash over several issues such as the approaches adopted to arrive at agreement terms and how to make outcomes address their concerns. Their disputes sometimes escalate and ultimately wreck the entire negotiation.

The risk of bargaining failure heightens especially when countries attempt to negotiate on matters which they have little prior experience at handling. It is because these actors may be unsure about how to embark on their new endeavours. As uncertainties mount, they may give up their efforts to cooperate altogether.

This phenomenon can be observed in many parts of the world. East Asia is no exception. We have witnessed several times that regional states struggled with such challenge. But against the odds, they sometimes successfully concluded their negotiations and launched cooperative projects. The Chiang Mai Initiative Multilateralization (CMIM), which is the most advanced financial agreement among the ASEAN+3 nations to date, represents such case.

Inspired by the preceding, this project is set out to analyse the negotiation processes of East Asian financial cooperation, which have been under-studied by the recent literatures. Using the making of the CMIM agreement as a case, it sought to examine bargaining strategies and tactics that help break an impasse, as well as the conditions under which such actions are likely to circumvent bargaining failure. Archival studies and interviews with involved negotiators and scholars were conducted, and process tracing was employed to reconstruct the successful making of the CMIM agreement.

The findings were arranged in four chapters: Chapter 3 on China, Chapter 4 on Japan, Chapter 5 on South Korea and Chapter 6 on Indonesia, Malaysia and Thailand. Focusing on individual countries does not intend to determine 'who won most from the CMIM negotiation' as it is difficult to make such claim. It is because different stakeholders sometimes possessed dissimilar goals they wanted to pursue, which partly stemmed from the situations at a bargaining table. For example, while South Korea attempted to raised its contribution quota amidst pressure from China and Japan to make the country do otherwise. In contrast, Thailand at one point aimed at making all ASEAN players agree on the temporary reduction of the Philippines' financial commitment. Rather, such chapter organization was purposed to highlight the roles played by individual states in evading stalemate and altering certain CMIM components.

Through 14 stories about how the involved stakeholders arrived at particular agreement details, this book has shown that the negotiators employ various kinds of strategies and tactics to avoid bargaining failure and shape final results. First, a sense of urgency (i.e. discount rate) not only helps close the negotiation but also significantly affect some agreement terms. Recall the case of South Korea's financial commitment portion. The country's stronger sense of urgency to settle the CMIM talks explained why it eventually retreated from its initial preference to make a contribution equal to that of China and Japan. In addition, because of Tokyo's lower sense of urgency, it was able to resist ASEAN nations' demands and continued with its course of action of enlarging the CMIM size before finalizing the other agreement terms.

Second, a back-up plan that actors can pursue should the negotiations collapse (i.e. a "best alternative to no agreement" or batna) has been found to enable states to evade a deadlock and influence agreement details. For example, the story of South Korea's contribution amount has demonstrated that the impact of the GFC on the state's economy turned out to worsen its batna vis-à-vis Japan. Consequently, Tokyo was able to convince Seoul to contribute less than itself. Likewise, due to their previous experiences with exchange rate crises and the IMF, the batnas of Indonesia, Malaysia and Thailand were worse than those of CLMVB. This ultimately affected the partition of the ASEAN's 20 per cent contribution quota between ASEAN5 and the latter.

Third, states can transform certain information into their bargaining leverage over the others. Knowledge about other actors in some cases help countries resolve their disputes and salvage the talks. For instance, by knowing Japan's preferences, China was able to reach an agreement with the former regarding the inclusion of Hong Kong into the CMIM framework, as well as the sharing of the three-year stint of the AMRO's first director. Likewise, leveraging on the data about its negotiating counterparts, Japan was able to gain an upper hand in settling the deal with South Korea over the latter's financial commitment, and with ASEAN over the decision to increase the CMIM fund size. Moreover, Tokyo took into account the different stakeholders' interests and concerns to compute a contribution proportion between the +3 and ASEAN (the 80:20 ratio) which was ultimately adopted by the latter. Moreover, South Korea utilized the preferences of China, Hong Kong and Japan to reconcile the Sino-Japanese conflict over the matter of Hong Kong participation, and finally determine the division of contributions and voting power among the +3 nations.

Another kind of information – knowledge about the issues being negotiated or 'expertise' – is found to help countries circumvent bargaining failure and arrive at their deals. For example, by knowing more about the technicalities of the CMIM, Japan gained some credibility in the other parties' eyes, making the country convince the latter to accept its proposed 80:20 ratio. Furthermore, as the writing procedure of the CMIM document has reflected, South Korea could boost the trustworthiness of its drafting team by hiring qualified legal and financial professionals and hence leveraging on the latter's expertise. As a result, the country effectively ameliorated conflicts over agreement details which emerged during the text-drafting phase.

Fourth, the analyses have unveiled the influence of a co-chair in settling disputes among the involved parties and altering negotiation details. Recall the decision to multilateralize the CMI. The Chinese co-chair significantly shaped this outcome by taking a lead in conducting studies and producing background papers for the discussions over the matter, and directly intervening to resolve the conflicts and bring the talk into a close. Likewise, the Japanese wielded its co-chairing authority to settle disagreements over the determination of the financial contributions between the +3 and ASEAN members. Moreover, when South Korea presided as a co-chair of the meeting, the country took advantage of this position to lobby the others to adopt its idea of a two-thirds (2/3) supermajority voting rule. In addition, exercising its co-chairing power, Thailand successfully pressured Singapore to allow the Philippines to temporarily reduce the latter's contribution amount.

Fifth, linking issues is another technique countries use to circumvent stalemate and cut their deals. For example, China's move to take up the first year of the AMRO first director's term was intentionally tied to the country's pledge of leaving the service immediately, allowing the Japanese individual to hold this post for the subsequent two years, which was longer than the Chinese one. By doing so, China was able to extract Tokyo's approval of the deal as well as achieve its goal of being the first country which national serves as the head of the CMIM's surveillance unit. Moreover, as the story of Hong Kong's CMIM membership has indicated, Japan linked its approval of the entity's participation to the issues of CMIM contributions and vote shares, and forced China to accept certain conditions set for Hong Kong.

Finally, preventing others from forming a coalition against oneself enables states to avoid a bargaining logjam and shape outcomes in their favour. As the case of a two-thirds (2/3) supermajority voting system has illustrated, South Korea strategically decided to side with neither China, Japan nor ASEAN. The former instead played a role of a balancing player in the middle of the trilateral conflict among the latter. As a result, South Korea able to convince the other parties to agree with its proposed two-thirds (2/3) majority voting principle, which ultimately gives the country an actual veto power to approve lending.

Beside the preceding insights, this negotiation research also offers some practical lessons. The policy makers involved in international financial negotiation and cooperation may find useful the following advice regarding how to prevent or break a negotiation from an impasse. First, as the drafting phase of the CMIM agreement has shown, experts are usually trusted by negotiators. Owing to their knowledge and adeptness of handling the matters, experts help lessen the probability of disputes which could arise at a bargaining table, thus expediting the progress of regional collaboration. This story also stresses the importance of Track 2 diplomacy[1] in advancing international cooperation. Via Track 2, professionals can assist government officers in carrying out fact-finding and problem-solving activities, as well as providing guidance for the decision making at the official level. Therefore, one should engage qualified personnel at certain stages of the negotiation, such as hiring them to conduct studies related to the negotiated topics or to enhance the drafting process of agreement texts.

Also, because a bargaining collapse is often borne out of diverging interests among different stakeholders, a prime challenge to the practitioners is to find ways to settle the conflicts. A compromise can be reached by, for example, knowing the others' preferences and addressing them. Hence, policy makers should attempt to tease out one another's interests by assessing the concerns or needs which underlie the arguments made, and search for solutions to fulfil those needs. Another way to arrive at an agreeable middle ground is to use issue linkage to create a package deal which yields benefits to the involved parties. Therefore, negotiators should identify different but reconcilable issues and incorporate them into an agreement which all actors can agree upon.

While my examination of the CMIM negotiation has disclosed several elements affecting international bargaining, I have not explored some of them in detail, which opens excellent opportunities for future research. First, to shed more light on East Asian financial cooperation and negotiation, scholars should move beyond the CMIM case to study other regional initiatives such as the Asian Bond Markets Initiative (ABMI) and the Asian Development Bank's "Strategy 2020."[2] Yet, I suspect that some factors shaping the outcomes of these initiatives may differ from those affecting the CMIM agreement terms. For instance, states' bargaining leverage in the CMIM partly stemmed from the amount of their reserve holdings. In contrast, their influence in altering the ABMI components may relate to the size and quality of their capital markets.

Another interesting case to be explored is the Asian Infrastructure Investment Bank (AIIB), which is a multilateral development bank with a main focus on financing infrastructure development in Asia. At the time of this writing, the AIIB has 57 founding member countries, the Articles of Agreement were finalized, and the members aimed to launch the entity's operation by the end of 2015. While many have anticipated that China, which initially announced the AIIB idea in October 2013, is likely to become the entity's largest shareholder, no detailed distributions of ownership among the players have been revealed. Likewise, little has been known about how the AIIB will be actually operated. What kinds of conditionalities are attached to the loan? Is lending activated by voting or consensus? If lending is approved by voting, what is the minimum amount of votes required to do so? How are the votes allocated among the member parties? Once these agreement terms are settled and released, interested analysts can scrutinize several issues. For instance, how are these rules made? And, what kinds of bargaining strategies and tactics the states use to settle their conflicts, conclude the AIIB negotiation, and shape the outcomes in their direction?

Second, because I have studied economic bargaining only among ASEAN+3 nations. Therefore, one should be cautious that some of my findings may not be found in negotiations in other regions. For instance, my analysis has unveiled the element of face-saving in preventing the CMIM talks from reaching a deadlock. While this factor is likely to be very critical in the East Asian context as these states take the concept of face seriously, it may be significantly less valued elsewhere. Thus, future studies should compare the results of my study with those in other locales such as Europe and Africa, to help account for variations across different settings. Doing so would help shed more light on our understanding of bargaining processes across regions and cultures.

Third, my analyses have surfaced the effects of domestic factors in influencing the outcomes at the international level. The fact that Japan's superior data collection and transfer systems turned out to shift the negotiation dynamics and results reminds us that one cannot exclude the roles of domestic elements from the study of international bargaining. This finding also suggests that these systems did not happen naturally. Rather, they stemmed from particular working disciplines and cultures the Japanese officers have embraced. Thus, future studies should probe more into how domestic conducts affect international negotiations, as well as identify "good practices" which can be cultivated at home to further enhance countries' clout at the international arenas.

Moreover, the story that Malaysia's learning of its neighbours' IMF experience shaped a country's stances in CMIM talks yields valuable insight. It is because it illustrates that an *indirect* experience can trigger a change in states' interests and bargaining positions. This warrants a study of international socialization, particularly how experiences are diffused across nations. As so far little has been known about the mechanisms behind such learning, interested scholars should explore how one state's experiences are absorbed by the others and shift the latter's bargaining stances, and the conditions under which these socialization processes are likely to occur.

The study of international socialization can be scrutinized from another angle. I have shown that the Thai co-chair's ability to use "issue exclusiveness" to handle the matter of the Philippines' contribution partly hinged on the +3 countries' acceptance of the practice of ASEAN Caucus in the CMIM negotiation. Therefore, those interested in studying the interactions between regional states (e.g. East Asian, African) and their extra-regional powers (e.g. the USA, the EU) should examine how certain regional principles and procedures socialize external players and affect their relationships, and the conditions under which this kind of learning is likely to take place.

Negotiation, as this book has demonstrated, is a challenging task. As different stakeholders have dissimilar priorities and interests, states often clash with one another over certain agreement details, which sometimes throw the negotiation on a verge of collapse. However, one should not be discouraged by such challenge and ultimately abandon one's pursuit of concluding an agreement. Among countries' differences lie the room for reconciliation and compromise, and some of that space has yet been fully explored. Admittedly, a successful negotiation is not easy. But, it is not entirely impossible.

Notes

1 In the realm of international interactions, Track 1 diplomacy often denotes to formal discussions among government personnel. In contrast, Track 2 diplomacy usually involves unofficial talks and problem-solving activities which assist the decision-making at Track 1. Track 2 in most cases involves academics and experts as key participants.
2 The ADB's Strategy 2020 was approved in April 2008. Strategy 2020 pursues three strategic agendas: (1) inclusive economic growth, (2) environmentally sustainable growth and (3) regional integration. The ADB promotes regional integration via sub-regional cooperation programs and capacity development on Asia Regional Integration Center (ARIC). The sub-regional programs supported by the ADB include Greater Mekong Sub-region (GMS) program; Indonesia, Malaysia, Thailand Growth Triangle (IMT-GT); and Brunei, Indonesia, Malaysia, Philippines East ASEAN Growth Area (BIMP-EAGA).

Appendix

List of the interviewees

A1   Dr Jayant Menon is Lead Economist, Office for Regional Economic Integration, Asian Development Bank, Philippines. Interviewed on 30 April 2014.

ASEC1   ASEAN Secretariat staff, ASEAN Secretariat, Jakarta, Indonesia. Interviewed on 15 March 2011.

ASEC2   A former ASEAN Secretariat staff. Interviewed on 16 November 2010.

C1   A Chinese expert, China Center for International Economic Exchanges (interview accounts were the interviewee's personal opinions). Interviewed on 13 May 2014.

C2   Professor Wang Yong, Peking University, China (interview accounts were the interviewee's personal opinions). Interviewed on 14 May 2014.

C3   Dr Gao Haihong, Institute of World Economics and Politics, Chinese Academy of Social Sciences, China (interview accounts were the interviewee's personal opinions). Interviewed on 14 May 2014.

I1   A government official, Ministry of Finance, Indonesia. Interviewed on 31 January 2011.

I2   An Indonesian negotiator. Interviewed on 31 January 2011.

J1   A Japanese negotiator. Interviewed on 17 November 2010.

J2   A Japanese negotiator. Interviewed on 15 November 2010.

J3   A government official, Ministry of Finance, Japan. Interviewed on 18 November 2010.

J4   A Japanese scholar. Interviewed on 17 November 2010.

J5   A Japanese negotiator. Interviewed on 15 November 2010.

M1   A Malaysian negotiator. Interviewed on 23 December 2010.

M2   A Malaysian negotiator. Interviewed on 23 December 2010.

M3   A government official, Bank Negara Malaysia. Interviewed on 15 October 2010.

M4   A government official, Ministry of Finance, Malaysia. Interviewed on 23 December 2010.

P1   A Filipino scholar. Interviewed on 16 November 2010.

SK1   Professor Junggun Oh, Korea University, South Korea. Interviewed on 15 November 2010.

SK2   A South Korean negotiator. Interviewed on 15 November 2010.

SK3   A Bank of Korea officer. Interviewed on 12 November 2010.

T1   A Thai negotiator. Interviewed on 30 September 2010.

T2   Mr Perames Vudthitornetiraks, a former official at the Ministry of Finance, Thailand. Interviewed on 30 September 2010.

T3   A government official, Bureau of International Economic Policy, Fiscal Policy Office official, Ministry of Finance, Thailand. Interviewed on 21 October 2010.

T4   A government official, Bank of Thailand. Interviewed on 4 October 2010.

T5   A former Thai negotiator. Interviewed on 7 October 2010.

T6   A former Thai finance minister. Interviewed on 16 February 2011.

T7   A Thai journalist. Interviewed on 29 September 2010.

T8   A Thai journalist. Interviewed on 30 September 2010.

T9   A government official, Bureau of International Economic Policy, Fiscal Policy Office official, Ministry of Finance, Thailand. Interviewed on 30 September 2011.

T10   A government official, Bank of Thailand. Interviewed on 20 October 2010.

T11   A Thai negotiator. Interviewed on 12 May 2015.

T12   A Thai scholar, Fiscal Policy Research Institute (FPRI), Thailand. Interviewed on 7 October 2010.

T13   A government official, Bank of Thailand. Interviewed on 23 December 2013.

T14   A government official, Ministry of Commerce, Thailand. Interviewed on 19 December 2013.

Bibliography

Afrol News. (2006). "China, Angola Sign 9 Cooperation Agreements." 7 March. www.afrol. com/articles/15848.

Aggarwal, V. (1985). *Liberal Protectionism: The International Politics of Organized Textile Trade*. Berkeley: University of California Press.

Aksoy, D. (2010). "Who Gets What, When, and How Revisited: Voting and Proposal Powers in the Allocation of the EU Budget." *European Union Politics*, 11: 171–194.

Altbach, E. (1997). "The Asian Monetary Fund Proposal: A Case Study of Japanese Regional Leadership." Japan Economic Institute Report, 47A: 1–12.

Amyx, J. (2005). "What Motivates Regional Financial Cooperation in East Asia Today?" *Asia Pacific*, 76: 1–8.

Antrim, L., and Sebenius, J. (1992). "Formal Individual Mediation and the Negotiators' Dilemma: Tommy Koh at the Law of the Sea Conference." In J. Bercovitch and J. Z. Rubin (eds), *Mediation in International Relations* (pp. 97–130). London: Macmillan.

APEC. (1997). "APEC Economic Leader Declaration: Connecting the APEC Community." Vancouver, Canada.

Arnon, K. (2011). "China, Japan Share Top Job at Financial Watchdog." ISN Hot News, 8 April. http://en.isnhotnews.com/?p=8770.

Asahi Shimbun. (2014) "China Expresses Readiness to Resume High-Level Economic Talks with Japan." 25 September. http://ajw.asahi.com/article/behind_news/politics/AJ2014 09250056.

Asami, T. (2005). "Chiang Mai Initiative as the Foundation of Financial Stability in East Asia." Institute for International Monetary Affairs, Japan, ASEAN +3 Research Group Studies 2004–2005, 1 March. www.asean.org/archive/17902.pdf.

ASEAN. (1997). "ASEAN Vision 2020." Kuala Lumpur, Malaysia, 15 December. www. asean.org/news/item/asean-vision-2020.

ASEAN+3. (2005). "Joint Ministerial Statement of the 8th ASEAN+3 Finance Ministers' Meeting." Istanbul, Turkey.

ASEAN+3. (2006). "Joint Ministerial Statement of the 9th ASEAN+3 Finance Ministers' Meeting." Hyderabad, India.

ASEAN+3. (2007). "Joint Ministerial Statement of the 10th ASEAN+3 Finance Ministers' Meeting." Kyoto, Japan.

ASEAN+3. (2008). "Joint Ministerial Statement of the 11th ASEAN+3 Finance Ministers' Meeting." Madrid, Spain.

ASEAN+3. (2009a). "Joint Media Statement: Action Plan to Restore Economic and Financial Stability of the Asian Region." Report from the AFMM+3 to Heads of States/ Government, 22 February.

ASEAN+3. (2009b). "Joint Ministerial Statement of the 12th ASEAN+3 Finance Ministers' Meeting." Phuket, Thailand.

ASEAN+3. (2011). "The Articles of Agreement in Respect of the ASEAN+3 Macroeconomic Research Office." January.

ASEAN+3. (2011). "Joint Ministerial Statement of the 14th ASEAN+3 Finance Ministers' Meeting." Ha Noi, Vietnam.

ASEAN+3. (2014). "Joint Ministerial Statement of the 17th ASEAN+3 Finance Ministers and Central Bank Governors' Meeting." Astana, Kazakhstan.

ASEAN+3 Macroeconomic Research Office (AMRO). (2011). "Press Release: Appointment of the AMRO Director." 6 April. www.amro-asia.org/wp-content/uploads/2011/11/AFDM+3-PR-2011–000–20110406-Appointmeent-of-the-AMRO-Director-PR2011 0503.pdf.

ASEAN+3 Macroeconomic Research Office (AMRO). (2015). "What We Do." www.amro-asia.org/what-we-do/.

Athukorala, P. C. (2008). "The Malaysian Capital Controls: A Success Story?" *Asian Economic Papers*, 7(1), 31–74.

Axelrod, R., and Keohane, R. O. (1985). "Achieving Cooperation under Anarchy: Strategies and Institutions." *World Politics*, 38(1): 226–254.

Balboa, J., Medalla, E. and Yap, J. T. (2007). "Closer Trade and Financial Co-operation in ASEAN Issues at the Regional and National Level with Focus on the Philippines." Philippines Institute for Development Studies, Discussion Paper Series No. 2007-03: 1–23.

Baldwin, D. A. (1985). *Economic Statecraft*. Princeton, NJ: Princeton University Press.

Bank of Korea. (2008). "Official Foreign Reserves." Press Release, 3 December.

Bank of Korea. (n.d.). "Stabilization of Foreign Exchange and Foreign Currency Funding Markets." www.bok.or.kr/broadcast.action?menuNaviId=1664.

BBC News. (1997). "South Korea: How the IMF Deal Works." 4 December. http://news.bbc.co.uk/2/hi/world/analysis/36736.stm.

Bennett, A. (2004). "Case Study Methods: Design, Use, and Comparative Advantages." In D. F. Sprinz and Y. Wolinsky (eds), *Models, Numbers, and Cases: Methods for Studying International Relations* (pp. 19–55). Ann Arbor: University of Michigan Press.

Bennett, A. (2008). "Process Tracing: A Bayesian Approach." In J. Box-Steffensemeir, H. Brady and D. Collier (eds), *Oxford Handbook of Political Methodology* (pp. 702–721). Oxford: Oxford University Press.

Bennett, A. (2010). "Process Tracing and Causal Inference." In H. Brady and D. Collier (eds), *Rethinking Social Inquiry: Diverse Tools, Shared Standards* (pp. 207–219). Plymouth, UK: Rowman and Littlefield.

Bennett, A., and Elman, C. (2006). "Qualitative Research: Recent Developments in Case Study Methods." *Annual Review of Political Science*, 9: 455–476.

Blavoukos, S., and Bourantonis, D. (2010). "Chairs as Policy Entrepreneurs in Multilateral Negotiations." *Review of International Studies*, 37(2): 1–20.

Bowles, P. (2002). "Asia's Post-crisis Regionalism: Bringing the State Back in, Keeping the (United) States Out." *Review of International Political Economy*, 9(2): 244–270.

Brett J. F., Pinkley, R. L. and Jackofsky, E. F. (1993). "Alternatives to Having a BATNA in Dyadic Negotiation: The Influence of Goals, Self-Efficacy, and Alternatives on Negotiated Outcomes." *International Journal of Conflict Management*, 7(2): 121–138.

Bunn, G., and Payne, R. A. (1988). "Tit-for-Tat and the Negotiation of Nuclear Arms Control." *Contemporary Security Policy*, 9(3): 207–233.

Busse, M., Huth, M. and Koopmann, G. (2000). "Preferential Trade Agreements: The Case of EU-Mexico." HWWA Discussion Paper 103. Hamburgisches Welt-Wirtschafts-Archiv (HWWA). http://ageconsearch.umn.edu/bitstream/26269/1/dp000103.pdf.

Cameron, M.A., and Tomlin, B.W. (2000). "Negotiating North American Free Trade." *International Negotiation*, 5(1): 43–68.

Campbell, D. (1979). "'Degrees of Freedom' and The Case Study." *Qualitative and Quantitative Methods in Evaluation Research*, 1: 49–67.

Carnevale, P.J., and Conlon, D.E. (1988). "Time Pressure and Strategic Choice in Mediation." *Organizational Behavior and Human Decision Processes*, 42(1): 111–133.

Carnevale, P.J., O'Connor, K.M. and McCusker, C. (1993). "Time Pressure in Negotiation and Mediation." In O. Svenson and A.J. Maule (eds), *Time Pressure and Stress in Human Judgment and Decision Making* (pp. 117–127). New York: Plenum Press.

Central Banking Publications. (2001). "Asian Monetary Fund Not a Bad Idea – US Official." www.centralbanking.com/central-banking/news/1427901/asian-monetary-fund-bad-idea-us-official.

Chaitrong, W. (2009). "Japan and China Vie to Be Top Contributor to Regional Fund." *The Nation*, 10 April.

Chan, G. (2012). "China's Response to the Global Financial Crisis and Its Regional Leadership in East Asia." *Asia Europe Journal*, 9(2–4): 197–209.

Chasek, P.S. (2005). "Margins of Power: Coalition Building and Coalition Maintenance of the South Pacific Island States and the Alliance of Small Island States." *Review of European Community and International Environmental Law*, 14(2): 125–137.

Chey, H. (2009). "The Changing Political Dynamics of East Asian Financial Cooperation: The Chiang Mai Initiative." *Asian Survey*, 49(3): 450–467.

China Daily. (2011). "China Issues 20b Yuan Treasury Bonds in HK." 17 August. www.chinadaily.com.cn/bizchina/likeqianghk/2011-08/17/content_13132687.htm.

China Post. (2008). "South Korea Establishes New Currency Swap Deals with Japan, China." 12 December. www.chinapost.com.tw/business/asia/korea/2008/12/12/187394/South-Korea.htm.

Cho, Y. (2014). "South Korea and the Pitfalls of East Asian Monetary Regionalism: Do Neighbors Mean Neighborly Behavior?" *Pacific Focus*, 29(1): 92–115.

Chow, P.C. (2013). *Economic Integration across the Taiwan Strait: Global Perspectives.* Northampton, MA: Edward Elgar.

Chung, C. (2013). "China and Japan in 'ASEAN Plus' Multilateral Agreements: Raining on the Other Guy's Parade." *Asian Survey*, 53(5): 801–824.

Chung, C.P. (2014). *Contentious Integration: Post–Cold War Japan–China Relations in the Asia-Pacific.* Burlington, VT: Ashgate.

Ciorciari, J.D. (2011). "Chiang Mai Initiative Multilateralization." *Asian Survey*, 51(5): 926–952.

Clark, S. (2015). "China's CIC Shifts Wealth Fund Focus to Emerging Markets." *Wall Street Journal*, 11 March. www.wsj.com/articles/chinas-cic-shifts-wealth-fund-focus-to-emerging-markets-1426090669.

Clark, W., Duchesne, E. and Meunier, S. (2000). "Domestic and International Asymmetries in United States-European Union Trade Negotiations." *International Negotiation*, 5(1): 69–95.

Cohen, H. (1980). *You Can Negotiate Anything.* Secaucus, NJ: Lyle Stuart.

Cohen, B.J. (1998). *The Geography of Money.* Ithaca, NY: Cornell University Press.

Cohen, B. (2003). "Are Monetary Unions Inevitable?" *International Studies Perspectives*, 4(3): 275–292.

Cohen, B.J. (2004). *The Future of Money.* Princeton, NJ: Princeton University Press.

Cohen, B.J. (2009). "Currency and State Power." Paper prepared for a conference to honor Stephen D. Krasner, Stanford University, 4–5 December. www.polsci.ucsb.edu/faculty/cohen/working/pdfs/krasner.pdf.

Cohen, B.J. (2010). "Finance and Security in East Asia." Department of Political Science, University of California, Santa Barbara. www.polsci.ucsb.edu/faculty/cohen/working/pdfs/East_Asia_Rev_2.pdf.

Cohen, B.J. (2012). "The Yuan Tomorrow? Evaluating China's Currency Internationalisation Strategy." *New Political Economy*, 17(3): 361–371.

Cohen, B.J. and Chiu, E.M. (2014). Introduction to *Power in a Changing World Economy: Lessons from East Asia*. Ed. B.J. Cohen and E.M. Chiu. New York: Routledge.

Constitution of the Kingdom of Thailand. (2007). "Unofficial Translation by Bureau of Technical and International Cooperation." Secretariat General of the Administrative Court, Thailand. www.isaanlawyers.com/constitution%20thailand%202007%20-%20 2550.pdf.

Costa, O., Couvidat, A. and Daloz, J. (2003). "The French Presidency of 2000: An Arrogant Leader?" In O. Elgström (ed.), *European Union Council Presidencies: A Comparative Perspective* (pp. 120–137). London: Routledge.

Da Conceição-Heldt, D. (2006). "Integrative and Distributive Bargaining Situations in the European Union: What Difference Does It Make?" *Negotiation Journal*, 22(2): 145–165.

Da Conceição-Heldt, D. (2011). *Negotiating Trade Liberalization at the WTO: Domestic Politics and Bargaining Dynamics*. Basingstoke, UK: Palgrave Macmillan.

De Dreu, C.K., Nijstad, B.A. and van Knippenberg, D. (2008). "Motivated Information Processing in Group Judgment and Decision Making." *Personality and Social Psychology Review*, 12(1): 22–49.

Dent, C.M. (2008). *China, Japan and Regional Leadership in East Asia*. Cheltenham, UK: Edward Elgar.

Desker, B. (2001). "Asian Developing Countries and the Next Round of WTO Negotiations." RSIS Working Paper, 18. Singapore: Nanyang Technological University.

Dolan, D. (2009). "ADB Meet Kicks Off as Asia Flexes Financial Muscle." 4 May. http://in.reuters.com/article/2009/05/04/idINIndia-39386820090504.

Downs, G., Rocke, D. and Siverson, R. (1985). "Arms Races and Cooperation." *World Politics*, 38(1): 118–146.

Drezner, D.W. (1999). *The Sanctions Paradox: Economic Statecraft and International Relations*. Cambridge: Cambridge University Press.

Drezner, D.W. (2007). *All Politics Is Global: Explaining International Regulatory Regimes*. Princeton, NJ: Princeton University Press.

Dupont, C. (1996). "Negotiation as Coalition Building." *International Negotiation*, 1(1): 47–64.

Eichengreen, B. (2009). "Can Asia Free Itself from the IMF?" www.eastasiaforum.org/2009/06/30/can-asia-free-itself-from-the-imf/.

Elliott, D.J., and Yan, K. (2013). "The Chinese Financial System: An Introduction and Overview." John L. Thornton China Center Monograph Series, 6. Washington, DC: Brookings Institution.

Enia, J. (2009). "Sequencing Negotiating Partners: Implications for the Two-Level Game?" *Negotiation Journal*, 25(3): 357–383.

Fearon, J. (1998). "Bargaining, Enforcement, and International Cooperation." *International Organization*, 52(2): 269–305.

Feinberg, R.E., ed. (2003). *APEC as an Institution: Multilateral Governance in the Asia-Pacific*. Singapore: Institute of Southeast Asian Studies.

Feldstein, M. (1998). "Refocusing the IMF." *Foreign Affairs*, 77: 20–33.

First Financial Daily. (2011). "Hua Wei Will Become the Asian Version of the IMF Department." 27 April. www.yicai.com/news/2011/04/749701.html.

Fischer, S. (2001). *Asia and the IMF*. Singapore: Institute of Policy Studies.

Fisher, R., and Ury, W. (1991). *Getting to Yes: Negotiating Agreement without Giving In*. New York: Penguin.

Ganesan, N. (2006). "Thai-Myanmar-ASEAN Relations: The Politics of Face and Grace." *Asian Affairs: An American Review*, 33(3): 131–149.

Gao, H., and Yu, Y. (2009). "Internationalization of the Renminbi." Paper presented at BoK-BIS Seminar in Seoul, South Korea, 19–20 March.

George, A., and Bennett, A. (2005). *Case Studies and Theory Development in the Social Sciences*. Cambridge, MA: MIT Press.

Gerring, J. (2004). "What Is a Case Study and What Is It Good For?" *American Political Science Review*, 98: 341–354.

Goldman, A., and Rojot, J. (2003). *Negotiation: Theory and Practice*. The Hague: Kluwer Law International.

Grimes, W. (2006). "East Asian Financial Regionalism in Support of the Global Financial Architecture? The Political Economy of Regional Nesting." *Journal of East Asian Studies*, 6(3): 353–380.

Grimes, W. (2009). *Currency and Contest in East Asia: The Great Power Politics of Financial Regionalism*. Ithaca, NY: Cornell University Press.

Grimes, W.W. (2011a). "The Asian Monetary Fund Reborn? Implications of Chiang Mai Initiative Multilateralization." *Asia Policy*, 11(1): 79–104.

Grimes, W.W. (2011b). "The Future of Regional Liquidity Arrangements in East Asia: Lessons from the Global Financial Crisis." *The Pacific Review*, 24(3): 291–310.

Grimes, W. (2014). "Sustainability of Regional Financial Cooperation in Asia: Chiang Mai Initiative Multilateralization and the Return of Politics." Research Institute of Economy, Trade and Industry, Japan. www.rieti.go.jp/en/special/p_a_w/042.html.

Haas, E. (1980). "Why Collaborate? Issue-linkage and International Regimes." *World Politics*, 32(3): 357–405.

Haggard, S. (2000). *The Political Economy of the Asian Financial Crisis*. Washington, DC: Peterson Institute for International Economics.

Hamilton, C., and Whalley, J. (1989). "Coalitions in the Uruguay Round." *Weltwirtschaftliches Archive*, 125(3): 547–562.

Hamner, W.C., and Baird, L.S. (1978). "The Effect of Strategy, Pressure to Reach Agreement and Relative Power on Bargaining Behavior." In H. Sauermann (Ed.), *Contributions to Experiment Economies* (Vol. 7, pp. XX–XX). Mohr: Tubingen.

Hampson, F., and Hart, M. (1995). *Multilateral Negotiations: Lessons from Arms Control, Trade, and the Environment*. Baltimore, MD: Johns Hopkins University Press.

Hassdorf, W. (2011). "Much Ado about Nothing? Chiang Mai Initiative Multilateralisation and East Asian Exchange Rate Cooperation." *Ritsumeikan Annual Review of International Studies*, 10: 128–130.

Henderson, M.D., Trope, Y. and Carnevale, P.J. (2006). "Negotiation from a Near and Distant Time Perspective." *Journal of Personality and Social Psychology*, 91(4): 712–729.

Henning, C. (2002). *East Asian Financial Cooperation*. Washington, DC: Peterson Institute for International Economics.

Henning, C. (2009). *The Future of the Chiang Mai Initiative: An Asian Monetary Fund?* Washington, DC: Peterson Institute for International Economics.

Hess, P. (2014). "China's Financial System: Past Reforms, Future Ambitions and Current State." In F. Rövekamp and H. G. Hilpert (eds), *Currency Cooperation in East Asia* (pp. 21–41). New York: Springer.

Hong Kong Monetary Authority (HKMA). (2014). "Hong Kong as Offshore Renminbi Centre – Past and Prospects." 18 February. www.hkma.gov.hk/eng/key-information/insight/20140218.shtml.

Hong Kong Special Administrative Region (HKSAR). (2015). "Hong Kong – The Facts: Financial Services." www.gov.hk/en/about/abouthk/factsheets/docs/financial_services.pdf.

Hopmann, P. (1978). "Asymmetrical Bargaining in the Conference on Security and Cooperation in Europe." *International Organization*, 32(1): 141–177.

Hopmann, P. (1996). *The Negotiation Process and the Resolution of International Conflicts.* Columbia: University of South Carolina Press.

Hook, G. D., Gilson, J., Hughes, C. W. and Dobson, H. (2002). "Japan and the East Asian Financial Crisis: Patterns, Motivations and Instrumentalisation of Japanese Regional Economic Diplomacy." *European Journal of East Asian Studies*, 1(2): 177–197.

Huotari, M. (2012). "Practices of Financial Regionalism and the Negotiation of Community in East Asia." Occasional Paper, 8. Federal Ministry of Education and Research. www.southeastasianstudies.uni-freiburg.de/Content/files/occasional-paper-series/op8_huotari_feb-2012_end.pdf.

Hurd, I. (2005). "The Strategic Use of Liberal Internationalism: Libya and the UN Sanctions, 1992–2003." *International Organization*, 59(3): 495–526.

Institute for International Monetary Affairs (IIMA). (2005). "Economic Surveillance and Policy Dialogue in East Asia." www.asean.org/archive/17889.pdf.

Ito, T. (2007). "Asian Currency Crisis and the International Monetary Fund, 10 Years Later: Overview." *Asian Economic Policy Review*, 2(1): 16–49.

Jensen, L. (1988). *Bargaining for National Security: The Postwar Disarmament Negotiations.* Columbia: University of South Carolina Press.

Jiang, Y. (2010). "Response and Responsibility: China in East Asian Financial Cooperation." *The Pacific Review*, 23(5): 603–623.

Jiang, Y. (2013). *China's Policymaking for Regional Economic Cooperation.* New York: Palgrave Macmillan.

Kaplan, E., and Rodrik, D. (2001). "Did the Malaysian Capital Controls Work?" Working Paper, 8142. Cambridge, MA: National Bureau of Economic Research.

Katada, S. N. (2008). "From a Supporter to a Challenger? Japan's Currency Leadership in Dollar-Dominated East Asia." *Review of International Political Economy*, 15(3): 399–417.

Katada, S. N., and Sohn, I. (2014). "Regionalism as Financial Statecraft: China and Japan's Pursuit of Counterweight Strategies." In *The Financial Statecraft of Emerging Powers: Shield and Sword in Asia and Latin America* (pp. 138–161). New York: Palgrave Macmillan.

Kawai, M. (2005). "East Asian Economic Regionalism: Progress and Challenges." *Journal of Asian Economics*, 16(1): 29–55.

Kawai, M. (2009). "From the Chiang Mai Initiative to an Asian Monetary Fund." Paper prepared for the conference on the "Future Global Reserve System" organized by Columbia University in partnership with ADB and ADBI, Tokyo, 17–18 March. http://aric.adb.org/grs/papers/Kawai%205.pdf.

Kawai, M. (2010). "Why Asia Needs Its Own Monetary Fund." In *The Euromoney Asia-Pacific Markets Handbook.* www.adbi.org/files/kawai.asia.monetary.fund.pdf.

Kawai, M., and Houser, C. (2007). *Evolving ASEAN+3 ERPD: Toward Peer Reviews or Due Diligence?* Tokyo: Asian Development Bank Institute.

Khong, Y. (1992). *Analogies at War: Korea, Munich, Dien Bien Phu and the Vietnam Decisions of 1965.* Princeton, NJ: Princeton University Press.

Kim, K. (2009). "Global Financial Crisis and the Korean Economy." Paper presented at the Asia Economic Policy Conference on "Asia and the Global Financial Crisis," Santa Barbara, CA, 19–20 October. www.frbsf.org/economic-research/events/2009/october/asia-global-financial-crisis/Panel_Kim.pdf.

King, G., Keohane, R. and Verba, S. (1994). *Designing Social Inquiry: Scientific Inference in Qualitative Research*. Princeton, NJ: Princeton University Press.

Klotz, A. (2008). "Case Selection." In A. Klotz and D. Prakash (eds), *Qualitative Methods in International Relations: A Pluralist Guide* (pp. 43–60). New York: Palgrave Macmillan.

Kollman, K. (2003). "The Rotating Presidency of the European Council as a Search for Good Policies." *European Union Politics*, 4(1): 51–74.

Komorita, S., and Barnes, M. (1969). "Effects of Pressures to Reach Agreement in Bargaining." *Journal of Personality and Social Psychology*, 13(3): 245–252.

Korea Times. (2008). "S. Korea Signs $30 Billion Currency Swap with US." 30 October. www.koreatimes.co.kr/www/news/biz/2008/10/123_33538.html.

Korea Trade-Investment Promotion Agency (KOTRA). (2010). "East Asia's Safety Net." *Invest Korea Journal*, May–June.

Krasner, S. (1983). *International Regimes*. Ithaca, NY: Cornell University Press.

Lane, M. T. D., Schulze-Gattas, M. M., Tsikata, M. T., Phillips, M. S., Ghosh, M. A. R. and Hamann, M. A. J. (1999). "IMF-Supported Programs in Indonesia, Korea and Thailand: A Preliminary Assessment." Occasional Paper, 178. Washington, DC: International Monetary Fund.

Lax, D., and Sebenius, J. (1986). *The Manager as Negotiator*. New York: Free Press.

Lee, S. (2009). "Korea, China, Japan Reach a Difficult Truce on CMI." *Joong-Ang Daily*, 14 May 14.

Lee, Y. J. (2010). "Financial Community Building in East Asia: The Chiang Mai Initiative – Its Causes and Evaluation." Paper presented at 2010 EPIK Young Leaders Conference organized by East Asia Institute, Seoul, South Korea, 17 August. www.eai.or.kr/data/bbs/kor_report/YoonJinLee.pdf.

Lewicki, R. J., Saunders, J. W. and Minton, J. W. (2000). *Negotiation*. Boston, MA: McGraw-Hill.

Lipscy, P. Y. (2003). "Japan's Asian Monetary Fund Proposal." *Stanford Journal of East Asian Affairs*, 3(1): 93–104.

Lohmann, S. (1997). "Linkage Politics." *Journal of Conflict Resolution*, 41(1): 38–67.

Majone, G. (2002). "The European Commission: The Limits of Centralization and the Perils of Parliamentarization." *Governance*, 15(3): 375–392.

Mannix, E. (1993). "Organizations as Resource Dilemmas: The Effects of Power Balance on Coalition Formation in Small Groups." *Organizational Behavior and Human Decision Processes*, 55(1): 1–22.

Mansfield, E. D., and Reinhardt, E. (2003). "Multilateral Determinants of Regionalism: The Effects of GATT/WTO on the Formation of Preferential Trading Arrangements." *International Organization*, 57(4): 829–862.

Martin, L. (1993). *Coercive Cooperation: Explaining Multilateral Economic Sanctions*. Princeton, NJ: Princeton University Press.

Mayntz, R. (2003). "Mechanisms in the Analysis of Macro-Social Phenomena." MPIfG Working Paper, 03/3. Cologne, Germany: Max Planck Institute for the Study of Societies.

Men, J. (2013). "China's Economic Diplomacy: Sino-EU Relations." Ekonomiaz, 82.

Menon, J. (2012). "Regional and Global Financial Safety Nets." Presentation to the Conference on the Evolving Global Architecture: From a Centralized to a Decentralized System, Nanyang Technological University and ADB Institute, Singapore, 26–27 March.

Milgrom, P., and Roberts, J. (1987). "Informational Asymmetries, Strategic Behavior, and Industrial Organization." *The American Economic Review*, 77(2): 184–193.

Ministry of Finance Japan (MOF Japan). (2014). "Press Release: The Agreement Establishing ASEAN+3 Macroeconomic Research Office ('AMRO Agreement') Was Signed." 10 October. www.mof.go.jp/english/international_policy/financial_cooperation_in_asia/amro/amro_20141010_e.pdf.

Ministry of Foreign Affairs of the People's Republic of China (FMPRC). (2002). "Vice Foreign Minister Wang Yi on the Achievements of Premier Zhu Rongji's Visit." Press Release, 7 November.

Moon, C. I. (1988). "Complex Interdependence and Transnational Lobbying: South Korea in the United States." *International Studies Quarterly*, 32(1): 67–89.

Moore, D. A. (2000). "Optimal Time Pressure Can Maximize Productivity in Solitary, Cooperative, and Competitive Tasks." Unpublished manuscript, Carnegie Mellon University, Pittsburgh, PA.

Moravcsik, A. (1993). "Preferences and Power in the European Community: A Liberal Intergovernmentalist Approach." *Journal of Common Market Studies*, 31(4): 473–473.

Moravcsik, A. (1998). *The Choice for Europe: Social Purpose and State Power from Messina to Maastricht*. Ithaca, NY: Cornell University Press.

Morrison, W. M. (2000). "The Growth of the Private Sector in China and Implications for China's Accession to the World Trade Organization." Washington, DC: Congressional Research Service.

Murnighan, J. K., Babcock, L., Thompson, L. and Pillutla, M. (1999). "The Information Dilemma in Negotiations: Effects of Experience, Incentives and Integrative Potential." *International Journal of Conflict Management*, 10(4): 313–339.

Nanto, D. (1998). "The 1997–98 Asian Financial Crisis." Congressional Research Service Report, 6 February. http://fas.org/man/crs/crs-asia2.htm.

Narlikar, A. (2003). *International Trade and Developing Countries: Bargaining Coalitions in the GATT and WTO*. New York: Routledge.

Narlikar, A., and Tussie, D. (2004). "The G20 at the Cancun Ministerial: Developing Countries and Their Evolving Coalitions at the WTO." *World Economy*, 27(7): 947–966.

Nathan, L. (2006). *No Ownership, No Peace: The Darfur Peace Agreement*. London: Crisis States Research Centre.

Neale, M. A., and Bazerman, M. H. (1992). "Negotiator Cognition and Rationality: A Behavioral Decision Theory Perspective." *Organizational Behavior and Human Decision Processes*, 51(2): 157–175.

Ng, G. (2011). "China Taking the Lead in Drive for Possible Common Asian Currency." *The China Post*, 24 May. www.chinapost.com.tw/business/asia/asian-market/2011/05/24/303488/China-taking.htm.

Noble, J. (2014). "China's Foreign Exchange Reserves Near Record $4tn." *Financial Times*, 15 April. www.ft.com/intl/cms/s/0/4768bd3c-c461–11e3–8dd4–00144feabdc0.html#axzz3YNIxGqE9.

Odell, J. (1980). "Latin American Trade Negotiations with the United States." *International Organization*, 34(2): 207–228.

Odell, J. (1985). "The Outcomes of International Trade Conflicts: The US and South Korea, 1960–1981." *International Studies Quarterly*, 29(3): 263–286.

Odell, J. (2000). *Negotiating the World Economy*. Ithaca, NY: Cornell University Press.

Odell, J. (2004). "Case Study Methods in International Political Economy." In D. Sprinz and Y. Wolinsky-Nahmias (eds), *Models, Numbers, and Cases: Methods for Studying International Relations* (pp. 56–80). Ann Arbor: University of Michigan Press.

Odell, J. (2005). "Chairing a WTO Negotiation." *Journal of International Economic Law*, 8(2): 425–448.

Odell, J. (2009). "Breaking Deadlocks in International Institutional Negotiations: The WTO, Seattle and Doha." *International Studies Quarterly*, 53(2): 1–47.

Park, J. (2013). "Political Rivals and Regional Leaders: Dual Identities and Sino-Japanese Relations within East Asian Cooperation." *Chinese Journal of International Politics*, 6(1): 85–107.

Pempel, T. J. (2008) "Restructuring Regional Ties." In A. Macintyre, T. J. Pempel and J. Ravenhill (eds), *Crisis as Catalyst: Asia's Dynamic Political Economy* (pp. 164–180). Ithaca, NY: Cornell University Press.

People's Bank of China Study Group (PBOC Study Group). (2006). "The Timing, Path, and Strategies of RMB Internationalization." *China Finance* 5: 12–13.

Permanent Mission of China to the UN at Geneva. (2004). "The 10th Conference of Chinese Diplomatic Envoys Stationed Abroad Held in Beijing." www.china-un.ch/eng/xwdt/t156047.htm.

Phongpaichit, P., and Baker, C. (2004). "Experience and Prospects of Financial Cooperation in ASEAN." Symposium on Co-Design for a New East Asia after the Crisis, Nagoya University.

Pinkley, R. (1995). "Impact of Knowledge Regarding Alternatives to Settlement in Dyadic Negotiations." *Journal of Applied Psychology*, 80(3): 403–417.

Pinkley, R., Neale, M. and Bennett, R. (1994). "The Impact of Alternatives to Settlement in Dyadic Negotiation." *Organizational Behavior and Human Decision Processes*, 57(1): 97–116.

Polzer, J., Mannix, E. and Neale, M. (1998). "Interest Alignment and Coalitions in Multi-party Negotiation." *The Academy of Management Journal*, 41(1): 42–54.

Pruitt, D. (1981). *Negotiation Behavior*. New York: Academic Press.

Pruitt, D., and Drews, J. (1969). "The Effect of Time Pressure, Time Elapsed, and the Opponent's Concession Rate on Behavior in Negotiation." *Journal of Experimental Social Psychology*, 5(1): 43–60.

Qiu, Q. (2012). "Yuan Gains Favour with Exporters." *China Daily*, 13 July. http://europe.chinadaily.com.cn/europe/cnbanksineuro/2012-07/13/content_15577515.htm.

Quaglia, L. (2009). "How Does Expertise Influence Negotiations in the EU?" Paper prepared for the EUSA conference, Los Angeles, CA.

Quaglia, L., and Moxon- Browne, E. (2006). "What Makes a Good EU Presidency? Italy and Ireland Compared." *Journal of Common Market Studies*, 44: 349–368.

Raiffa, H. (1982). *The Art and Science of Negotiation*. Cambridge, MA: Harvard University Press.

Rajan, R. (2002). "Study on Monetary and Financial Cooperation in East Asia (Summary Report)." Manila: Asian Development Bank.

Rana, P. B. (2002) "Monetary and Financial Cooperation in East Asia: The Chiang Mai Initiative and Beyond." ERD Working Paper, 6. Manila: Asian Development Bank.

Rapkin, D. P. (2001). "The United States, Japan, and the Power to Block: The APEC and AMF Cases." *The Pacific Review*, 14(3): 373–410.

Rapoport, A., Weg, E. and Felsenthal, D. (1990). "Effects of Fixed Costs in Two-Person Sequential Bargaining." *Theory and Decision*, 28(1): 47–71.

Rathus, J. (2009). "The Chiang Mai Initiative: China, Japan and Financial Regionalism." www.eastasiaforum.org/2009/05/11/the-chiang-mai-initiative-china-japan-and-financial-regionalism/.

Rathus, J. (2010). "Affordable Delays for the Chiang Mai Initiative?" www.eastasiaforum.org/2010/12/24/affordable-delays-for-the-chiang-mai-initiative/.

Rathus, J. (2011). "Chiang Mai Initiative: China Takes the Leader's Seat." *East Asia Forum*, 30 June. www.eastasiaforum.org/2011/06/30/chiang-mai-initiative-china-takes-the-leader-s-seat/.

Ravenhill, J. (2002). "A Three Bloc World? The New East Asian Regionalism." *International Relations of the Asia-Pacific*, 2(2): 167–195.

Rowley, A. (2008). "Japan Hosts First of Regular Tripartite Summits." *Business Times Singapore*, 13 December.

Sachs, J. D. (1997). "The Wrong Medicine for Asia." *New York Times,* 3 November.

Saputro, E. (2011). "Where to for ASEAN+3's Macroeconomic Research Office?" *East Asia Forum*, 18 June. www.eastasiaforum.org/2011/06/18/where-to-for-asean3-s-macroeconomic-research-office/.

Schalk, J., Torenvlied, R., Weesie, J. and Stokman, F. (2007). "The Power of the Presidency in EU Council Decision-Making." *European Union Politics*, 8(2): 229–250.

Schei, V., and Rognes, J. (1993). "Knowing Me, Knowing You: Own Orientation and Information about the Opponent's Orientation in Negotiation." *International Journal of Conflict Management*, 14(1): 43–59.

Schelling, T. (1960). *The Strategy of Conflict*. Boston: Harvard Business School Press.

Schoemaker, P. (1990). "Strategy, Complexity and Economic Rent." *Management Science*, 36(10): 1178–1192.

Schotter, J., and Wildau, G. (2014). "China and Switzerland Sign Bilateral Currency Swap Line." *Financial Times*, 21 July.

Schout, A. (1998). "The Presidency as Juggler: Managing Conflicting Expectations." *Eipascope*, 2: 1–9.

Sebenius, J. (1983). "Negotiation Arithmetic: Adding and Subtracting Issues and Parties." *International Organization*, 37(2): 281–316.

Sebenius, J. (1996). "Sequencing to Build Coalitions: With Whom Should I Talk First?" In R. Zeckhauser, R. Keeney and J. Sebenius (eds), *Wise Choices: Decisions, Games, and Negotiations* (pp. 324–348). Cambridge, MA: Harvard Business Press.

Sell, S., and Odell, J. (2003). "Reframing the Issue: The Coalition on Intellectual Property and Public Health in the WTO, 2001." In J. Odell (ed.), *Negotiating Trade: Developing Countries in the TWO and NAFTA* (pp. 85–114). Cambridge: Cambridge University Press.

Setboonsarng, S., and Lim, H. (2012). *ASEAN-Hong Kong: The Case for Cooperation*. Singapore: Institute of Asian Affairs.

Shoji, T. (2009). "Pursuing a Multi-dimensional Relationship: Rising China and Japan's Southeast Asia Policy." In J. Tsunekawa (ed.), *The Rise of China: Responses from Southeast Asia and Japan* (pp. 157–84). NIDS Joint Research Series, 4. Tokyo: National Institute for Defense Studies.

Singh, J. P. (2003, November). "Wiggle Rooms: New Issues and North-South Negotiations during the Uruguay Round." In *Conference on Developing Countries and the Trade Negotiation Process (6–7 November)*. UNCTAD, Palais des Nations, Room XXVII, Geneva.

Skocpol, T. (2007). *States and Social Revolutions: A Comparative Analysis of France, Russia, and China*. Cambridge: Cambridge University Press.

Smith, D. L., Pruitt, D. G. and Carnevale, P. J. (1982). "Matching and Mismatching: The Effect of Own Limit, Other's Toughness, and Time Pressure on Concession Rate in Negotiation." *Journal of Personal and Social Psychology*, 42: 876–883.

So, A. Y. (2004). "Hong Kong's Pathway to Becoming a Global City." In J. Gugler (ed.), *World Cities beyond the West: Globalization, Development and Inequality* (pp. 212–239). Cambridge: Cambridge University Press.

Sohn, I. (2005). "Asian Financial Cooperation: The Problem of Legitimacy in Global Financial Governance." *Global Governance*, 11(4): 487–504.

Sohn, I. (2007). "East Asia's Counterweight Strategy: Asian Financial Cooperation and Evolving International Monetary Order." G-24 Discussion Paper Series, 1–11. New York: United Nations.

Sohn, I. (2008). "Learning to Co-operate: China's Multilateral Approach to Asian Financial Co-operation." *China Quarterly*, 194: 309–326.

Sohn, I. (2012). "Toward Normative Fragmentation: An East Asian Financial Architecture in the Post–Global Crisis World." *Review of International Political Economy*, 19(4): 586–608.

Song, G. (2013). "Building Friends Nearby: China's Economic Relations with Neighboring Countries." China Institute of International Studies, 25 November. www.ciis.org.cn/english/2013–11/25/content_6486720.htm.

Stake, R. (1995). *The Art of Case Study Research*. Thousand Oaks, CA: SAGE.

Stubbs, R. (2014). "ASEAN's Leadership in East Asian Region-Building: Strength in Weakness." *Pacific Review*, 27(4): 523–541.

Stuhlmacher, A., and Champagne, M. (2000). "The Impact of Time Pressure and Information on Negotiation Process and Decisions." *Group Decision and Negotiation*, 9(6): 471–491.

Stuhlmacher, A., Gillespie, T. and Champagne, M. (1998). "The Impact of Time Pressure in Negotiation: A Meta-Analysis." *International Journal of Conflict Management*, 9(2): 97–116.

Sung, Y., and Song, E. (1991). *The China–Hong Kong Connection: The Key to China's Open Door Policy*. Hong Kong: Cambridge University Press.

Sussangkarn, C. (2011a). "Chiang Mai Initiative Multilateralization: Origin, Development, and Outlook." *Asian Economic Policy Review*, 6(2): 203–220.

Sussangkarn, C. (2011b). "Institution Building for Macroeconomic and Financial Cooperation in East Asia." *International Economy*, 15: 1–14. www.jsie.jp/Annual_Conferences/Spring_1st/pdf/Paper_Sussangkarn.pdf.

Sussangkarn, C. (2012). "Development of Foreign Exchange Liquidity Support Mechanism in East Asia." *Regionalismo financiero y estabilidad macroeconómica*, 74–86. http://eprints.soas.ac.uk/17390/1/6420_Papers_and_proceedings_2012_COMPLETO.pdf#page=89.

Sussangkarn, C., and Manupipatpong, W. (2015). "A View from ASEAN." In M. Kawai, Y. C. Park and C. Wyplosz (eds), *Monetary and Financial Cooperation in East Asia: The State of Affairs after the Global and European Crises* (pp. 102–32). Oxford: Oxford University Press.

Sussangkarn, C., and Vichyanond, P. (2007). "Directions of East Asian Regional Financial Cooperation." *Asian Economic Papers*, 5(3): 25–55.

Takano, Y. (2009). "Tokyo Aims to Push Ten over Yuan in Asia." *Asahi Shimbun*, 5 May.

Tallberg, J. (2002). "The Power of the Chair in International Bargaining." Paper prepared for presentation at the 2002 ISA Annual Convention.

Tallberg, J. (2006). *Leadership and Negotiation in the European Union*. Cambridge: Cambridge University Press.

Tallberg, J. (2008). "Bargaining Power in the European Council." *Journal of Common Market Studies*, 46(3): 685–708.

Tallberg, J. (2010). "The Power of the Chair: Formal Leadership in International Cooperation." *International Studies Quarterly*, 54(1): 241–265.

Talley, I., and Wei, L. (2015). "Momentum Builds to Label Chinese Yuan a Reserve Currency." *Wall Street Journal*, 1 April. www.wsj.com/articles/momentum-builds-to-label-chinese-yuan-a-reserve-currency-1427926918.

Thompson, L. (2001). *The Mind and Heart of the Negotiator.* 2nd ed. Upper Saddle River, NJ: Prentice Hall.

Tollison, R., and Willett, T. (1979). "An Economic Theory of Mutually Advantageous Issue Linkages in International Negotiations." *International Organization,* 33(4): 425–449.

Touval, S., and Zartman, I.W. (1985). *International Mediation in Theory and Practice.* Boulder, CO: Westview Press.

Tso, C.D., and Yeh, K.C. (2013). "China's Role in Chiang Mai Initiative Multilateralization (CMIM): A Reluctant and Constrained Leadership." In B. J. Cohen and M. Chiu (eds), *Power in a Changing World Economy: Lessons from East Asia* (pp. 111–124). New York: Routledge.

Wagner, L.M. (2008). *Problem-Solving and Bargaining in International Negotiations.* Vol. 5. Leiden: Martinus Nijhoff.

Wall, J.A., Jr., and Rude, D.E. (1991). "The Judge as Mediator." *Journal of Applied Psychology,* 76(1): 54–59.

Wallace, W. (1976). "Issue Linkage among Atlantic Governments." *International Affairs,* 52(2): 163–179.

Waltz, K. (1959). *Man, the State and War.* New York: Columbia University Press.

Wang, H. (2014). "From 'Taoguang Yanghui' to 'Yousuo Zuowei': China's Engagement in Financial Minilateralism." CIGI Papers, 52. Waterloo, ON: Centre for International Governance Innovation.

Warntjen, A. (2007). "Steering the Union: The Impact of the EU Presidency on Legislative Activity in the Council." *Journal of Common Market Studies* 45: 1135–1157.

Weatherbee, D.E. (2015). *International Relations in Southeast Asia: The Struggle for Autonomy.* New York: Rowman and Littlefield.

Wei, L. (2015). "China's CIC Gearing Up Investment in Overseas Assets." *Wall Street Journal,* 27 March. www.wsj.com/articles/chinas-cic-gearing-up-investment-in-overseas-assets-1427456722.

Wen, J. (2003). "Composing a New Chapter for East Asia Cooperation." A speech given at the 7th ASEAN Summit, Bali, Indonesia, 7 October.

Wen, J. (2004). "Strengthening Cooperation for Mutual Benefit and a Win-win Result." A speech given at the 8th ASEAN+3 Summit, Vientiane, Laos, 29 November.

Wheatly, A. (2009). "Crisis Spurs Asia to Hasten Cooperation, a Little." 13 October. http://in.reuters.com/article/2009/10/12/us-asia-economy-cooperation-analysis-idUSTRE59B56G20091012.

Winham, G.R. (1977). "Negotiation as a Management Process." *World Politics,* 30(1): 87–114.

Wolfe, R., and McGinn, K. (2005). "Perceived Relative Power and Its Influence on Negotiations." *Group Decision and Negotiation,* 14(1): 3–20.

Wriggins, W. (1976). "Up for Auction: Malta Bargains with Great Britain, 1971." In W. Zartman (ed.), *The 50% Solution: How to Bargain Successfully with Hijackers, Strikers, Bosses, Oil Magnates, Arabs, Russians, and Other Worthy Opponents in This Modern World* (pp. 208–234). Garden City, NY: Anchor Press/Doubleday.

Xia, L. (2007). "East Asian Multilateral Cooperation and the Prospect of China-Japan Relations." In M. Heazle and N. Knight (eds), *China-Japan Relations in the Twenty-First Century: Creating a Future Past?* (pp. 35–53). Cheltenham, UK: Edward Elgar.

Xinhua. (2012). "Chinese Mainland, HK Sign New Supplement to CEPA." *China Daily,* 6 July. http://usa.chinadaily.com.cn/business/2012-06/29/content_15537247.htm.

Xinhua. (2015). "China, Suriname Sign Currency Swap Deal." 18 March. http://en.people.cn/business/n/2015/0318/c90778-8865223.html.

Yang, Y. (1998). "China in the Middle of the East Asian Crisis: Export Growth and the Exchange Rate." Asia Pacific Press, Australian National University. https://digitalcollections.anu.edu.au/bitstream/1885/40420/3/cu98-4.pdf

Yin, R. (2009). *Case Study Research: Design and Methods*. Thousand Oaks, CA: Sage.

Yoshida, T. (2004). "East Asian Regionalism and Japan." Working Paper, 9. Institute of Developing Economies, APEC Study Centre.

You, N., Fu, J. and Wang, B. (2009). "Nation Should Play Greater Role in G20, Says Expert." *China Daily*, 19 March. www.chinadaily.com.cn/bizchina/2009-03/19/content_7594063.htm.

Young, O. (1991). "Political Leadership and Regime Formation: On the Development of Institutions in International Society." *International Organization*, 45(3): 281–308.

Yu, Y. (2008). "Panda Bonds Could Help China Avoid the Risks of US Treasury Bonds." *East Asia Forum*, 19 December. www.eastasiaforum.org/2008/12/19/panda-bonds-could-help-china-avoid-the-risks-of-us-treasury-bonds/.

Yukl, G., Malone, M., Hayslip, B. and Pamin, T. (1976). "The Effects of Time Pressure and Issue Settlement Order on Integrative Bargaining." *Sociometry*, 39(3): 277–281.

Zartman, W. (1994). "Two's Company and More's a Crowd: The Complexities of Multilateral Negotiation." In W. Zartman (ed.), *International Multilateral Negotiation: Approaches to the Management of Complexity* (pp. 1–10). San Francisco, CA: Jossey-Bass.

Zartman, W., and Berman, M. (1983). *The Practical Negotiator*. New Haven, CT: Yale University Press.

Zartman, W., and Rubin, J. (2002). *Power and Negotiation*. Ann Arbor: University of Michigan Press.

Zhang, Y. (2012). "China's Regional and Global Power." *East Asia Forum*, 6 February. www.eastasiaforum.org/2012/02/06/chinas-regional-and-global-power/.

Zhu, R. (2000). "Speech by His Excellency Zhu Rongji Premier of the State Council of the People's Republic of China at the Fourth Meeting of Heads of State/Government of ASEAN, China, Japan and the Republic of Korea (10+3)." www.fmprc.gov.cn/eng/topics/zgcydyhz/dsiczgdm/t25976.htm.

Index

Note: Page numbers in *italics* followed by *b* indicate boxes, by *f* indicate figures, and by *t* indicate tables. Page numbers followed by n indicate notes.

For Product Safety Concerns and Information please contact our EU
representative GPSR@taylorandfrancis.com
Taylor & Francis Verlag GmbH, Kaufingerstraße 24, 80331 München, Germany

www.ingramcontent.com/pod-product-compliance
Ingram Content Group UK Ltd.
Pitfield, Milton Keynes, MK11 3LW, UK
UKHW020953180425
457613UK00019B/662